D0464710

The Revolt Against the Masses

How Liberalism Has Undermined the Middle Class

The Revolt Against the Masses

How Liberalism Has Undermined the Middle Class

Fred Siegel

Encounter Books
New York • London

First American edition published in 2013 by Encounter Books, an activity of Encounter for Culture and Education, Inc., a nonprofit, tax-exempt corporation.
Encounter Books website address: www.encounterbooks.com

Manufactured in the United States and printed on acid-free paper. The paper used in this publication meets the minimum requirements of ANSI/NISO Z39.48-1992 (R 1997) (Permanence of Paper).

FIRST AMERICAN EDITION

LIBRARY OF CONGRESS CATALOGING-IN-PUBLICATION DATA

Siegel, Frederick F., 1945–
The revolt against the masses : how liberalism has undermined the middle class / by Fred Siegel.
pages cm
Includes bibliographical references and index.
ISBN 978-1-59403-698-9 (hardcover : alk. paper) — ISBN 978-1-59403-699-6 (ebook)
1. Middle class—United States—History—20th century. 2. Liberalism—United States—History—20th century. 3. United States—Politics and government—20th century. I. Title.
HT684.S54 2013
320.51′30973—dc23

2013007444

Dedicated to the memory of Frank Macchiarola
1941–2012
Catholic Democrat, mensch, great Brooklynite

Contents

★ ★ ★

Introduction

This short book is not a comprehensive history of American liberalism. A number of important figures and episodes are merely glossed over. Instead, it rewrites the history of modern American liberalism. It shows that what we think of liberalism today—the top-and-bottom coalition we associate with President Obama—began not with Progressivism or the New Deal but rather in the wake of the post–World War I disillusionment with American society. In the Twenties, the first writers and thinkers to call themselves liberals adopted the hostility to bourgeois life that had long characterized European intellectuals of both the left and the right. The aim of liberalism's founding writers and thinkers—such as Herbert Croly, Randolph Bourne, H.G. Wells, Sinclair Lewis, and H.L. Mencken—was to create an American aristocracy of sorts, to provide the same sense of hierarchy and order long associated with European statism.

Like communism, Fabianism, and fascism, modern liberalism was a vanguard movement born of a new class of politically self-conscious intellectuals. Critical of mass democracy and middle-class capitalism, liberals despised the individual businessman's pursuit of profit as well as the conventional individual's self-interested pursuit of success, both of which were made possible by the lineaments of the limited nineteenth-century state.

Snobbery is not new to liberalism. But the actual history of liberalism will be new to most readers, which is my reason for writing this book. The history of liberalism as written by liberal historians begins either with the pre-WWI Progressive movement or, more likely, with the New Deal of the 1930s. In the plumb-line account usually wholesaled, there is a direct ascent from the Progressives to the social salvation represented by the New Deal to the Great Society and on up to the present. The Progressives, it's said, were the first to show that big non-constitutional government could be used to solve big problems. After the yahoos of the 1920s put the country to sleep for a decade, leading to the stock-market crash, the New Deal rode to the rescue to establish the beau ideal for future governance. Conservatives tell a similar story, but theirs is an account of descent, from liberty into "statism."

But the story isn't quite true at beginning, middle, or end. The story of liberalism is more than an account of how the administrative state broke free of its constitutional bonds. Liberalism, like its rivals, including communism, fascism, and social democracy, emerged as part of the early twentieth century's intellectual response to the newly emergent realities of mass production, mass politics, and mass culture. Like fascism and communism, liberalism was strongly influenced by the Nietzschean ideal of a true aristocracy that might serve as a corrective to the perceived debasements of modern commercial society shorn of traditional hierarchies. It was liberals' claim to be an aristocracy based on talent and sensibility that helped define the 1960s and '70s. It was then that highly educated liberals—acting, they said, on behalf of African Americans—pushed aside the social-democratic trade unionists within the Democratic Party.

Liberalism was far more intellectually permeable, and far more politically adaptable, than most of its competitors and more willing than all but the trade-union-tied social democrats to work through the existing government structures. These qualities brought it to the forefront of American life. But it nonetheless represents a distinct ethos, a stylized set of political postures often at odds with America's democratic, capitalist, and egalitarian traditions.

The set of cultural and emotional attachments, the political libido of liberalism, so to speak, coalesced in the wake of WWI in an angry repudiation of Progressivism and Woodrow Wilson. Modern liberalism preceded the New Deal by more than a decade. The very term "liberal," in its modern usage, was coined by writers and intellectuals who defined themselves by their hostility to the middle class and the moralistic Progressives who had imposed Prohibition in 1919. As *The Revolt Against the Masses* will show, liberalism began as a fervent reaction to wartime Wilsonian Progressivism, and it took its still current cultural shape in the 1920s well before the Great Depression came crashing down on the country. It was in the seminal 1920s that the strong strain of snobbery, so pervasive among today's gentry liberals, first defined the then nascent ideology of liberalism.

The best short credo of liberalism came from the pen of the once canonical left-wing literary historian Vernon Parrington in the late 1920s. "Rid society of the dictatorship of the middle class," Parrington insisted, referring to both democracy and capitalism, "and the artist and the scientist will erect in America a civilization that may become, what civilization was in earlier days, a thing to be respected." Alienated from middle-class American life, liberalism drew on an idealized image of "organic" pre-modern folkways and rhapsodized about a future harmony that would reestablish the proper hierarchy of virtue in a post-bourgeois, post-democratic world. In the mid-1950s during a brief reconciliation between liberals and their country, the literary critic Lionel Trilling noted that "for the first time in the history of the modern American intellectual, America is not to be conceived of as a priori the vulgarest and stupidest nation of the world." This novelty soon passed.

The ideals of the 1920s liberals were, by way of the statist and technocratic elements of the 1930s, carried forward into the 1960s. It was in the 1960s that liberals, even more than conservatives, laid siege to the social-solidarity heritage of the New Deal. In the name of good causes such as opposition to racism and the war in Vietnam, post–New Deal upper-middle-class liberals looked to remake America in their own image by enhancing their own power. They defined middle-class Americans, including those who made it into modest prosperity through unionized work, as the unenlightened objects of their enmity. Much of the middle and lower-middle class, subject to liberal experiments in schooling, crime, and gender relations, reciprocated the animosity. Liberal social programs to combat poverty and reform the schools, their failures now long institutionalized, have produced a government whose grasp far exceeds its competence and whose costs are carried by the private-sector middle class. Like corrupt Harlem congressman Charley Rangel, who did his best to keep new businesses out of Harlem so that he could fend off rivals and accumulate anti-poverty money for his political friends and allies, liberalism has been dedicated to preserving the problems for which it presents itself as the solution.

In today's America, those who claim to be morally superior all too often enjoy both neo–Gilded Age wealth and close ties to government. After the government-driven failures and excesses of the past forty years, liberalism has become an ugly blend of sanctimony, self-interest, and social connections. When the editor-in-chief of the popular liberal website *Slate*, frustrated with opposition to Obama's expansion of the federal government, entitled an article "Down with the People," he echoed the assumption that has driven liberalism since its inception.

Liberalism, as a search for status, is sufficiently adaptable that even in failure, self-satisfaction trumps self-examination. As the critic Edmund Wilson noted without irony, the liberal (or "progressive reformer," in his term) has "evolved a psychological mechanism which enables him to turn moral judgments against himself into moral judgments against society."

This is a book about the inner life of American liberalism over the past ninety years and its love affair with its own ambitions and emotional impulses. Liberals believe that they deserve more power because they act on behalf of people's best interests—even if the darn fools don't know it.

CHAPTER 1

★ ★ ★

Progenitors

Modern liberalism has often been defined as the experimental method applied to politics and as the mentality that insists that culture, not nature, puts the future of humanity in its own hands. In terms of American history, modern liberalism is conventionally presented as an adaptation of nineteenth-century laissez-faire liberal individualism to the growth of big business, and as an updated expression of Jacksonian animus to vested interests. There is something substantial in all of these definitions, but, even taken together, they leave out a great deal.

American liberals don't like to compare themselves with other twentieth-century ideologues. But, like all the ideologies that emerged in the early twentieth century—from communism and fascism to socialism, social democracy, and its first cousin, British Fabianism—liberalism was created by intellectuals and writers who were rebelling against the failings of the rising middle class. They had a quarrel with the industry, immigration, and economic growth that produced unprecedented prosperity in the United States. They recoiled at what they saw as the ugly bustling cacophony of the urban masses loudly staking their claim to capitalism's bounty.

In America, the founding fathers of liberalism emerged at the turn of the twentieth century, looking both backward to the more orderly virtues of pre-industrial society and forward to the promise of a future that would use science to transcend the crass culture created by a largely unregulated capitalism. At a time when millions were reaping the benefits of a stunning array of new inventions—the telephone, motion pictures, the washing machine, the gramophone—America seemed ripe for reshaping. Autos, airplanes, and radios were altering received notions of time and space. On the one hand, we were reveling in the new: the most dynamic economy in the world that was generating vast national oligopolies. On the other, we were mired in the old: a provincial political culture rooted in practices that had taken hold well before the Civil War. The disparity was striking.

The politics of the countryside were organized around courthouse cliques pursuing petty preferences and ethnic squabbles, while urban centers were ravished by the "pigs at the trough" character of the big-city political machines, which replaced the rule of law with the politics of patronage. By European standards, there was no central government in America to speak of. Most social and economic policy originated in the states, where the political parties (organized around ethnic, cultural, and regional issues) dominated government. Nationally, the president spent as much time on patronage as policy, and he competed with Congress for control of the departments of the Treasury, Agriculture, and the Interior. Far from regal, presidents in this era were known to answer the White House doorbell. Shortly after the famed British author H.G. Wells visited the U.S. in 1905, he described the American federal government as "marooned, twisted up into knots, bound with safeguards, and altogether impotently stranded."

In the aftermath of the Civil War, anti-slavery journalists and intellectuals felt besmirched by the "great barbecue" of getting and spending unleashed by the breakneck expansion of the economy. James Russell Lowell's 1876 "Ode for the Fourth of July" captured the sense of displacement:

> And if the nobler passions wane,
> Distorted to base use, if the near goal
> Of insubstantial gain
> Tempt from the proper race-course of the soul...
> Is this the country we dreamed in youth,
> Where wisdom and not numbers should have weight...?

E.L. Godkin, the founding editor of *The Nation* and a forerunner of liberalism, similarly complained about ignoble Americans: "A gaudy stream of bespangled, belaced, and beruffled barbarians" were flocking to New York to spend their recently acquired fortunes. "Who knows how to be rich in America?" he asked. "Plenty of people know how to get money; but…to be rich properly is indeed a fine art. It requires culture, imagination, and character." Godkin and his allies, hoping for leaders of superior intelligence and virtue, looked to Charles Francis Adams Jr. as a possible leader. He was the grandson of president John Adams and the son of President John Quincy Adams, and, like Godkin, he thought that businessmen lacked the temperament to govern; what we needed in office were aristocrats like him.

It was Charles Francis Adams's brother Henry who, through his book *The Education of Henry Adams* (first published privately in 1907), became an inspiration to liberals. *The Education* described Henry Adams's disappointment with an American society that did not pay him due deference. Adams's disaffection created the model for much of what became left-wing intellectual life. Adams turned his sour complaints of being bypassed and his sense of himself as a failure into a judgment against the American people. The hustle and bustle of American life were so dismaying to him that he once said he "should have been a Marxist."

"To the gradually cohering body of dissenters from the orthodoxies of American life," explained Lionel Trilling, "*The Education of Henry Adams* was a sacred book . . . despite, or because of, its hieratic esoteric irony and its reiterated note of patrician condescension." Henry Adams grounded the intellectual's alienation from American life in the resentment that superior men feel when they are insufficiently appreciated in America's common-man culture. Adams's disdain for the modern and the mechanical and his distrust of the ideal of progress would become leitmotifs of American liberalism and important elements of the environmental movement. Reissued, *The Education of Henry Adams* won the Pulitzer Prize in 1919. In the wake of WWI, the book was read as prophecy that had foretold the damage done by democracy in the Great War.

Adams resented the new men—the economists, physicians, and chemists whose science-based authority had displaced literary men such as himself. H.G. Wells and the American architecture critic Herbert Croly, two of modern liberalism's founders, shared Adams's anti-capitalist sentiments. But Wells and Croly argued in their seminal works that the very experts Adams had despised had a crucial role to play: They could help displace the freewheeling capitalism the literary elites scorned.

H.G. Wells is today best remembered as the author of such late-nineteenth-century best-selling socio-scientific fantasies as *The Time Machine*, *The War of the Worlds*, and *The Invisible Man*, all still read today, if only as entertainment or fodder for Hollywood scripts. But he was much more than a fantasist. At the turn of the twentieth century, Wells set forth the two central tropes of liberalism: a sense of superiority and a claim on the future. Liberals thought themselves smarter than other people because they had seen through the supposed Victorian verities to a future not yet born.

"Thinking people who were born about the beginning of this century are in some sense Wells's own creation," George Orwell explained in 1941. "There you were, in a world of pedants, clergymen and golfers…and here was this wonderful man who could tell you about the inhabitants of planets and the bottom of the sea, and who knew that the future was not going to be what respectable people imagined."

Wells's 1901 nonfiction book *Anticipations of the Reaction of Mechanical and Scientific Progress upon Human Life and Thought* was credited with "the discovery of the future." He described the book as the "keystone to the main arch of my work." His programs for deploying scientific remedies to cure social diseases turned the already esteemed author into a social and political seer in England and also in America, where *Anticipations* had already been serialized in *The North American Review.*

The story of the shift from the "old" nineteenth-century Victorian liberalism of laissez-faire to the "new liberalism" that is the modern statist variety has almost exclusively focused on how the growth of giant industries undercut the old assumptions about individual sovereignty. But there was a parallel shift induced by the concussive intellectual impact of Darwinism. Darwin's location of human origins in the natural world rather than the spiritual realm begged for prophets of a secular humanity. Wells, who more than any other intellectual understood both shifts, saw himself and was seen by his devotees as just such a prophet.

Anticipations seemed to endow the author with omniscience and made Wells an intellectual hero for reform-minded writers anxious to break with what they saw as the stale orthodoxies of nineteenth-century laissez-faire capitalism, with its business-centered morality and embrace of democracy. "The book," Wells explained, "was designed to undermine and destroy...monogamy, faith in God & respectability, all under the guise of a speculation about motor cars and electrical heating." For many young American intellectuals, Wells's writings were a passport out of provincialism.

Looking back on the century of material and mechanical progress that had just passed, numerous fin de siècle writers commented on both its achievements and its running sore, the seemingly permanent immiseration of the urban working class. But Wells looked ahead and asserted that there was as much a pattern to the future as there was to the past. He not only argued inductively about the likely nature of what was to come based on the way the telephone and telegraph and railroad had shrunk the world, but he also conjured up a dramatic cast of characters. His account was peopled with those he loathed, such as the idle, parasitic rich and the "vicious helpless pauper masses," whom he described as "the people of the abyss." He similarly despised the yapping politicians and yellow journalists who were, in his view, instruments of patriotism and war.

But if these were the people who were leading the world on the path to hell, there were also the redeemers, the "New Republicans," "the capable men" of vision who might own the future. These scientist-poets and engineers could, he thought, seize the reins in the Darwinian struggle; rather than descending into savagery, we would follow their lead toward a new and higher ground. They were the heroes of the drama. "Written in the language of sociology," explain his biographers Norman and Jeanne McKenzie, his fictions were morality plays about the Last Judgment. If the redeemers, the anti-global-warming crusaders of their day, were rejected, then civilization would perish.

For the randy Wells, the choice was clear. On one hand, he could join the ranks of the new men of science—who aimed to discard Anglo-American family mores and replace the politicians—and freely pursue a richly textured life. On the other hand, if he adhered to stale Victorian morality, his life would be one of bleakly conventional routines. Compared with the "normal, ordinary world which is on the whole satisfied with itself" and that encompasses "the great mass of men," he wrote, "there is the ever advancing better world, pushing through this outworn husk in the minds and wills of creative humanity." This was the difference between the bovine "Normal Life" of workers, clerks, and small businessmen and the "Great State" led by the creative class. The conflicts between these classes were "not economic but psychological," he said. The advent of the machine created the possibility of what he called, anticipating Herbert Marcuse, "surplus life." It was a realm of expanded imagination available to those who eschewed "the normal scheme" and engaged in what John Stuart Mill had portrayed as "life experiments."

Wells gave an account of his first trip to these shores, in 1906, in *The Future in America*, which was serialized in U.S. and British magazines. In it, we see that Wells was heartened by the absence of a traditional aristocracy in America but also chagrined that Americans lagged in creating a new aristocratic class of scientists and intellectuals, who were the key to a shining future. "All Americans are, from the English point of view, Liberals of one sort or another," he wrote. "The American community...does not correspond to an entire European community at all, but only to the middle masses of it—to the trading and manufacturing class between the dimensions of the magnate and the clerk and the skilled artisan. It is the central part of the European organism without either the dreaming head or the subjugated feet." In England, he noted approvingly, modern men of money "had become part of a responsible ruling class." But the absence of an aristocracy in the U.S. had a debilitating underside because it left the country without the sense of "state responsibility," which was needed "to give significance to the whole." The typical American "has no sense of the state," Wells complained. "He has no perception that his business activities, his private employments, are constituents in a larger collective process."

Wells was appalled by the decentralized nature of America's locally oriented party and country-courthouse politics. He was aghast at the flamboyantly corrupt political machines of the big cities, unchecked by a gentry that might uphold civilized standards. He thought American democracy went too far in providing leeway to the poltroons who ran the political machines and the "fools" who supported them. The "immigrants are being given votes," but "that does not free them, it only enslaves the country," he said. In the North, he complained, even "the negroes were given votes." This was no small matter for Wells, because as an Englishman he saw his country's path as thoroughly intertwined with America's. "One cannot look ten years ahead in England, without glancing across the Atlantic," he wrote in *The Future in America*. "Our future is extraordinarily bound up in America's, and in a sense dependent on it." Not that he embraced it: "I would as soon go to live in a pen in a stockyard as into American politics," he wrote.

The federal government in Washington, suffering from "state blindness," from "a want of concentration," sent Wells into further hyperbole. "The place seems to me to reflect…that dispersal of power, the evasion of simple conclusiveness" produced by "a legislature that fails to legislate, a government that cannot govern." Demonstrating his limited knowledge of European governments, he rated the American government as the bottom of the barrel: "Congress as it is constituted at present is the feeblest, least accessible, and most inefficient central government of any civilized nation in the world West of Russia."

At a time when "collectivism" and "individualism" were new words that reflected the twin challenge to the Victorian ideal of laissez-faire government, Wells saw the absence of an American collective will as the nation's greatest weakness. "The greatest work which the coming century has to do…is to build up an aristocracy of thought and feeling which shall hold its own against the aristocracy of mercantilism" and its allies "materialism and Philistinism." Wells had discarded the Calvinism of his youth but clung fondly to its concept of a deserving elect.

Limning what would become modern American liberalism, Wells saw three social streams that might converge to form the headwaters of the great river of statism. Speaking of "salvation by schools," he was greatly encouraged by the growth of scientific and professional knowledge in American academia, which was well ahead of its English counterpart that was still struggling, in his view, to shake off the cobwebs of classical learning. Like his teacher Thomas Huxley, who had become famous as "Darwin's bulldog," Wells believed that only the intelligentsia could save industrial civilization from self-destruction. Presciently, Wells told his readers, "I write of the universities as the central intellectual organ of a modern state."

Wells was also inspired by the early-twentieth-century muckrakers who, with their allies in the Progressive movement, led a sharp shift away from America's ethnic and regional politics. The muckrakers challenged the traditional American sense of certainty and self-satisfaction. Aided by the growth of the penny newspapers and monthly ten-cent magazines, such as those that serialized Wells's novels, the muckrakers' assault on the great monopolies and political machines helped create an increasingly national political identity. "The Americans," Wells wrote, "have become suddenly self-critical, are hot with an unwonted fever for reform and constructive effort." Can-do commercialism, he argued, was "crushing and maiming a great multitude of souls." Progressivism, or what Wells innocently called "the revolt of the competent," pointed to the creation of a Wellsian managerial elite similar to the "voluntary nobility" he idealized as samurai in his 1905 dialogue novel, *A Modern Utopia*.

In the course of Wells's 1906 visit to the U.S., Jane Addams, Upton Sinclair, and Lincoln Steffens befriended him. He became part of their world, and it was Steffens who arranged Wells's first visit to the White House. And though they disagreed on some scores, Wells placed his greatest hopes in the person of President Theodore Roosevelt.

TR, an avid reader, was delighted to sit down at the White House and talk for hours with Wells, who was already an international celebrity at age thirty-nine. Like Wells and Charles Francis Adams Jr., Roosevelt (the warrior President made famous by his role as the leader of the Rough Riders in the Spanish–American War) thought businessmen incapable of political leadership. The president saw them as having the "ideals of pawnbrokers."

Roosevelt recognized that the confluence of rapid industrialization and high levels of immigration had exacerbated class divisions in America, but he felt that class barriers could be overcome. The eugenically minded Wells, who compared mass immigration to the earlier slave trade, was doubtful. "In the 'colored population,' America has already ten million descendants of unassimilated and perhaps unassimilable labor immigrants," he wrote. "These people are not only half civilized and ignorant, but they have infected the white population with a kindred ignorance." Roosevelt had read *The Time Machine*, and he rightly saw it as an anticipation of deepened class divisions hardened over time into an overworld and an underworld; he disagreed with Wells's pessimism. Discussing the significance of *The Time Machine*, Roosevelt became "gesticulatory," his voice "straining." Roosevelt, as Wells recalled it, considered Wells's notion that "America must presently lose the impetus of her ascent, that she and all mankind must culminate and pass" one day: " 'Suppose after all,' [TR] said slowly, 'that it should prove to be right, and it all ends in butterflies and morlocks. That doesn't matter now. The [reform] effort's real. It's worth going on with it. It's worth it—even then.' "

"My hero in the confused drama of human life is intelligence; intelligence inspired by constructive passion," Wells wrote in *The Future in America*. "There is a demigod imprisoned in mankind." Three years before Herbert Croly's pathbreaking book *The Promise of American Life*, in which Croly offered Roosevelt as the embodiment of a new liberal politics, Wells presented TR as a demigod incarnate, the very symbol of "the creative will in man." "His range of reading is amazing, and he has receptivity to the pitch of genius," Wells wrote of Roosevelt. Here was the man of the future—"traditions have no hold on him"—the very model of the philosopher-samurai, seemingly stepped out of one of his own novels. "I know of no other a tithe [tenth] so representative of the creative purpose, the goodwill in men as he."

The American thinkers who did the most to carve out the enduring assumptions and mental gestures that streamed into liberalism as an ideology were Herbert Croly, editor and co-founder of *The New Republic*, and Randolph Bourne, a spirited young prophet full of righteous anger. Croly had a slow-fire political piety, and Bourne a tendency to not so much live as burn intensely, but both argued eloquently in the tradition of John Stuart Mill and H.G. Wells for a secular priesthood that could Europeanize America. Their legacy not only endured; it thrives down to the present.

Herbert Croly, whose 1909 book *The Promise of American Life* was the first political manifesto of modern American liberalism, was admired by both Teddy and Franklin Roosevelt. His approach to liberalism, as his economically oriented colleague George Soule explained, was "more fundamental" than that of others who, like Croly, wanted to reshape public institutions. What Croly wanted was to remake American life "for the purpose of liberating a large quantity and higher quality of American manhood and womanhood," Soule wrote. "What was important was the process of liberation of the personality, not mere achievement of honest city government, regulation of monopolies, or better conditions for labor."

Croly and Bourne hoped for a re-founded regime that would break with the "monarchism" of a totemic Constitution. "Disinterested" intellectuals, as well as poet-leaders, experts, and social scientists such as themselves would lead the new regime. They saw such men and women as possessing a third eye that allowed them to see not only more of the world but also the world in its proper perspective. And if their talents were not to be wasted or frustrated, it was imperative to constrain the conventional and often corrupt politics of middle-class capitalists so that these far-seeing leaders might obtain the recognition and power that was their due.

Croly had little use for Hamilton's ideal of a commercial republic and even less for Jefferson's yeoman individualists; they were the bêtes noires of his philosophy. "To achieve a better future," he argued, Americans had to be "emancipate[d] from their past." He rejected American tradition, with its faith in the Constitution and its politics of parties and courts, and argued for rebuilding America's foundation on higher spiritual and political principles that would transcend traditional ideas of democracy and self-government. Like Wells, Croly called for centralized power that might be, he acknowledged, "injurious to certain aspects of traditional American democracy." But this was no great loss, because "the average American individual is morally and intellectually inadequate to serious and consistent conceptions of his responsibilities as a democrat." The "erroneous and misleading" democratic tradition, he concluded, "must yield before the march of a constructive national democracy" remodeled along French lines

Croly had studied in Paris and had "an addiction to French political philosophy," in the words of his friend, the literary critic Edmund Wilson. Croly, said Wilson, "considered his culture mainly French." Croly's aim was to restructure the Republic on a Francophile footing. His argument in *The Promise of American Life* and its successor, *Progressive Democracy* (1915), two books so tightly connected that Croly said he wished he had written them as one, is best described as a plan for achieving (Auguste) Comtian ends—that is, the worship of society—by Rousseauian means, i.e., a plebiscitary democracy led by enlightened experts. As Croly himself explained it, he was "applying ideas, long familiar to foreign political thinkers, to the subject matter of American life."

If liberals have a hard time understanding their own history, it's at least in part because they've so successfully avoided dealing with Herbert Croly—who he was and what he hoped to achieve. Croly's moralistic streak led his detractors to describe him as "Crolier than thou," but his was an unconventional kind of morality. He was born in 1869 to David Croly and Jane Cunningham Croly, both successful New York journalists. David Croly, a sexual reformer who believed that copulatory repression bred social disorder, was a founding member of the Church of Humanity, an institution dedicated to propagating the ideas of the French sociologist Auguste Comte. David Croly's wife, known professionally as "Jennie June," was a caustic critic of marriage and a leading feminist writer. Their son was among the first in America to be baptized into the Comtian faith. Comte, a utopian socialist of sorts, attributed the troubles of the modern world to the "spiritual disorganization of society." He wanted to deploy positivist science to restore the unity lost in the Protestant Reformation, and thus create a modern version of the "moral communism of medieval Christendom."

The young Herbert Croly was raised to be a prodigy, but he developed slowly. He left Harvard before graduating and went to work for the *Architectural Record*, during which time he wrote *Stately Homes in America from Colonial Times to the Present Day.* At the age of forty, he took the underlying themes of his architectural writing, the tension between the artist and the marketplace, and translated them into politics, in *The Promise of American Life*. The book sold poorly but propelled him onto the national stage, where he drew the interest of former president Theodore Roosevelt. Croly would influence TR, just as TR, whom Croly saw as an American Bismarck, had already influenced him.

Bismarck was much on Croly's mind. In *The Promise*, Croly, like John Stuart Mill, showed nothing but contempt for English liberalism. He saw it leading to "economic individualism . . . faith in compromise . . . [and a] dread of ideas." These had, he wrote, made "the English system a hopelessly confused bundle of semi-efficiency and semi-inefficiency." Croly much preferred the greater efficiency and, as he saw it, the greater equality of Germany, where "little by little the fertile seed of Bismarck's

Prussian patriotism grew into a semi-democratic nationalism." Its great virtue was organization: "In every direction, German activity was organized and placed under skilled professional leadership, while...each of these special lines of work was subordinated to its particular place in a comprehensive scheme of national economy. ... The German national organization means increased security, happiness and opportunity of development for the whole German people."

Liberals came to accept as a given Croly's insistence that, in America, the German path could be achieved only by using higher education to create the "skilled professional leadership" necessary to run society. Entrusting public affairs to this educated class would, Croly believed, have "a leavening effect on human nature." "Democracy must stand or fall on a platform of possible human perfectibility," he said. These were the words of a radical, not a reformer—a man who, like Marx and Comte, saw himself as leading humanity to a higher and more refined stage of civilization.

For Croly, businessmen and their allies—the jack-of-all-trades latter-day Jeffersonians—were blocking the path to the bright future he envisioned for the specialists of the rising professional classes. America's business culture, he warned, threatened individuality, because businessmen "have a way of becoming fundamentally very much alike," despite their differences. "Their individualities are forced into a common mold because the ultimate measure of the value of their work is the same, and is nothing but its results in cash. ... In so far as the economic motive prevails, individuality is not developed; it is stifled."

The flip side of Croly's hostility to self-interested businessmen was his adoration of the new class of American intellectuals and artists. This class had the virtue, he said, of having a "disinterested" take on public affairs, which allowed it to rise above the petty peculiarities of the marketplace and serve all of humanity, in the manner of Plato's guardians. Unfortunately, "the popular interest in Higher Education has not served to make Americans attach much importance to the advice of the highly educated man," Croly lamented. "He is less of a practical power in the U.S. than he is in any European country." Like H.G. Wells in England, Mussolini in Italy, and Lenin in Russia, Croly wanted the collective power of society put "at the service of its ablest members," who would take the lead roles in the drama of social re-creation.

Croly's Progressive-era audience was stirred by his insistence that the "ablest" deserved a more interesting world. "The opportunities, which during the past few years the reformers have enjoyed to make their personal lives more interesting, would be nothing compared to the opportunities for all sorts of stirring and responsible work, which would be demanded of individuals under the proposed plan for political and economic reorganization," he wrote in *The Promise.*

Croly concludes *The Promise* with the insistence that "the common citizen can become something of a saint and something of a hero, not by growing to heroic portions in his own person, but by the sincere and enthusiastic imitation of heroes and saints." This will depend, he argued in the book's final sentence, on "the ability of his exceptional fellow-countrymen to offer him acceptable examples of heroism and saintliness." Croly's critique of industrial-era inequality had by its conclusion become a call for, in his own words, the "creation of a political, economic, and social aristocracy."

In recent years, the terms "progressive" and "liberal" have become interchangeable. But while the Progressives and the founding fathers of liberalism shared a hostility to various groups—big-city political bosses, the immigrant masses, pharisaical plutocrats, and laggard legislatures—their sensibilities were fundamentally at odds. Wells and Croly sought transcendence; they looked to the creation of a new elite, a separate caste with the wisdom to lead society to social salvation by breaking with the conventions of middle-class Victorian morality. Progressivism, which embraced a conventional morality, sought social control over the unruly passions. It was a largely middle-class Protestant movement that wanted to outlaw alcohol, gambling, and prostitution. Broadly speaking, Progressives hoped to tame the big corporations and big-city political machines so as to restore the traditional promise of American life. The Progressives who were important in both the Republican and Democratic Parties were in the business of "moral uplift." They had no use for the saloon, sexuality, or socialism. In the words of President Theodore Roosevelt, they wanted to curb the power of big business so that the "worthy man" had the "chance to show the worth that is in him." Influenced by the social gospel, they aimed to diminish class divisions by outlawing child labor and instituting an income tax. They wanted to build what philosopher William James described as a "middle-class paradise."

After the 1912 election, the Progressives, led by a segregationist, Democrat Woodrow Wilson, placed their faith in pragmatic reason and the better natures of the American people. Expanded government, even if it skirted the limits of constitutionally permitted powers, they insisted, would serve as an efficacious engine of popular goodwill that could soften the harsh rigors of industrial capitalism. After the unfortunate interregnum of the 1920s, so the story goes, Progressivism, faced with the Great Depression, matured into the full-blown liberalism of the New Deal.

But that is not what happened. The first articulation of what we would today recognize as modern liberalism was shaped by the lyrical left of pre-WWI Greenwich Village and also by the split within the Progressive movement between those who supported American involvement in WWI and the philo-German opponents of the war.

For the Greenwich Villagers of 1915, H.G. Wells was a seer. The influential literary critic Van Wyck Brooks, who coined the terms "highbrow," "lowbrow," and "middlebrow" to demarcate the levels of taste in American life, was the first American to write a book on Wells. "Without doubt," wrote Brooks, "Wells has altered the air we breathe and made a conscious fact in many minds the excellence that resides in certain kinds of men and modes of living and odiousness that resides in others." Hope for the Wellsian future, Brooks argued, was to found in "the rudiments of a socialist state," which he located "in the Rockefeller Institute, the Carnegie and Russell Sage Foundations, the endowed universities and bureaus of research, and in the type of men they breed."

Village rebel Floyd Dell similarly found Wells to be a spiritual and political guide to the future. For Dell, Wells was a revelation:

> And suddenly there came into our minds the magnificent and well-nigh incredible conception of Change. … gigantic, miraculous change, an overwhelming of the old in ruin and an emergence of the new. Into our eternal and changeless world came H.G. Wells prophesying its ending,

> and the kingdom of heaven come on earth; the heavens shall be rolled up like a scroll, and all the familiar things of earth pass away utterly—so he seemed to cry out to our astounded ears.

Alongside Wells there arose Randolph Bourne, the first prophet of what in the 1960s would be called youth culture. Bourne came of age in the Greenwich Village of the pre-WWI years when the lyrical left was besotted with utopian ideas of a new revolutionary culture that would break down the barriers between art and politics. Bourne's "political discussions were actually lit by a spiritual viewpoint," explained his friend and fellow mystic Waldo Frank. "They took into account the content of the human soul, the individual souls, the values of *being*."

Bourne's premature death in 1918 from influenza at age thirty-two came as he reached the height of his fame. His scathing attacks on "Mr. Wilson's War" had already secured his political immortality. Bourne's anti-war writing would be repeatedly revived, first in the late 1930s and early 1940s, and again with tremendous force in the Vietnam War era; most recently he's been recast in the light of Foucault and postmodernism as an intellectual pioneer who introduced Nietzschean themes into American intellectual life. But unlike the Bourne of legend, the real man was never persecuted for his anti-war views and in fact was not anti-war as such; rather, in WWI he was anti-American and culturally philo-German. It was Bourne who pioneered the use of moral equivalence when, in a defense of Germany, he emphasized the parity between "the horrors of capitalistic peace at home" with the "horrors of war in Belgium."

Bourne, said his friend and biographer Van Wyck Brooks, wanted to "think emotions" and "feel ideas." The young prophet of multiculturalism established a number of conceptual tropes that took an unrelenting hold among liberals. They found in his writings their own irresolvable tensions and anomalies raised to a literary level.

Bourne was the ideologist of Youth, always with the capital Y, as source of wisdom. He asserted, by way of Nietzsche, that the older generation's puritanical calls for service and selflessness were in fact either empty rhetoric or a veiled version of selfishness in which good deeds were merely the basis for boasting and "the will to power." In his collection of essay published in 1913 as *Youth and Life*, he electrified his contemporaries by presenting Youth as an alternative to the Christian virtues. "The world has nothing to lose but its chains—and its own soul to gain," he wrote. "Youth…has no right to be humble. The ideals it forms will be the highest it will ever have, the insight the clearest, the ideas the most stimulating. . . . Youth's attitude is really the scientific attitude. . . . Our times give no check to the Radical tendencies of Youth." The goal of "my religion," he explained, was "the bringing of a fuller, richer life to more people on this earth. "Perpetual youth" would be "salvation."

Bourne wanted to enlist "a vast army of young men and women who felt a fluttering in their souls that call them to some great impersonal adventure." He envisioned a modernized version of the Catholic priest, "a new type of teacher-engineer-community worker," who could aestheticize society and redeem slovenly America. "I begin to wonder whether there aren't advantages in having administration of the State taken care of by a scientific body of men with a social sense, or perhaps an aesthetic-scientific idea of a desirable urban life," he wrote. "There really may be something in the German claim that this liberates energies for real freedom of thought."

His other cat's-paw was what he saw as the pre modern energies of the new immigrants from southern and eastern Europe not yet corrupted by capitalist modernity. He called for them to create a "Trans-National America"—in effect, to practice multiculturalism avant la lettre in order to free the country from the shackles of puritanical Protestant culture. In its place, he hoped for a "beloved community" in which the young would replace bourgeois individualism with an organic culture that encouraged people to flourish as individuals and yet absorbed them into a loving whole. Bourne would be read on some of the communes of the 1960s as the prophet of their founding.

Randolph Bourne, the pioneer of generational politics and an aestheticized society, was born in 1866 to a genteel middle-class Presbyterian family of Bloomfield, New Jersey, descended from Protestant ministers and lawyers. He entered the world in literally the worst manner possible, suffering from what he once described as a "terribly messy birth." Tuberculosis of the spine turned him into a dwarfed hunchback. His face was contorted, his ear misshapen, his breathing difficult and audible.

Yet he made his mark as a student at Columbia, where he studied with John Dewey, Franz Boas, and Charles Beard and was seen by his fellow students as already the equal of these giants. As an undergraduate, he published in *The Atlantic* and would soon become a staff writer at Croly's *New Republic*. He shared Croly's hopes for improving America's tastes by reshaping individual Americans in the collective image created by a great national project. Writing in a utopian vein similar to Croly's, Bourne explained:

> What the primitive man had easily, through the compactness of his society, and what every compact groups gets easily—the exaltation of the individual by concerted social expression of the common desires, ideas and ideals—we are reaching out for with great pain and striving . . . we are feeling for a complete social consciousness which must eventually raise the whole world to a kingdom of Heaven.

But while the Kingdom of Heaven was within reach, its prophets were mired in the muck of America, a land of "appalling slovenliness" and "ignorance." The urban masses, as Bourne saw them, were "without taste, without standards but those of the mob." The recent immigrants, once exposed to their new country's commercial culture, became, Bourne argued, "the flotsam and jetsam of American life, the downward undertow of our civilization with its leering cheapness and falseness of taste and spiritual outlook, the absence of mind and sincere feeling we see in our slovenly towns, our vapid moving pictures, our popular novels, and in the vacuous faces of crowds on the city street."

Bourne, his ideas already well developed, was an important part of New York's bohemian cultural and literary scene and a spokesman for youth when he won a fellowship in 1913 to tour Europe. Traveling in continental Europe on the eve of World War I, Bourne was awed by "the joyous masses" that have "evolved a folk-culture." His first stop was England, which "was always exasperating me and shocking my instincts," he wrote to a friend. With few exceptions, such as the suffragettes and the writings and personality of George Bernard Shaw, England's commonsense politics repelled him. Already alienated from the middle class of his native Bloomfield, he found in Britain the "hard inhumanity" and "crusted hypocrisy" he associated with Anglophile America.

France and Germany were another matter. Most Americans thought of Europe as old and decadent and America as holding out youthful promise; Bourne reversed those assumptions. "To cross the seas," he wrote, "and come upon my own enthusiasms and ideals vibrating with so intense a glow seemed an amazing fortune." He was drawn to *unanimisme*, a literary movement devoted to unearthing the French folk-consciousness that had been buried in France's cities. He admired the "group mind" that had been forged in French peasant culture and that resisted American-style modernity. Describing Paris, he said, "I soon felt an intellectual vivacity, a sincerity and candor, a tendency to think emotions and feel ideas that wiped out those facetiousnesses and puzzle-interests and sporting attitudes towards life that so got on one's nerves in England." To a friend he wrote, "The irony and vivacity of the French temperament delight me." Clearly enamored, he believed that, unlike in England, class distinctions barely existed in France.

He found reading Rousseau a revelation. Assessing Rousseau's arguments about the need for a General Will, Bourne exclaimed: "Yes, that is what I would have felt, done, said! I could not judge him and his work by those standards that the hopelessly moral and complacent English have imposed upon our American mind. It was a sort of moral bath; it cleared up for me a whole new democratic morality, and put the last touch upon the old English way of looking at the world in which I was brought up and which I had such a struggle to get rid of."

Bourne was also drawn to the French proto-fascist Maurice Barrès, who believed an all-encompassing nationalism should replace bourgeois individuality. In France, "the search for the *nationalisme intégral* of Barrès, the youth of today, one feels, are seeking the nourishing quality of...the richness of a common culture, which has a right to make traditionalism seem seductive and beautiful." Writing in *The Atlantic* in an article titled "Maurice Barrès and the Youth of France," he found in Barrès "a traditionalism from which all the blind, compressing forces of the social groups have been withdrawn, so that one feels only the nourishing influence of a rich common culture in which our individual souls are steeped." "This is a gospel to which one could give one's self with wistfulness and love!" he enthused. Bourne was drawn to Barrès's evocation of the " 'communion of saints'—the ideal collective life where the hunger of '*moi individuel*' is satisfied by the '*moi social*.' " In this glorious France, "the land and its dead" along with its "worshipers" would be "bound together in interwoven links of *amitiés*, a consciousness of a common background of living truth."

"The new national consciousness" of Barrès, he argued, was "not a mere chauvinism, but sounds deeper notes of genuine social reform at home." Bourne—whose most famous and enduring essay, "War Is the Health of the State," was a denunciation of American involvement in WWI—wholeheartedly approved of French preparations for war with Germany. He saw them as contributing to the health of the French state:

> The hard decivilizing life of the *caserne* [barracks] is accepted . . . as a necessary sacrifice against the threats of the foe to the east. Politically, a restlessness seems to be evident, a discontent with the feebleness and colorlessness of the republican state, and a curious drawing together of the extreme Left and the extreme Right, in an equal hatred . . . of the smug capitalism of the day—a *rapprochement* for the founding of the Great State, which shall bind the nation together in a sort of imperial democracy, ministering to the needs of the people and raising them to its ideals of splendor, honor, and national defense.

Drawn as he was to France, he found Germany even more captivating. Arriving in Germany just as the Kaiserreich ignited World War I, Bourne was in the Berlin crowd when Wilhelm II, speaking from his balcony, declared war. Bourne was enthralled by an entire nation in Kultural revolt against the values of Anglo-America Zivilization. "German ideals," he believed, were the only broad and captivating ones for his generation. He was moved by "the feel of their sheer heroic power" compared with the pale fare of the Anglo-Saxon world. "Whatever the outcome of the war," he insisted, anticipating Charles Lindbergh, "all the opposing countries will be forced to adopt German organization [and] German collectivism."

Although not drawn to German militarism, he compared Germany very favorably with "shabby and sordid" America and its "frowsy towns." He found that in Germany "war on squalor and ugliness was being waged on every hand," because "taste is, after all, the only morality." Taken by the beauty of German architecture and town planning, he anticipated the arguments made on behalf of the USSR in the 1930s: "The *Stadtbaurat* [head of municipal planning and building] went over for us the development of the city, and gave us considerable insight into the government, policy and spirit of a typical little German municipality. Undemocratic in political form, yet ultra-democratic in policy and spirit, scientific, impartial, giving the populace—who seemed to have no sense of being excluded from 'rights'—what they really wanted, far more truly than our democracies seem to be able to secure."

In America, he felt oppressed by the "blind compressing forces of conventionality" he had experienced in his New Jersey hometown. In America, he wrote, "social pressures warp and conventionalize and harden the personality," inhibiting truly creative people. American society was "one vast conspiracy for carving one into the kind of statue it likes." He preferred the "spirit" of "the open road, with the spirit always traveling . . . always escaping the pressures that threaten its integrity."

Bourne occasionally spoke of the open road, which invokes individuality, but he also spoke and wrote often of his hunger to be swept up in something larger than himself, of "vibrating in camaraderie with the beloved society, given new powers, lifted out of himself, transformed through the enriching stimulation of his fellows—the communion of saints—into a new being, spiritual because no longer individual."

Enthralled by Germany, he bracketed its militarism as being of limited importance; after all, Germany offered its people the possibility of being absorbed into an oceanic spirit of oneness. In 1915, a few months after German submarines sank the *Lusitania*, a British passenger ship with a large number of Americans on board, Bourne opened an article for *The New Republic* with the following words: "German ideals are the only broad and seizing ones that have lived in the world in our generation. Mad and barbarous as they must seem to minds accustomed to much thinner and nicer fare, one must have withdrawn far within a provincial Anglo-Saxon shell not to feel the thrill of their sheer heroic power."

While praising the imposing tastefulness of German sculpture and town planning, with its "clean, massive and soaring lines," he wrote that "the cosmic heroisms of the German ideal fall . . . strangely on our ears." "It comes to us as a shock to find a people who believe in national spirits which are heroic, and through the German spirit, in a world-spirit; for the 'world spirit,' says one of their professor-warriors, 'speaks today through Germany.'" In fighting Germania, the British and the French, stuck in the aesthetic status quo, were rejecting "the most overwhelming and fecund group of ideas and forms in the modern world, ideas which draw all nations after them in imitation, while the nations pour out their lifeblood to crush the generator."

Bourne identified deeply with Germany, which he saw as a victim, not unlike himself, of those with inferior taste who were waging war on superior beings. Just as he saw himself as a victim of his traumatic birth and uncomprehending bourgeois family, so Germany in his eyes had become a victim of its troubled origins and philistine neighbors. "It has been the tragedy of the German spirit that [it] has had to dwell in a perverse universe, so that what from within looked always like the most beneficent working-out of a world-idea seemed from without like the very running-amuck of voracious power." He was taken by the promise of a German victory:

> From the prospect of German hegemony, we can at least foreshadow the Pax Romana. With its lulling truce, its shelter for the recuperation of the world, its enforced learning of the ideas of order, neatness, prosperity to which the British and Latin civilizations seem as yet relatively indifferent. A Germanized England or France would be an England or France immensely furbished, immensely modernized. Germanization would be the rough massage that would bring the red blood to the surface and a new glow of health to these two nations.

"The world," he went on, explaining why taste was morality, "will never be safe until it has learned a high and brave materiality that will demand cleanliness, order, comfort, beauty, and welfare as the indispensable soil in which the virtues of mutual respect, intelligence, and good will may flourish."

Like his fellow Greenwich Village lyrical leftist Max Eastman, Bourne had little interest in either Germany's political culture or the conduct of the war. Eastman spoke approvingly of Germany's "state-socialism attended by paternal discipline," and he admired the "candor" of Germany's expression of its war aims, which, he thought, reflected the authenticity of German culture. The German attempts to encourage a Mexican invasion of the United States; German sabotage in America, such as the explosion of Black Tom Island in New York Harbor; and Germany's pursuit of unrestricted submarine warfare—these were beneath concern for both Eastman and Bourne.

After three years of war, *The New Republic* reversed course and supported American entry into the conflict, in part on the grounds that American involvement could help stem German militarism and also accelerate domestic reform. The reversal led Bourne to break with Croly and his mentor John Dewey, as well as with Walter Lippmann of *The New Republic*. In Bourne's influential essays "War and the Intellectuals" and "War Is the Health of the State," written in 1917 for *Seven Arts*, he lamented that the entire pre-war period had been "spiritually wasted." "The real enemy" he insisted, as he had not when in France and Germany, "was war itself." He said little of Wilson except to argue cursorily that he could have used American powers to "force a just peace." And he had few disagreements with Wilson's war aims except to argue that democracy could have been expanded peacefully.

He decried "a war deliberately made by intellectuals," referring not to the Nietzschean strand in Germany that he much admired, but to American intellectuals. Equating Germany's Prussian political life with that of the U.S., he compared pro-war writers at *The New Republic* to the Prussian general and theorist of war Friedrich von Bernhardi. His old friends at *The New Republic* had betrayed their calling, he insisted, by bowing before the British like "colonials" in thrall to their masters. Appealing to the instincts of "the herd," they had incited the "sluggish masses" to go to war. He seems never to have asked why unconventional souls such as Thorsten Veblen, his good friend Van Wyck Brooks, and Upton Sinclair felt sufficiently menaced by Prussian militarism to reluctantly support, as did Wilson, American entry into the war.

When Bourne succumbed to influenza in 1918, he was deeply mourned by his many friends. Brooks remembered his "quick bird like steps and the long, black student's cape he had brought back with him from Paris." In his celebrated novel *1919*, John Dos Passos wrote that if ever a man had a ghost, it was Bourne: "A tiny twisted unscared ghost in a black cloak hopping along the grimy old brick and brownstone streets still left in downtown New York, crying out in a shrill soundless giggle: *War is the health of the state*."

But that wasn't quite right. The American state shrank rapidly under Wilson's successor, Republican Warren G. Harding. The new president had the good graces to free Socialist Eugene Debs, whom Woodrow Wilson had jailed for vocally opposing the war. Harding's slogan was "not nostrums but normality." The main stem of the GOP, historian Morton Keller writes, "sloughed off its older support for active government and redefined itself as the party of laissez-faire and the old America."

While Bourne was dying, H.L. Mencken, described by the *New York Times* as "the premier social critic of the first half of the twentieth century," was coming to fame as a bitter German-American critic of "Mr. Wilson's War." At the height of his influence in the 1920s, Mencken's reputation fattened on the inanities of Prohibition, blue-nosed book-banning, and the Ku Klux Klan, all of which he saw as works of the "boobus Americanus." His broadsides against Prohibition, posturing preachers, and anti-evolutionists made him a hero to generations of liberals and college students. But his true quarry was American democracy and the American people, whom he defined as a "rabble of ignorant peasants."

Henry Louis Mencken, born in 1880 to a moderately successful German-American cigar manufacturer, adopted his father's prejudices. Father and son disdained do-gooders, socialists, and Democrats. Terry Teachout, in his book on Mencken, *The Skeptic,* quotes Mencken's description of his father: "All mankind, in his sight, was divided into two great races: those who paid their bills, and those who didn't. The former were virtuous, despite any evidence that could be adduced to the contrary; the latter were unanimously and incurably scoundrels." His father's death freed the young Henry, age eighteen, to become a newspaperman.

A self-educated man, Mencken developed himself by writing books, at the age of twenty-six and twenty-seven, on the plays of George Bernard Shaw and the philosophy of Friedrich Nietzsche, his two chief intellectual influences. His was the first book on Nietzsche published in America. Neither book was successful, but both represented the first flowerings of an audacious talent.

Mencken's style drew heavily on Shaw, particularly his propensity for "stating the obvious in terms of the scandalous." Mencken, the confident son of a burgher, was little interested in Shaw's Fabian Socialism, but he was enthralled by the Irishman's insistence on "the selective breeding of man." In his 1903 play *Man and Superman*, Shaw wrote that "we must eliminate the Yahoo, or his vote will wreck the Commonwealth," and these words became a signpost of Mencken's career. In a sense, each writer paved the way for the other. Thanks in part to Mencken, Shaw became a popular playwright in America even before he established himself as a fixture on the London stage. *The Devil's Disciple* and *Caesar and Cleopatra* were first presented in America, not England.

Shaw the transplanted Irishman and Mencken the displaced Deutschlander shared an abiding hatred of Anglo-American culture. And like the Napoleonists (the British radical Whigs who hoped for a Napoleonic victory that could clear out the detritus of the English aristocracy), Mencken and Shaw strongly admired powerful rulers who could defeat democracy in the name of a more orderly and culturally hierarchical set of social arrangements.

The Americans learned from Shaw how to be narrow-minded in a witty, superior way. Shaw pioneered the path whereby an author could simultaneously insult the middle class and yet be embraced by it on the grounds that receptivity to criticism signified someone who was a cut above. Both men mined the ore that was usually the moral strength but sometime the self-defeating vulnerability of Western culture: its capacity for self-criticism.

The content of Mencken's writings drew on Shaw's Social Darwinist, Nietzschean, and eugenicist thinking. "Through Shaw," Mencken later wrote, " I found my vocation at last." In the introduction to his essays on Shaw's plays, Mencken wrote, "Darwin made this war between the faithful and the scoffers the chief concern of the time, and the sham-smashing that is going on might be compared to the crusades that engrossed the world in the middle ages." And Shaw was "the premier scoffer and dominant heretic of the day," declared Mencken. For all the differences between the meat-eating, beer-drinking Mencken and the asexual, anti-vaccine, vegetarian teetotaler Shaw, they were both, acknowledged the American, "working the same side of the street." Both men rose to the height of their influence in the midst of the carnage of World War I. Shaw as a pacifist (for the time being) and Mencken as paladin of free speech became icons of opposition to conventional Anglo-American values.

Mencken had genuine cause for bitterness during World War I, when the excesses of zealous Americanism left him fearful for the safety of his family. But while Mencken was touting the genius of Teutonic militarism,

German saboteurs blew up the munitions depot at Black Tom Island off Manhattan. That strike, until 9/11 the most violent action by a hostile force in the history of New York City, caused $20 million (in 1916 dollars) of damage, sinking the peninsula and its contents into the sea. The Kaiser's plans to invade New York Harbor and his plot to bring Mexico into the war against the United States never came off, but not from a lack of interest.

Mencken's World War I writings on behalf of imperial Germany have been largely forgotten. Opposed to American intervention on the side of the Allies in the Great War, Mencken had no objection to war per se. Drawing on Nietzsche's notion of the "will to power," he wrote: "War is a good thing, because it is honest, it admits the central fact of human nature. . . . A nation too long at peace becomes a sort of gigantic old maid." What he opposed were British, and then American, efforts at defeating German militarism.

The war, notes Mencken biographer Fred Hobson, "focused his thoughts" and created a clear position. Mencken explained:

> I, too, like the leaders of Germany, had grave doubts about democracy. . . . It suddenly dawned on me, somewhat to my surprise, that the whole body of doctrine that I had been preaching was fundamentally anti–Anglo Saxon, and that if I had any spiritual home at all, it must be in the land of my ancestors. When World War I actually started, I began forthwith to whoop for the Kaiser, and I kept up that whooping so long as there was any free speech left.

This wasn't a brief episode, but the very core of Mencken's political being. He proudly proclaimed in his columns for the *Baltimore Sun* papers that in the battle between autocracy and democracy, he wanted to see democracy go down. Mencken was enamored not only of the Kaiser's autocratic rule but also with "the whole war machine." He mocked Allied outrage over German killings of Belgian civilians, as well as the sinking of the *Lusitania*, which brought the death of 124 Americans. Mencken advised Theodore Dreiser, a fellow German American: "There can never be any compromise in future men of German blood and the common run of 'good,' 'right thinking' Americans. We must stand against them forever, and do what damage we can do to them, and to their tin-pot democracy."

During the course of the war, he was censored by the *Sun* papers but wrote three revealing articles for *The Atlantic*. The first, "The Mailed Fist and Its Prophet," celebrated Nietzsche as the inspiration for the new Germany, which was "contemptuous of weakness." Germany was a "hard" nation with no patience for politics because it was governed by the superior men of its "superbly efficient ruling caste," he wrote admiringly, adding: "Germany becomes Nietzsche; Nietzsche becomes Germany." Mencken approvingly quoted Nietzsche to the effect that "the weak and the botched must perish. . . . *I tell you that a good war hallows every cause.*"

The second *Atlantic* article, based on Mencken's own reporting from the Eastern Front in 1917, was a piece of hero worship that exalted General Erich Ludendorff as Germany's "national messiah." Mencken treasured the Kaiser, but he thought Ludendorff was worth "forty kaisers" and was the man to lead German *Kultur* in its total war against Anglo-Saxon civilization. According to Mencken, the general's greatness revealed itself in the way that he had stamped out people's individuality so that "the whole energy of the German people [could] be concentrated on the war."

The third, and most intriguing, essay—"After Germany's Conquest of the United States"—talked about the benefits to America of being ruled by the hard men of a superior *Kultur*. Known only because of the exchange of letters between Mencken and the editor of *The Atlantic*, the article was withdrawn and never published. Interestingly, despite Mencken's extraordinary efforts to document his own life, the manuscript, according to Vincent Fitzpatrick, curator of the Mencken collection, cannot be found. Mencken's reputation, it seems, was saved by wartime self-censorship—in Boston, home of *The Atlantic*.

CHAPTER 2

★ ★ ★

1919: Betrayal and the Birth of Modern Liberalism

The years before the U.S. entered World War I were a golden age for American utopian reformers. Known as the Progressive era, they were "the years of Great Expectation when the Millennium, Woodrovian fostered, seemed just around the corner," wrote the young reformer John Chamberlain. Speaking of his fellow young intellectuals, Lewis Mumford exclaimed: "There was scarcely one who did not assume that mankind either was permanently good or might sooner or later reach such a state of universal beatitude."

By 1919, the sweet melody of hope had been replaced among writers and intellectuals by the anger and resentment born of a cataclysmic war, a failed peace, and a country wracked by what came to be known as the Red Scare. Hope survived for some, however, in the form of the Bolshevik Revolution. These were the conditions under which the Wilson-led Progressives of 1916, preaching social redemption for all, were reborn as the liberals of 1919, now suffused with scorn not only for President Wilson but also for American society.

Modern state-oriented liberalism, so the standard tale goes, was the inevitable extension of the pre–World War I tradition of Progressivism. But this is true only in a limited sense. The economic mobilization of WWI did provide the administrative model for the early years of the

New Deal. But culturally, socially, and politically, liberalism represented a sharp break from Progressivism.

Progressivism was a middle-class Protestant movement that hoped to adapt to the strains of big corporations and big-city political machines in order to restore the traditional promise of American life. The Progressives, who were important in both the Republican and Democratic Parties, were in the business of moral reform. They were largely middle-class Victorians committed to the purification of politics, which they hoped to achieve by remolding the country's polyglot population into a unified whole. Progressivism reached its apogee during WWI when its advocates won Prohibition and women's suffrage while shutting down brothels and imposing "one hundred percent Americanism."

In the standard accounts of American liberalism, both left and right argue that after the 1920s, Progressivism faced the Great Depression and as a result matured into the fully flowered liberalism of the New Deal. As I suggested in the previous chapter, this is fundamentally mistaken. While "winning the war abroad," the Progressives "lost their war at home," notes historian Michael McGerr. "Amid race riots, strikes, high inflation, and a frenzied Red Scare, Americans turned against the Progressive blueprint for the nation. The climax of Progressivism, World War I, was also its death knell." Modern Republicanism—as incarnated in the 1920s by Presidents Harding, Coolidge, and Hoover—and modern liberalism were both reactions to the excesses of Progressivism.

Modern liberalism was born of discontinuity, a rejection of Progressivism—a wrenching betrayal and a shift in sensibility so profound that it still resonates today. More precisely, the cultural tone of modern liberalism was, in significant measure, set by a political love affair gone horribly wrong between Woodrow Wilson and a liberal left unable to grapple with the realities of power politics. For Progressives, reformers, and Socialists, the years from 1918 through 1920 were traumatic. During the presidential election of 1916, many leftists had embraced Woodrow Wilson as a thaumaturgical leader of near messianic promise, but in the wake of repression at home and revolution and diplomatic disappointment abroad, he came to be seen as a Judas, and his numinous rhetoric was despised as mere mummery.

For the ardent Progressive Frederick Howe, who had been Wilson's Commissioner of Immigration, the pre-war promise of the benign state built on reasoned reform had turned to ashes. "I hated," he wrote, "the new state that had arisen" from the war. "I hated its brutalities, its ignorance, its unpatriotic patriotism that made profit from our sacrifices and used it to suppress criticism of its acts. . . . I wanted to protest against the destruction of my government, my democracy, my America." As part of his protest, the thoroughly alienated Howe distanced himself from Progressivism. Liberals were those Progressives who had renamed themselves so as to repudiate Wilson. "The word *liberalism*," wrote Walter Lippmann in 1919, "was introduced into the jargon of American politics by that group who were Progressives in 1912 and Wilson Democrats from 1916 to 1918." The new liberalism was a decisive cultural break with Wilson and Progressivism. While the Progressives had been inspired by a faith in democratic reforms as a salve for the wounds of both industrial civilization and power politics, liberals saw the American democratic ethos as a danger to freedom at home and abroad.

Wilson, a devout Presbyterian, was the first—and until President Obama the only—president to have systematically studied socialism. In 1887, as a young man, he responded to the growth of vast industrial monopolies that threatened individual freedom with this argument:

> It is clear that in fundamental theory socialism and democracy are almost if not quite one and the same. They both rest at bottom upon the absolute right of the community to determine its own destiny and that of its members. Men as communities are supreme over men as individuals.

In the midst of the 1912 presidential race, Wilson reiterated his sense of the kinship between democracy, which he saw as having roots in Christianity and socialism: "When you do socialism justice," he said, "it is hardly different from the heart of Christianity itself." In 1916, Wilson, a former college professor, not only brushed aside intense opposition to make the unprecedented appointments of two pro-labor-union justices to the Supreme Court, but he also backed the railroad workers in their fight for an eight-hour day. In addition he imposed a surtax on the wealthy, which earned him the support of prominent Socialists such as Upton Sinclair and Helen Keller.

To the lyrical left of Greenwich Village, Wilson's 1916 campaign slogan, "He kept us out of war," opened the way for the emergence of a more vibrant American culture. With talk of a "New Renaissance" in the background, Villager Floyd Dell spoke of an "exalted present pregnant with possibilities." For Dell and his friends Randolph Bourne and Max Eastman, the war in Europe seemed far away. For the moment, they were imbued with an impregnable optimism. "It was," said Dell, "our future."

The administration's critique of European power politics and its talk of the need for international law gave pacifist Jane Addams "unlimited faith in the president." When Meyer London, the anti-war Socialist congressman from New York's Lower East Side, and Socialist Party leader Morris Hillquit visited the White House to talk about the prospects for peace in Europe, they came away concluding, "[Wilson's] sympathies are entirely with us." Similarly, as Thomas Knock recounts in his book *To End All Wars*, after visiting the White House, the leaders of the American Union Against Militarism left feeling that "the President had taken us into his bosom." Wilson, they noted, facing increased pressure to enter the war, "always referred to the Union Against Militarism as though he were a member of it" and talked about how "we" had to lay out a case for creating "a family of nations."

The mutual courtship between Wilson and the leftists flourished during the hard-fought 1916 presidential election. In his campaign for reelection, Wilson faced a Republican Party that had recovered from its 1912 split between Teddy Roosevelt's breakaway Bull Moose Progressives and the party's anti-reform regulars; the revitalized GOP had coalesced around Supreme Court Justice Charles Evan Hughes. In the midst of the war in Europe, Wilson scraped out a victory by bringing into his "peace camp" sizable numbers of those who had supported TR's intensely moralistic Bull Moosers (who admired Germany's proto-welfare state), as well as Eugene Debs's Socialists.

When Wilson gave his "peace without victory" speech in January 1917, proposing a democratic and anti-imperialist path out of the brambles of bloodshed, the revolutionary leftist Eastman was "enraptured." In the next fifteen months, the faith of Eastman and the Progressives seemed well justified. But Germany's declaration of unrestricted submarine warfare and the public revelation of the Kaiser's plans for an alliance with Mexico to conquer the Southwest pushed the country toward war. Most Progressives backed America's entry. The Progressive animus toward corrupt and overmighty party bosses and autocratic monarchists was, notes historian Morton Keller, "readily transferred to an overbearing Kaiser and his war machine as a continuation of the fight against tyranny at home." Reforms at home and abroad were melded, as when *The New Republic*'s Walter Lippmann warned, "We shall call that man un-American and no patriot who prates of liberty in Europe and resists it as home.

Not even America's reluctant entry into WWI in April of 1917 sundered Wilson's strong ties with the largely anti-war left. In the very speech in which he had asked for a congressional declaration of war, Wilson welcomed the February Revolution of 1917 in Russia, which had overthrown the czar and put the Socialist Alexander Kerensky in power. The American president effusively, if inaccurately, described the Russian Revolution as the fulfillment of the Russian people's long struggle for democracy. The revolution, explained Secretary of State Robert Lansing, "had removed the one objection to affirming that the European War was a war between Democracy and [Prussian] Absolutism."

With American entry, Wilson, as always of two minds, made a point of keeping U.S. forces strictly under American command, which rankled the British and the French, whom he regarded as imperialists. He insisted on referring to the U.S. not as an ally of England and France but rather as an "Associated Power." Wilson, like the isolationists, didn't want to get tangled in Europe's affairs, noted Walter Weyl of *The New Republic*; rather, he wanted to rise above them and impose a new vision from on high.

Eight months later, shortly after Lenin overthrew Kerensky, Wilson expressed his ambivalence toward Bolshevism, exclaiming, "My heart is with them, but my mind has a contempt for them." Conceptually, Wilson saw Bolshevism as a legitimate response to economic inequality, notes historian Georg Schild. In practice, as an alternative to capitalism, he found it both unworkable and unacceptably autocratic.

"The Fourteen Points, [Wilson's] message of good luck to the 'republic of labor unions' in Russia and his warning to the Allied powers that their treatment of Bolshevik Russia would be the 'acid test' of their 'good will . . . intelligence, and unselfish sympathy': These moves were immensely impressive to us," explained Max Eastman, speaking for many leftists and Progressives. This was the extraordinary moment when Russia's War Commissar Leon Trotsky, referring to Wilson, coined the now famous concept of the "fellow traveler." The metaphor was based on Trotsky's belief that the American president and the Bolsheviks shared a critique of European imperialism; both the newly Soviet Russia and a reformed, less capitalist U.S., in Trotsky's view, were travelling on parallel tracks into a brighter future.

While Wilson increasingly spoke of an international comity between nations, comity between not-so-assimilated ethnic groups in the U.S. was breaking down. The German aggressions in eastern Europe produced pitched battles between Germans and Slavs in the streets of Chicago. At the same time, nearly a half million Germans in America returned to fight for the fatherland. Charles John Hexamer, president of the National German-American Alliance, financed in part by the German government, urged Germans in the U.S. to maintain their separate identity so they wouldn't "descend to the level of an inferior culture."

The most important example of German sabotage was the spectacular explosion on Black Tom Island in the summer of 1916, which shook a sizable swath of New York City and New Jersey; the force was the equivalent of an earthquake measuring 5.5 on the Richter scale. It shattered windows in Times Square, and people as far away as Philadelphia felt the blast. The man-made peninsula, situated in the mouth of New York Harbor, was a key storage and shipping point for munitions sales to the British and French. The peninsula sank into the sea as seven were killed and the Statue of Liberty was damaged. After the attack, President Roosevelt denounced Germany's supporters in America as "creatures" of "disloyalty and anarchy [who] must be crushed."

The American entrance into the war triggered hysteria, one result of which was the Sedition Act of 1918. The legislation was so broad in its assessment of what constituted a danger that it allowed violators to be sent to prison for ten years for saying that they preferred the Kaiser to President Wilson. Others were jailed for mocking salesmen who sold Liberty Bonds to support the war. Most famously, Socialist leader Eugene Debs was jailed for criticizing conscription. The disparity between Wilson's call for extending liberty abroad and his suppression of liberty at home became a running wound for disenchanted Progressives.

Wilson placed George Creel, a journalist and Socialist who had strongly supported child-labor laws and women's suffrage, in charge of the Committee for Pubic Information, an agency intended to sustain morale during wartime. But the committee, which Creel described as "the world's greatest adventure in advertising," wildly overshot its mark. Creel wanted "no mere surface unity, but a passionate belief in the justice of America's cause that should weld the people of the United States into one white-hot mass instinct with fraternity, devotion, courage, and deathless determination."

Everything German, from Beethoven to sauerkraut to teaching the German language, was barred. When black leaders protested the federal failure to respond to the wave of lynching that accompanied the war, they were accused of aiding the German enemy by criticizing the U.S. The Justice Department and the attorney general went so far as to encourage loyal vigilantism. The American Protective League (APL), a quarter-of-a-million-strong nativist organization, obtained semi-official status in order to spy on those suspected of disloyalty. The League also went out of its way to protect the national interest by breaking up strikes while branding its critics Reds.

Wilson, responding to the excesses of the American Protective League, exclaimed, "I'd rather the blamed place should be blown up than persecute innocent people." Yet Wilson also declared, "Woe be to the man or group of men that seeks to stand in our way." Despite misgivings about the APL, Wilson deferred to the judgment of Attorney General Thomas Gregory and refused to restrain the group's vigilantism. Only after the armistice ended the war in November of 1918 did Wilson, heeding the advice of incoming Attorney General A. Mitchell Palmer, move to end government cooperation with the APL.

The armistice largely ended the fighting in Europe, but it opened a new chapter in the hostilities at home. In America, fear of the Germans was seamlessly succeeded by the Red Scare. The Bolsheviks' effectively unconditional surrender to the Germans in March of 1918 had created a cat's cradle of anti-Communist fears that intertwined with hostility to the Huns. With the Soviet surrender at Brest-Litovsk, Germany won control of the Baltic states (Poland, Belarus, and the Ukraine), with their attendant coal and oil resources, freeing the Kaiser's army to focus on the Western Front with deadly effect. In this context, Lenin's return to Russia in April 1917 by way of a sealed railroad car supplied by Berlin was seen as proof, and not only by conspiracists, that the Bolshevik leader was a German agent.

Progressives and leftists, counseled by Raymond Robbins, who had worked for Wilson in 1912 and served as an unofficial ambassador to the Bolsheviks, adopted a counter-conspiracy, echoes of which persist to this day. Robbins, smitten by Bolshevism, wrote to Lenin, "It has been my eager desire . . . to be of some use in interpreting this new democracy to the people of America." Robbins also mistakenly blamed the U.S. for forcing Lenin to agree to Germany's harsh terms at Brest-Litovsk. During the next few years, explains historian Peter Filene, Robbins's efforts shaped the opinions of a vast circle of American Progressives. The Progressives were enraged when Wilson succumbed to pressure from the French and the English, both suffering massive casualties on the Western Front, and gave half-hearted American military support to a campaign that tried to force the Bolsheviks back into the war. Most Americans accused the Bolsheviks of betrayal, in their abject surrender to the Germans, but the Progressives, Filene notes, saw this "betrayal," the American intervention, as an American perfidy.

Here too, Wilson, juggling principle and practicality, proved strikingly inconstant. In the words of historian Georg Schild: "The Wilson who agreed to the Allied intervention [against the Soviets] in the summer of 1918" and the Wilson who "one year later at the Paris Peace Conference" helped save the Soviet Union by insisting that the Germans relinquish their conquests on the Eastern Front "almost seemed like two different people." Wilson the Progressive went to the Paris Peace Conference of 1919 with the understanding that "we are running a race with Bolshevism and the world is on fire." "From the eastern border of France all the way through Asia to the Sea of Japan," notes historian Anthony Read, "not a single pre-war government remained in power." From Berlin to Seattle, strikes and in some cases pro-Bolshevik revolutionary movements seemed like the wave of the future. Comintern chief Zinoviev confidently predicted, "In a year's time, the whole of Europe will be Communist." The leaders looking to remake the world at Versailles were confounded by Bolshevism; they didn't know exactly what it was, much less how to contain it.

The leaders gathered at Versailles, notes Read, saw themselves as men dancing on a live volcano that had destroyed the old Europe and was threatening continued eruptions. Harry Kessler, an Anglo-German count and a Soviet sympathizer, captured the scene: "The wave of Bolshevism surging in from the East resembles somewhat the invasion by Islam in the seventh century," he wrote. "Fanaticism and power in the service of a nebulous fresh hope are faced, far and wide, by nothing more than the fragments of old ideologies. The banner of the prophets waves at the head of Lenin's armies too." Faced with the Soviet challenge, Wilson, who came bearing the new ideology of universal democracy, floated the idea that the Bolsheviks should be invited to the Paris Peace Conference. Churchill, who saw in Communism something akin to "legalized sodomy," blocked the suggestion. Wilson the Progressive took a different tact: "War won't defeat Bolshevism, food will," he said. Capitalism had to reform itself, he argued, to stave off Bolshevik barbarism.

Wilson's efforts to reconstruct Europe largely failed, not only because the U.S. declined to join the League of Nations, but more significantly because the task at hand was impossible; what the war had sundered could not be put back together. Many former Wilson supporters were angry and disillusioned with the meager fruits of a war that had failed to make the world safe for democracy. But people across the political spectrum shared those feelings widely. Those who were soon to call themselves liberals were particularly incensed by wartime conscription, the repression of civil liberties, Prohibition, and the overwrought fears of Bolshevism in America.

In 1918, with war still raging, the unions, emboldened by a surge in membership and squeezed by an inflation-borne decline in living standards, engaged in a wave of strikes, some of which were forcibly repressed by Pinkerton detectives, the APL, and local police forces. The walkouts led by the revolutionary Industrial Workers of the World, well known for work sabotage, seemed particularly ominous. The IWW, which sometimes called itself "Lenin's advanced guard," was led in part by "Big" Bill Haywood, who would soon be deported to the USSR. At the end of the year, in the wake of the armistice, the mayor of New York City, John Hylan, banned the Socialist red flag at public gatherings. Shortly thereafter, 500 soldiers and sailors broke up a Socialist rally at Madison Square Garden. The bad blood endured. In a November 11, 1919, celebration of the first anniversary of the war's end, American Legionnaires and members of the IWW, (known as "Wobblies") clashed in Centralia, Washington. Six Wobblies were killed in the name of combating the Red Scare.

Communism was as yet ill defined in America. Wilson himself thought it might be merely a temporary way station on the road to liberal democracy. But every strike, confrontation, and racial incident was taken, on both left and right, as a manifestation of Bolshevism. Every challenge to the existing social order, no matter how justified, was attributed to the Red Scare. The new so-called African-American uppityness, meaning insufficient deference to whites, was attributed to homegrown Bolshevism. "Uppityness" was met with a wave of lynching and a resurgence of the KKK. White attacks on blacks set off riots in Chicago and Washington that required federal troops to suppress.

The Red Scare intensified in June of 1919 when Attorney General A. Mitchell Palmer was nearly killed by a terrorist bomb planted in his Georgetown home. Bombs went off in seven other cities that same night. The bombers were probably, notes historian Beverley Gage, from the Galleanisti group of Italian anarchists that included the as yet unknown Nicola Sacco and Bartolomeo Vanzetti. But the attacks were attributed to their conceptual cousins, the Russian Bolsheviki. The attacks reignited the intense nationalism of the war years and stoked a renewed hysteria. Palmer, who subsequently claimed to have a list of 60,000 subversives, engaged in a series of warrantless raids aimed at capturing the mostly immigrant "red radicals," some of whom were jailed or shipped back to Russia. In the process, Palmer, with no reproach from Wilson, widely trampled on civil liberties and harassed the innocent as well as the likely guilty.

The pre-war Progressives had hoped to transcend a politics based on ethnic and regional peculiarities to forge a reformed national polity grounded in Protestant moral uplift. But the attempt to forge national unity in order to prosecute the war heightened the ethnic tensions wrought by mass immigration. One of the arguments put forth for enacting Prohibition in 1919 was that it might help Americanize the booze-swilling immigrants who were in need of moral improvement through assimilation.

Progressives, who had broadly supported Prohibition, saw it primarily as a means to protect working-class families from the economic depredations of drink. But the newly minted liberals were infuriated by what they saw as cultural continuation of wartime repression. "Like most sensible people," shouted liberal Harold Stearns, "I regard Prohibition as an outrage and a direct invitation to revolution."

An aggressive nationalism and an accelerated Americanization became political twins. Both demanded something that, with the partial exception of the Civil War North, had never existed before: a coherent, irrefragable governmental power. In Europe, war had become intertwined with revolution; in the U.S., the war and the Bolshevik challenge called up the seemingly un-American concept of a General Will, a 100 percent Americanism that brooked no opposition.

Palmer had hoped to ride the Red Scare into the White House. But within a year, the amiable Republican Warren G. Harding of Ohio was ensconced in Washington, along with his card-playing cronies. The crusade that had ended abroad finally wound down at home. Harding, who in a conciliatory gesture freed Socialist leader Eugene Debs from jail, championed what he dubbed a return to "normalcy" in public life.

The silver lining of the wartime repression was that it laid the groundwork for the modern interpretation of the First Amendment, which would eventually extend free-speech rights to individuals harassed by not only federal authorities but state and local government as well. The expansion of free speech evolved from the 1918 case of Jacob Abrams, a Russian-Jewish immigrant bookbinder. Abrams had printed anarchist leaflets in English and Yiddish and distributed them on New York's Lower East Side by dropping them from buildings. The pamphlets bitterly denounced Wilson's half-hearted attempts to cooperate with England and France in pressuring Russia back into the war against Germany. Zealous prosecutors saw the leaflets as violations of the Espionage Act, which made it a crime to undermine American wartime policy. Abrams was sentenced to twenty years in jail and eventually deported.

In 1919, the Supreme Court upheld Abrams's conviction. But in his dissent, Supreme Court Justice Oliver Wendell Holmes laid the basis for the modern First Amendment. Holmes found that "speech that produces or is intended to produce a clear and *imminent* danger" can be prosecuted. But he saw no such "imminent" danger in Abrams's leaflets, which he described as "silly" writings by an "unknown man." More important was Holmes's underlying reasoning. Like the British philosopher John Stuart Mill, Holmes determined that a maximum of free speech was essential for a successful society. America, he reasoned, had an interest in discovering truth available only through "the marketplace of ideas," where proponents of competing viewpoints must strive to make their best case.

The spirit of Justice Holmes, with his emphasis on a carefully calibrated consideration of conflicting imperatives, has not always been in evidence on the part of historians. In the years since the Red Scare, most left and liberal chroniclers of that period, whether due to inadequate imagination or parochial political motives, have simply argued away the existence of Communists and anarchists who sought to inflict real harm upon America. Sacco, based on the ballistic evidence, was most certainly guilty; and Vanzetti was convicted of an earlier violent crime; in the hands of sympathizers, both were turned into injured innocents whose legend became part of a martyrology.

The fears of those years were wildly exaggerated, but they were not manufactured out of whole cloth. Lenin's emissary in New York, Ludwig Martens, wasn't unjustly persecuted and deported. Martens, notes historian Beverley Gage, referring to internal Russian documents, was one of the conduits Lenin used to smuggle 3 million rubles (largely in gold, jewels, and silver) into the U.S. to finance Communist Party activities. The famed Wall Street bombing of September 1920 aimed at banker J.P. Morgan, which claimed the lives of thirty-eight ordinary New Yorkers and injured 400, was probably the work of radical anarchists. The post-WWI Red Scare inaugurated an ongoing dynamic in which the excesses induced by the response to an internal enemy allowed liberals to pretend that the only danger at hand was the American reaction to imagined enemies.

For the intellectuals and writers who saw the bright sun of optimism just over the horizon in 1916, the end of the war years brought anger and intensified alienation. WWI, said Floyd Dell, discredited "the schemes and instruments of idealism" and produced a generation of young minds "trained in disillusion." Many Americans felt that they had been let down by their leader, their country, and their countrymen, and they had little interest in the intractable dilemmas of how to deal with Prussianism and Bolshevism. They felt betrayed by Wilson on Russia, betrayed by Wilson on the failures and compromises of the Versailles Treaty, betrayed by Wilson in his willingness to suppress civil liberties, and confirmed in their disdain for the society that had supported both the Red Scare and Prohibition. They placed blame for "the sanctimonious swindle" of WWI not on America's enemies but on the middle-class nature of American society. In the words of Harold Stearns, an influential young liberal: "We crushed German militarism only to find that we ourselves had adopted many of its worst features."

The pre-war faith in progress, noted Bertrand Russell's son Conrad, had been "gunned down" in World War I. In *This Side of Paradise*, F. Scott Fitzgerald describes the effect of WWI: "all Gods dead, all wars fought, all faith in man shaken." President Wilson in particular was accused by one former Progressive as having "produced more cynics than any other figure in modern history."

Stearns, soon to exile himself to France, wrote bitterly about the post-war U.S. in his seminal 1919 book, *Liberalism in America*: "In Soviet countries there is in fact no freedom of the press and no pretense that there is. In America today there is in fact no freedom of the press and we only make the matter worse by pretending that there is." The man who had been President Wilson's Commissioner of Immigration, Frederick Howe, was equally bitter. America "seemed to want to hurt people," he said. "It showed no concern for innocence. . . . It was not my America, it was something else."

Between January of 1920 and July of 1922 when the Twenties began to roar, the country endured an economic collapse nearly as steep as that between 1929 and 1933. But the plummet was followed by a rapid recovery under Harding, who was devoted to less government through lower taxes and less regulation. This might have seemed a vindication of the American way, particularly as compared with Europe's ongoing woes. But the short, sharp downturn, resolved without government intervention, drew only passing intellectual attention. Literary elites soon returned to their central themes.

A 1922 follow-up book edited by Stearns, *Civilization in the United States: An Inquiry by Thirty Americans*, might better have been titled "Why There Is No Civilization in America." The theme repeated by the various authors was that people just do things better in Europe. Stearns, the man who had done the most to explain why liberalism was different from the Progressivism that had preceded it, conceived of the book's essays as a collective denunciation of a supposedly Puritan America. "Life in this country," explained one of the contributors, "is joyless and colorless, universally standardized, tawdry, uncreative, given over to the worship of wealth and machinery." America's material success, one essayist noted, was a reflection of its spiritual failure. The wife of the American man, another contributor explained, quoting George Cabot Lodge, "finds him so sexually inapt that she refuses to bear his children." Before his death in 1918, Randolph Bourne, always a lodestar to Stearns and other young liberals, had noted: "The modern radical opposes the present social system not because it does not give him 'rights' but because it warps and stunts the potentialities of society and of human nature."

The contributors to *Civilization in the United States*, many of them Harvard men, were driven by resentment. The so-called lost generation, explained Malcolm Cowley, was "extremely class conscious." Like Bourne, they had "a vague belief in aristocracy and in the possibility of producing real aristocrats through education," Cowley said. They went to Europe "to free themselves from organized stupidity, to win their deserved place in the hierarchy of intellect." They felt that their status in America's business culture was grossly inadequate, given their obviously exceptional intelligence and extraordinary talent. Their simmering anger at what they saw as the mediocrity of democratic life led them to pioneer the now commonplace stance of blaming society for their personal failings. Animated by patrician spirit, they found the leveling egalitarianism of the United States an insult to their sense of self-importance.

What followed was not so much protest as slow-burning scorn. In 1919, the Germanophile H.L. Mencken, writing in the *New Republic*, called for "honoring" the civilian heroes who had so hysterically suppressed Beethoven out of misguided patriotism; these ignoramuses, he urged, should be bedizened with bronze badges and golden crosses. Mencken branded the mass of Americans who had backed "Wilson's War" as "boobs" and "peasants." They were nothing more than a "timorous, sniveling, poltroonish, ignominious mob." Mencken, a great admirer of the Kaiser, characterized American democracy as "the worship of jackals by jackasses."

Taking its cue from Mencken, the liberalism that emerged from 1919 was contemptuous of American culture and politics. For the liberals, the war years had revealed that American society and democracy were themselves agents of repression. These sentiments deepened during the 1920s and have been an ongoing current in liberalism ever since.

In picking their fights with Prohibition and their Pecksniffian former hero Wilson, liberals encouraged the tolerance and appreciation of differences that would over time mature into what came to be called pluralism. "The root of liberalism," as opposed to the Progressivism that preceded it, wrote Stearns, "is hatred of compulsion, for the liberal has respect for the individual and his conscience and reason which the employment of coercion necessarily destroys." Although not always observed by liberals themselves—who were willing to put free speech, pluralism, and the resistance to regimentation aside in the 1930s—the call for an urbane temper would then and in the future be the mark of liberalism at its best.

The underside of this new sensibility was both an inverted moralism and a hauteur that have dogged political liberalism down to the present. "Something oppressed" the liberals, wrote literary critic Malcolm Cowley, "some force was preventing them from doing their best work." Between 1920 and 1934, when Cowley wrote those words, that "something" oppressing liberals "was the stupidity of the crowd, it was hurry and haste, it was Mass Production, Babbittry, Our Business Civilization, or perhaps it was the machine."

Woodrow Wilson had insisted that mass society, properly led, could produce an "autonomous life in every part yet a common life & purpose." But, for Wilson's critics, World War I had set fire to that optimism. The "sanctimonious swindle," as they now described American involvement in WWI, produced a rolling wave of hostility to middle-class society, which they blamed for the bloodshed. In Greenwich Village,

Floyd Dell described the fall from the heights of pre-war idealism: "Humanity seems to have climbed painfully up from the primeval slime and reached out its hands toward the stars in vain. Its arts and sciences . . . have provided it with the full means of self-destruction. . . . There are evidently flaws in our human nature which make our idealism a tragic joke." America had failed the liberals, and they would never forgive it.

CHAPTER 3

★ ★ ★

"Randolph Bourne Writing Novels" About Main Street

In the 1920s, D.H. Lawrence was following a well-trodden path in England and Europe when he wrote one of his most anthologized poems, "How Beastly the Bourgeois Is." In it, Lawrence compares the middle class, "especially the male of the species," to "a fungus, living on the remains of a bygone life/sucking his life out of the dead leaves of greater life than his own." In the nineteenth century, English aesthetes such as John Ruskin and Oscar Wilde, German thinkers such as Adam Muller and Ferdinand Tönnies, who mourned the lost glory of the medieval world, and French litterateurs, most notably Charles Baudelaire and Gustave Flaubert, had made careers of flaying the bourgeoisie. Lawrence joined this European tradition in his hatred for the middle class as the bearer of reason, democracy, and capitalism. In the words of the great French historian of Communism François Furet, the middle class was "petty, ugly, miserly, laborious, stick-in-the-muds, while artists were great, beautiful, brilliant, and bohemian." Flaubert, for his part, argued that politically, "the only rational thing . . . is a government of Mandarins," and that "the whole dream of democracy is to raise the proletarian to the level of stupidity attained by the bourgeois."

But it was only in the 1920s that this contempt for the bourgeoisie—and with it a hostility to America as the quintessentially middle-class, democratic, and capitalist nation—was brought to a wide readership on these shores by a new generation of writers, including Sinclair Lewis, F. Scott Fitzgerald, and H.L. Mencken. Critiques of popular culture were nothing new in twentieth-century America. Americans pioneered popular culture because big-city entertainments had to appeal to uprooted people who came from a bewildering diversity of cultures ranging from rural America to the peasant backwaters of eastern and southern Europe. In the World War I era, the rise of illustrated newspapers, radio, and movies—media that appealed to the immigrant masses, assumed to be of a low IQ—produced a hard rain of criticism. Genteel traditionalists charged that popular recreations not only pandered to the most brutish instincts of America's "primitive blockheads" and urban peasants, but also threatened to swamp high culture in a wave of brackish effusions. The Progressives of the early twentieth century blamed the corrupt capitalists for turning popular entertainment into a moral swamp in which business interests submerged the worthy folk cultures of earlier eras.

But while the Progressives had hoped to redeem America's virtue, the mass-culture critics of the 1920s hoped to remake America in the image of Europe. The leading literary critic Van Wyck Brooks, who idealized Europe, decried the growing separation between highbrow and lowbrow cultures. A self-styled Socialist, Brooks yearned for an "organic" society and scorned the common man as a "simple moron" who needed the leadership of artists and writers.

For liberals, the great revelation of 1919 that they carried into the 1920s was that middle-class society at large, and not just the Bible Belters with their restrictive mores, was to blame for their subjugation. Their disdain for Main Street was matched by their contempt for the detritus of urban popular culture. Referring to most Americans as "the herd," they saw the industrialism that raised standards of living as a pernicious "degradation" imposed by a country organized around the needs of the middle class. The new popular culture of Broadway shows, movies, baseball, and Coney Island were all "makeshifts of despair," part of the proof that America was a "joyless" land. Brooks compared the United States to a "primeval monster" that was "relentlessly concentrated in the appetite of the moment" and that knew "nothing of its own vast, inert nerveless body, encrusted with parasites and half-indistinguishable from the slime in which it moves."

In the 1920s, the first decade in which women could vote, what looked like freedom and progress to most white Americans was an affront to liberal intellectuals, who were cultivating their own alienation. Increasingly conscious of themselves as a group, liberal writers and intellectuals, though more widely read than at any time in the past, experienced the Twenties as a time when their art was stymied by American philistinism. The public mood of the decade was upbeat, buoyed by prosperity and also by the dramatic arrival of electricity, the automobile, and the radio, which brought classical and commercial music to the masses. To the intellectual coterie, this mood was a Calvary. The creative class was being crucified, asserted Mencken, by the inferior breeds of humanity who had presumptuously betrayed their proper role as peasants by crossing the Atlantic from Europe and breeding each other into New World idiocy.

"These writers," wrote their chronicler Malcolm Cowley, "were united into one crusading army by their revolt" against the American tradition as they understood it. "In the exciting years 1919–1920," wrote Cowley, "they seized power in the literary world . . . almost like the Bolsheviks in Russia." Edmund Wilson concurred; he took pride in the belief that his generation of critics and writers had launched an unprecedented and continuous attack on their own culture. Edmund Wilson's bitterness over President Wilson and World War I corroded like acid on the skin. Speaking of the war, which he had experienced firsthand as a medical-corps stretcher bearer, Wilson hissed: "I should be insincere to make it appear that the deaths of this 'poor white trash' of the South and the rest made me feel half so bitter as the mere conscription or enlistment of any of my friends."

The cultural qualities associated with political liberalism were best expressed in the writings of Minnesota-born and Yale-educated Sinclair Lewis. "Shaped by the Herbert Croly age in American thinking," Lewis was "Randolph Bourne writing novels," explained the historian, novelist, and literary critic Bernard DeVoto. Lewis's novels of his native Midwest were "stocked . . . with unforgettable symbols of business domination," noted historian Arthur Schlesinger wrote. "They fixed the image of America, not just for the intellectuals of his own generation, but for the world in the next half century."

Main Street was Sinclair Lewis's first bestseller. A sardonic sally at the small-town American middle class and its commercial culture, the book was published just before "the back-slapping, glad-handing" Warren G. Harding brought his cronies and their card games (but not his mistress) into the White House. Contemporaries saw *Main Street* as more than a novel: It was the true account of American life. The novel's impact was compared to that of *Uncle Tom's Cabin*. The literary historian and Lewis biographer Mark Schorer described it as the "most sensational event in twentieth-century American publishing history." More than any other book, *Main Street* gave the political label "liberal" its cultural content.

Lewis presented himself as a man of the prairies who knew America intimately. But Schorer noted that he knew little of the United States and almost nothing of its history. Rather, he was a literary man through and through—though some would describe him as an academic manqué because he made up for his lack of experience by doing detailed research—and he drew on the fiction of H.G. Wells (after whom he had named a son) for the themes of his early writings. His worldview came from reading the arguments of the German Darwinist Ernest Haeckel on evolution, the Hungarian theorist of social degeneration Max Nordau, and the Belgian symbolist playwright Comte Maeterlinck, who won the Nobel Prize in 1911. He was not very interested in politics per se, but, while still at Yale, the twenty-one-year-old Lewis was drawn to Upton Sinclair's utopian Community Helicon Hall, in then bucolic Englewood, New Jersey. In its brief history, Helicon Hall—purchased with the money Upton Sinclair made from *The Jungle*—drew in such luminaries as William James, Lincoln Steffens, and Emma Goldman. A few years later, in 1909, Lewis lived for a time in another would-be utopia, Jack London's Carmel commune. While there, he sold story plots to London, whose imagination had begun to run dry. From 1909 to his triumph with *Main Street* in 1920, Lewis was immersed in the literary world.

Main Street caught the post-war literary mood of disillusion perfectly. It distilled and amplified the sentiments of Americans who thought of themselves as members of a creative class stifled by the conventions of provincial life. It's the story of Carol Kennicott, a sensitive young woman from the big city who is trapped by a nearly loveless marriage with a stodgy middle-class husband. She's also imprisoned by small-town life in Gopher Prairie, a dreary midwestern settlement dominated by Rotarians. Carol, like Randolph Bourne, was repelled by the "grayness" and "dullness" of "shabby" town life in America. Unlike the towns of an idealized Europe, characterized by "noble aspiration" and a "fine aristocratic pride," Gopher Prairie (modeled on Lewis's Minnesota hometown of Sauk Centre) was defined by the "men of the cash-register...who make the town a sterile oligarchy."

Carol is tormented by the self-satisfied mediocrity that surrounds her. She dreams of a "better life," of "a more conscious life," though she is never able to define it. In his notes for *Main Street*, Lewis wrote of Carol Kennicott: "Her desire for beauty in prairie towns was but one tiny aspect of a world-wide demand [for] alteration of all our modes of being and doing business."

Carol and the people she's drawn to, such as Guy Pollock, a lawyer twenty years her senior, provided a stock of tropes for the next half century's commentaries about the conformity of American life. "I had decided to leave here," Guy tells Carol. "Then I found that the Village Virus had me. . . That's all of the biography of a living dead man." "The Village Virus," as Carol explains it to herself, is contentment: "The contentment of the quiet dead, who are scornful of the living for their restless walking. It is negation canonized as the one positive virtue. It is the prohibition of happiness. It is slavery self-sought and self-defended. It is dullness made God." Americans, Carol says, are "a savorless people, gulping tasteless food, and sitting afterward, coatless and thoughtless, in rocking-chairs prickly with inane decorations, listening to mechanical music, saying mechanical things about the excellence of Ford automobiles, and viewing themselves as the greatest race in the world."

In 1922, Lewis followed *Main Street* with the satire *Babbitt*, which outsold *Main Street*. Here again the book's strength was what Schorer described as Lewis's "gift for imitating the speaking American voice" in all its forced joviality. George Babbitt is the standard-issue hail-fellow-well-met businessman. He lives in a single-family suburban home and makes his money by "selling houses for more than people could afford to pay." Lewis had fun with Babbitt's energetic but barren boosterism for his midsized midwestern city of Zenith. Paving the way for the Frankfurt School and the mass-culture critiques of the 1950s, Lewis writes of Babbitt: "These standard advertised wares—toothpastes, socks, tires, cameras, instantaneous hot-water heaters—were his symbols and proofs of excellence; at first the signs, then the substitutes, for joy and passion and wisdom." Babbitt haplessly rebels against his surroundings only to return to the comfortable fold. Yet the book closes with his regret, as Joseph Campbell would later put it, that "he didn't follow his bliss." On the last page, Babbitt says, "I've never done a single thing I want to in my whole life! I don't know's I've accomplished anything except to just get along."

The book was generally received with plaudits as much sociological as literary. "Babbitry," noted Malcolm Cowley, anticipating Herbert Marcuse, became the moniker for "this pecuniary vision of repressive progress." Mencken was enthusiastic about the book and described it as "fiction only by a sort of courtesy." Lewis Mumford, a utopian and an architecture critic, saw Babbitt as less a fictional character than a "flesh and blood" commentary on the materialism of American life. But Walter Lippmann struck a different note. He saw both the depth that Lewis achieved at times and the formation of a new set of clichés.

Carol Kennicott and George Babbitt, wrote Lippmann, "are driven by they know not what compulsions, they are ungoverned and yet unfree, the sap of life does not reach them, their taproots having been cut." Lewis's writings have "prospered by inventing and marketing useful" stereotypes that "express the new, disillusioned sense of America," said Lippmann. His books, he added, have become "source books for the new prejudices." Speaking of "Babbittry" became a form of knowingness that allowed someone to live conventionally while expressing his superiority. "The old reformer has become the Tired Radical, and his sons and daughters drink at the fountain of [Mencken's] *American Mercury*," noted Socialist Norman Thomas in 1926. "They have no illusions but one. And that is that they can live like Babbitt and think like Mencken." Here began what David Brooks would later describe as the world of "Bobos," meaning bourgeois bohemians.

The Puritan pioneers, according to Croly and Mencken, were supposed to have imposed a stifling democratic uniformity that trampled the talent of individual artists. Staggering under the weight of the country's repressive prosperity, America, so the coterie argued, failed to produce great literature. This cenacle, the critic DeVoto noted, spoke of a materialist "conspiracy against the good life," much as their heirs in the Thirties would speak of a "capitalist conspiracy." In the style of the European modernists, the cultural vanguard of the 1920s adopted the metaphor of the masses as a means of denying others the individuality they claimed for themselves. They had no doubt that the American masses were culturally diseased people, playthings in the hands of America's philistine plutocrats. For the critics of mass culture, World War I had discredited, not the Kaiser and German militarism, but democracy. "When work lets out," wrote *New Republic* writer Waldo Frank, a native New Yorker who had been born to wealth, Gotham's "streets rise with the poured human waste" that descends into the subways where, when the doors open, "the brackish human flow pours through."

Waldo Frank's widely discussed 1927 *New Republic* essay "The Drug on the Market" depicted an America "enslaved" by the idea of progress. "We are proud," said a mocking Frank, "of the short-cuts...the newspapers, telephones, and radios" with which "we clutter and sterilize our world." Like Europe's reactionary modernists, such as D.H. Lawrence and Wyndham Lewis, he was angered by the encroachment of the masses onto the social stage. "In a democracy," Frank complained, "where castes are vague, where money-power has few manifest badges of dress or standard of living; where indeed millionaire and clerk go to the same movie, read the same books, travel the same roads, and where intellectual distinctions must be carefully concealed," it is the "herd" that rules. In a similar vein, he wrote of the "secretly controlled affair of baseball" in which Babe Ruth's home runs are "an effort on the part of the machine to *connect* with the crowd." "Babe Ruth," he concluded "is the demagogue of the game." A few years later, after side trips into mysticism and Hispanic and Native American cultures, Frank would become an ardent Communist.

Looking back on the '20s from the perspective of WWII, DeVoto, once an admirer of Sinclair Lewis, came to see his writings "as an exercise in expressing the contemptibility of small town American life." But what, DeVoto asked, was Lewis's point? Lewis was never able to extract an ethic from his negative aesthetics other than to imply that those who recognized the ugliness of American life thereby acquired a higher morality that entitled them to lead. "It appears," wrote DeVoto, "that the Village Virus which has poisoned America consists of the failure of small towns to support productions of the one-act plays of Eugene O'Neill, to provide candlelight at dinner, and to sanction lounging pajamas as evening wear for housewives."

Carol Kennicott and George Babbitt may have sought a secular salvation, but what they created was an expansion of consumer culture. Lewis and his acolytes wanted no part of the old Puritan ethic and what they saw as its cramped aesthetics. The new ethic, as Malcolm Cowley noted, would be organized around consumption. The heirs of Carol and George embraced a "self-expression" that "encouraged a demand for all kinds of products"—like pajamas or modern furniture or that Greenwich Village innovation, the party—in which a group of friends gathered to dance to the Victrola and drink liquor in the era of Prohibition. "Escape from the mass was becoming a mass movement," Cowley noted wryly, because with the help of business, "the Villaging of the middle class had spread through the country." Bohemianism, he mistakenly observed, was "dying of success."

George and Carol had a hard time figuring out what they were for, but by the mid-Twenties, a series of celebrated court cases helped them define what they were against.

CHAPTER 4

★ ★ ★

Three Trials

The sensational 1924 Leopold and Loeb case in which the judge's verdict was broadcast over the air, the 1925 Scopes "Monkey Trial" about the teaching of evolution, and the 1926–27 trial and execution of Sacco and Vanzetti, two anarchists accused of killing a payroll guard, helped shape liberal attitudes on human agency, religion, and capital punishment. Each produced poems, polemics, plays, novels, essays, and movies that became part of American culture down to the present. Each deeply resonated with the emerging liberal ethos.

The facts of the Leopold and Loeb case were not in dispute. Nathan Leopold and Richard Loeb were both preternaturally brilliant young men from very wealthy Chicago Jewish families who had entered college at ages fourteen and fifteen respectively. Bored with their lives and inspired to read Nietzsche after coming across a reference to him in Jack London's *Sea-Wolf,* they saw crime as a means of breaking free from conventional morality. They committed burglaries, set fires, and smashed storefront windows to no effect, as none of their offenses drew attention. They then decided to commit a Nietzschean transgression that would not only draw the world's notice but also show that they stood beyond good and evil. The eighteen- and nineteen-year-old planned what they thought was a perfect murder. Their victim, chosen haphazardly, was Bobby Franks, a fourteen-year-old boy from their social world. They killed him by driving a chisel into his skull, then they dumped the body into a drainage ditch.

When they came to trial, their parents had the boys represented by "the Great Defender," liberal hero Clarence Darrow. Darrow had his own theories that he trotted out in court, not to argue for their innocence but to show why their lives should be spared. The Leopold and Loeb case allowed Darrow to present a liberal view of criminal justice, a view based on what he saw as science rather than biblical proscription. It became a seminar for the citizenry on the new field of psychiatry.

Darrow, a man of great courage, was not afraid to tackle unpopular causes. In the 1890s, Darrow had successfully defended the railway workers' leader Eugene Debs and kept "Big" Bill Haywood, of the International Workers of the World, from the gallows. Crime, he had argued for many decades, was created by economic conditions that were akin to sickness and disease. "There is no such thing as crime as the word is generally understood," he contended. "I do not believe that people are in jail because they deserve to be."

But over time—influenced, like many liberals, by the eugenics movement and the rise of Freudian psychiatry—Darrow modified his views. As a modern man who believed in moral progress, he still didn't see criminals as responsible for their acts. But instead of continuing to emphasize material motivations, he argued by way of Darwin that people are basically animals shaped by their heredity and upbringing, so their choices can be explained scientifically. "Science and evolution," Darrow wrote, "teach us that man is an animal, a little higher than the other orders of animals; that he is governed by the same natural laws that govern the rest of the universe." Rather than an expression of free will, individual choices were predetermined, which made crime a medical problem. The courts therefore needed to prescribe treatment rather than punishment. Speaking of Loeb and his murder of Bobby Franks, Darrow said, "This terrible crime was inherent in his organism, and came from some ancestor."

The defense, notes historian Simon Baatz, called on Freudians who explained, in the name of science, that violent behavior was the product of crippling childhood traumas that only psychotherapy could remedy. Darrow also played the biochemical card. The expert endocrinologists whom he called to testify attributed Leopold and Loeb's behavior to defective glands. In his plea to the judge, Darrow asked, "Why did they kill Bobby Franks?" After a dramatic pause, he answered:

> Not for money, not for spite, not for hate. They killed him as they might kill a spider or a fly, for the experience. They killed him because they were made that way. Because somewhere in the infinite processes that go to the making up of a boy or the man something slipped, and these unfortunate lads sit here, hated, despised, outcasts, with the community shouting.

In other words, Leopold and Loeb were victims, and to sentence them to death would be to reject science and give in to the mob with its puritanical contempt for new experiences. This was a plea as much to America as to the judge who was a known opponent of capital punishment. The killers were sentenced to two life sentences on the grounds that they were too young to be executed.

The famed preacher Billy Sunday weighed in on the murder: It could be "traced to the moral miasma that contaminates some of our 'young intellectuals,'" he said. "It is now considered fashionable for higher education to scoff at God. . . . Precocious brains, salacious books, infidel minds—all these helped to produce this murder."

Leopold and Loeb were not the only young men entranced by Nietzsche in this era. The German thinker was a subject of great interest on college campuses of the 1920s. But the two killers' curiosity was more than intellectual. According to a friend of both men, Leopold "believed Nietzsche literally" and saw in Loeb, whom he adored, the Übermensch that the philosopher had written about. Leopold wrote to a receptive Loeb: "A superman…is, on account of certain superior qualities inherent in him, exempted from the ordinary laws which govern men. He is not liable for anything he may do." Leopold spoke freely of wanting to become the "perfect Nietzschean." Both youths saw anything that gave them pleasure as morally justified. The murder, as the two freely admitted, was their attempt to act out the Nietzschean ideal. Nietzsche would return in Darrow's next great case, the Scopes Trial, when science and an imagined mob again played central roles in the liberals' version of the story.

No one incident or event contributed more to the self-understanding of liberals or the way they conceived of their political rivals over the past half century than the Scopes "Monkey Trial," or more precisely the version of the trial rendered in the wake of McCarthyism by the 1955 Broadway hit *Inherit the Wind*. The trial, which took place in the rural backwater of Dayton, Tennessee, in 1925, featured a clash of the titans. The "Great Defender" Darrow represented John Scopes, the high school teacher being tried for teaching Darwin's theory of evolution. The titular leader of the prosecution was the "Great Commoner" William Jennings Bryan, three-time Democratic Party presidential nominee and devout Christian. Beginning in the 1950s, the play *Inherit the Wind* and the two film versions of the stage production suffused the liberal imagination. The play's meaning was engraved into the minds of the many teenage students whose schools made the paperback edition of the stage production required reading for generations of high school juniors and seniors. As late as 2006 through 2010, the aging liberal activist Edward Asner toured the country with a revival of the 1955 play.

In the dramatized version of the case, which took considerable liberties with the historical record, the trial was initiated when Scopes, a high school biology teacher, was dragged out of his classroom by a mob and thrown into jail. In reality, as historian Edward Larson showed in his scrupulous rendering of the case based on primary sources, there was no mob, nor was there a jailing. Evolution had long been part of the Tennessee high school curriculum, and there had been no attempt to enforce the symbolic law—the Butler Act—that barred its teaching. In an era when science was seen as wondrous, this law was meant more as a matter of symbolism than substance. It was a period in which eugenics, which had first been introduced by Darwin's cousin Francis Galton, won strong support from liberals who supported both family planning and economic planning. Thirty-five states had enacted laws to restrain the ability of the genetically "unfit" to reproduce themselves.

The case was a contrivance from the outset. The American Civil Liberties Union, founded in the wake of WWI's repression, had initiated the case, which it saw as an opportunity to repeal the Butler Act while also making a name for itself. The ACLU ran newspaper ads across the state looking for a teacher who would be willing to cooperate with them in challenging the state law. They needed a defendant who would agree to be tried for violating the Butler Act. The town fathers of Dayton envisioned the trial as a potential boon that could put them on the map, and they convinced Scopes, a local high school teacher, to intentionally incriminate himself so that he would qualify as a defendant and the state's case could go forward. His arrest was a friendly affair arranged by local boosters as a prelude to the show, which would make history by being the first trial broadcast on radio.

William Jennings Bryan, who came to represent the prosecution in the public mind, spoke for the suffering of "the producing classes," the workaday citizens who wanted to see the traditional promise of American life maintained in an economy dominated by giant corporations. This representative of economic populism repeatedly clashed with the prophets of the new liberal order. Herbert Croly accused Constitution-fetishizing Jeffersonians such as Bryan of "suppressing fruitful social and economic inequalities…in favor of intellectual and moral conformity." In his 1909 *Promise of American Life*, Croly characterized the wordy and not always intellectually rigorous Bryan as a man born "too late." Bryan's "dislike of organization and of the faith in expert skill, in specialized training, and in large personal opportunities and responsibilities which are implied by a trust in organization," Croly insisted, "disqualified him for effective leadership of the party of reform."

Mencken, who wrote about the trial for the *Baltimore Sun*, gilded the liberal disdain for Bryan by depicting him as a buffoonish bigot and the "idol of morondom." Mencken, a eugenicist, despised Bryan as a demagogue "animated by the ambition of a common man to get his hand upon the collar of his superiors, or failing that, to get his thumb into their eyes." He mocked the locals as "Babbits," "morons," "peasants," and "yokels," which, to be fair, was no less caustic than his usual characterizations of the immigrant masses.

Bryan saw the Scopes trial as in part a matter of self-government. The trial, he wrote, raised the question of "whether the people . . . have a right to control the educational system which they have created and which they tax themselves to support." By contrast, Mencken saw the trial, and Bryan in particular, as the living proof of why democracy was a despicable form of government. Mencken's *Notes on Democracy* (1926) argued that democracy was both impossible and undesirable. Kaiser Wilhelm II, by then dethroned, praised the book highly, but a friend sighed that he wished

Mencken hadn't written it, "because it reveals too much about him." It was a tedious, repetitious performance by an intellectual vaudevillian whose writing never rose above his resentments.

But Bryan, Mencken's avatar of dreadful democracy, was far from a bigoted provincial man. A well-read world traveler, Bryan had read *On the Origin of Species* in 1905 and had engaged in an ongoing debate about the book with eugenicist Henry Fairfield Osborn, the president of the American Museum of Natural History. The Great Commoner treated his talented wife as a partner and decried the sin of religious prejudice. He roundly criticized his supporters who attributed his 1908 defeat at the hands of William Howard Taft to a Catholic conspiracy, and he would later take Henry Ford publicly to task for publishing *The Protocols of the Elders of Zion*.

A Presbyterian who often attended Methodist services, Bryan was not interested in theological disputes. He was an adept of the social gospel and insisted that the only authentic Christianity was "applied Christianity." Bryan wanted a politics based on "principles which are eternal," and he found these principles in his three lodestars: the Bible, the Constitution, and Thomas Jefferson. He was never a backwoods Bible thumper, and even though mistaken about human evolution, he was never a biblical literalist. Long before the trial, Bryan saw Darrow's Darwinism and its central tenet of natural selection as "the merciless law by which the strong crowd out and kill off the weak." As Bryan understood it, Darwinism was a license for unbridled capitalism.

For his part, Darrow had nothing but ridicule for Christian beliefs, and he considered the Christian doctrine of salvation dangerous. "It is not the bad people I fear so much as the good people," he said. "When a person is sure that he is good, he is nearly hopeless; he gets cruel—he believes in punishment."

In his closing statement, which because of the peculiarities of the case he handed out rather than reading aloud, Bryan mapped out the differing spheres he envisioned for religion and science:

> Science is a magnificent force, but it is not a teacher of morals. It can perfect machinery, but it adds no moral restraints to protect society from the misuse of the machine. It can also build gigantic intellectual ships, but it constructs no moral rudders for the control of storm-tossed

> human vessel. It not only fails to supply the spiritual element needed but some of its unproven hypotheses rob the ship of its compass and thus endanger its cargo. In war, science has proven itself an evil genius; it has made war more terrible than it ever was before. . . . Science has made war so hellish that civilization was about to commit suicide; and now we are told that newly discovered instruments of destruction will make the cruelties of the late war seem trivial in comparison with the cruelties of wars that may come in the future. If civilization is to be saved from the wreckage threatened by intelligence not consecrated by love, it must be saved by the moral code of the meek and lowly Nazarene. His teachings, and His teachings alone, can solve the problems that vex the heart and perplex the world.

In an effort to demonstrate that learning about evolution had not harmed Scopes's students, Darrow called some of them to the witness stand and asked: "Did it hurt you any? Do you still believe in church although you were told all life comes from a single cell?" To counter this, Bryan recalled the logic that Darrow had used so forcefully the year before in the Leopold and Loeb case. He played off Darrow's famous dodge for the two young killers and turned Darrow's logic against him by citing his comment from that case: "Is there any blame attached because somebody took Nietzsche's philosophy seriously and fashioned his life on it? . . . Your Honor, it is hardly fair to hang a nineteen-year-old boy for the philosophy that was taught him at the university." If Nietzsche's doctrine could have hideous consequences, Bryan went on, why couldn't the dog-eat-dog worldview of Social Darwinism have a similar impact?

Regardless of what happened in Dayton, the effect of the case was clear: European-like divisions, largely absent thus far in America, opened up between science and revealed religion—it was a chasm never to be closed. Absent the Scopes controversy, some of the fundamentalists might have drifted into the position already adopted by a few of their leaders that evolution was but another name for God's creation.

When the trial ended, the fundamentalists believed that Bryan had won, but much of the country saw Darrow as the clear winner. Bryan died shortly after the trial, leaving the fundamentalists leaderless, and they went into a long political hibernation until the 1970s, when they reemerged as political force in American life. After Scopes, and the case's revival with *Inherit the Wind*, fundamentalists were seen by many Americans as not just wrong about evolution, which was clear enough, but so psychologically deranged that they needed to be barred from the public square.

The irony of the Scopes trial, notes historian Michael Kazin, was that it led liberals to tag Bryan, who in many ways was a proto–New Dealer, as a "right-wing authoritarian." At the same time, it helped position Mencken—the rabidly anti-democratic and sometimes anti-Semitic supporter of eugenics who admired both the Kaiser and 1930s Germany—as "the champion of liberalism." But this is less of an irony than it appears to Kazin. Modern liberalism, before, during, and since the New Deal, has been based in large measure on Croly's "exceptional fellow countrymen," the professionals who feel contempt or pity for the unwashed and who are resentful that many business people are better off than they are. Bryan's humiliation became a central event in the liberal story of modern America; it linked together the post-WWI persecutions by rednecks, the execution of Saco and Vanzetti, and Sinclair Lewis's ever-popular *It Can't Happen Here*, the 1935 novel in which a Bryan-like leader established a dictatorship in America. It's a story whose echoes can still be heard during dinner-table conversations in America's hipper precincts.

Nicola Sacco and Bartolomeo Vanzetti were two Italian-American anarchists who met in Mexico during WWI while they were evading the draft. After the war, they returned to the U.S., and in 1920, during the waning days of the Red Scare, they were arrested for the murder of two men in the course of a factory-payroll holdup in Braintree, Massachusetts. The case initially evoked minimal public interest. Joseph Ettor and Arturo Giovannitti, two anarchist comrades who had been framed for murder during the famed 1912 strike in Lawrence, Massachusetts, argued, to scant effect, that Sacco and Vanzetti had been similarly set up. A Socialist reporter famously asserted: "There's no story in it. Just two wops in a jam." The Communists were equally dismissive at the time, but seven years later, when Sacco and Vanzetti were facing execution, Stalin called their case the most important event since the October Revolution of 1917.

Anarchist bombings, including one in Paris that killed twenty, did little to arouse support for the doomed men. But in 1925, the American Communist Party took up the case of the guilty (as shown by the ballistics evidence) Sacco and the questionably guilty Vanzetti (who was already in jail after a conviction for an earlier robbery). They turned it into an international cause célèbre in part by orchestrating passionate support from American liberals who saw in the case an opportunity to redress the many injustices imposed by the Red Scare of 1919–20. The defense cleverly placed first the Red Scare itself and then the Commonwealth of Massachusetts on trial. That strategy united virtually all liberals, Communists, working-class anarchists, and upper-class reformers in what was the first example of a top-bottom political alliance of the sort that came to characterize post-1960s politics.

Sacco and Vanzetti, playing their part well, were turned into characters in a passion play: "Dago Christs" persecuted by the "White Terror's" machinery of repression and mass hysteria, not for a crime but for their radical beliefs. Sacco and Vanzetti were the victims of a vast plot organized by both local and federal authorities, or so their lawyers argued in a conspiracy theory for which there was a conspicuous lack of substantiation. Their committed defenders, such as the future Supreme Court Justice Felix Frankfurter, rightly noted examples of judicial and prosecutorial misconduct, and many liberals rallied behind them to oppose the supposed misconduct rather than to defend Sacco and Vanzetti's innocence narrowly defined. Nonetheless, a passionate counter-frenzy emerged proclaiming their innocence as revealed truth. The talented writer Heywood Hale Broun, who had chafed under the empty "hullabaloo" of the roaring Twenties, became one of many leftists who relished the opportunity for an ideological battle. Writing about himself in the third person, he said: "For years [Broun] had complained with some reason of an inability to work up a satisfactory amount of hate. And now [with the Sacco and Vanzetti case] he had it."

Willi Münzenberg, the Comintern's master propagandist, also saw an opportunity in the Sacco and Vanzetti case. Drawing on declassified Comintern documents, Stephen Koch, in his *Double Lives: Spies and Writers in the Secret Soviet War of Ideas Against the West*, explains that Münzenberg's insight was to recognize that cultural attitudes could be converted into political capital for the Communist cause. Münzenberg's goal, Koch writes, was "to create for the right-thinking non-Communist West . . . the belief that . . . to criticize or challenge Soviet policy was the unfailing mark of a bad, bigoted, and probably stupid person, while support was equally infallible proof of a forward-looking mind committed to all that was best for humanity and mankind by an uplifting refinement of sensibility." Münzenberg also recognized that the principal counter-myth to the Russian Revolution was "the *idea* of America." Thus, Soviet sympathizers seized upon sensational events such as the Sacco-Vanzetti case not with a view toward establishing the innocence of the accused, but "to instill a reflexive loathing of the United States and its people," Koch notes. "To undermine the myth of the Land of Opportunity, the United States would be shown as an almost insanely xenophobic place, murderously hostile to foreigners."

Münzenberg helped Sacco and Vanzetti's supporters overlook the evidence that anarchist bomb threats had been used to intimidate witnesses. In addition, Münzenberg downplayed Vanzetti's revealing statement to Alvan Fuller, the Massachusetts governor, that his sort of violence was morally justified: "Only the slaves have the right to violence to free themselves," Vanzetti insisted, referring to the workers. "Only the violence that frees is legitimate and holy."

H.G. Wells and George Bernard Shaw were among the liberal icons who petitioned for Sacco and Vanzetti's release. One of the rare liberal dissenters from what soon became quasi-religious dogma was the revered Justice Oliver Wendell Holmes, who had been saved by postal inspectors from a bomb mailed to him. When liberals implored him to throw his judicial weight into halting the impending executions, Holmes commented tartly: "My prejudices are against the convictions . . . they are stronger still against the run of the shriekers. The lovers of justice have emphasized their love by blowing up a building or two." As for the intellectuals, their case "wasn't a matter of reason but simply shrieking because the world is not the world they want—a trouble most of us feel in some way." The intellectuals, he concluded, "seem to have gotten hysterical and to have lost their sense of proportion."

The consequences of the case were profound. Emotionally and politically it was the determining factor that led many liberals to swing toward Communism after the 1929 crash. The liberal Robert Morss Lovett, who would become a fellow traveler in the 1930s, wrote that nothing since the disillusionment following World War I had "so shaken the liberal's belief in the workings for equal justice of free institutions." Sacco and Vanzetti's execution made it impossible, Lovett said, "to deny the existence of the Class War in the United States." The literary critic Granville Hicks drew a related inference. He noted, "It was practically all my neighbors in Northampton [Massachusetts] except for the other members of the college faculty" who thought the verdict justified. "The battle," Hicks concluded, "was between the intellectuals and everybody else." But intellectuals soon found powerful new allies and a compelling foreign alternative to the American Dream.

CHAPTER 5

★ ★ ★

Giants in Decline

Herbert Croly's break with Wilson after the war, says his biographer David Levy, "featured all the unrestraint of those who feel a personal betrayal." In the early 1920s, a depressed Croly turned away from his deep involvement in politics and returned to his Comtean roots. He wrote of his despair in *The Breach in Civilization*, a manuscript that he withdrew from publication at the last moment. In it he argued that the subjectivism of the Protestant Reformation was the source of the world's ills: The "materialism and individualism" of the modern world thrived "at the expense of a unified authoritative moral system." And that, he argued, produced a disaster: "the fumbling experiment…of an essentially secular civilization."

In the wake of the 1924 presidential election and the defeat of Croly's favored candidate, Robert LaFollette, of the Farmer-Labor Party, Croly turned to the spiritual succor offered by "psychosynthesis." This was the New Age spirituality served up by the English guru A.R. Orage, who for a time became a fixture at *The New Republic*. During this phase of his life, Croly argued that, more than social justice, "liberalism should work toward a religious regeneration that could not be realized through the traditional efforts of reformers."

In 1927, intellectually adrift, Croly found hope in Mussolini's Italy, explaining that "whatever the dangers of Fascism, it has at any rate substituted movement for stagnation, purposive behavior for drifting, and visions of great future for collective pettiness and discouragement." Despite his distaste for the suppression of civil liberties, Croly saw in Mussolini a kindred spirit dedicated to pragmatic experimentation. He warned his anti-Mussolini liberal colleagues at *The New Republic* and elsewhere against "outlawing a political experiment which aroused in a whole nation an increased moral energy and dignified its activities by subordinating them to a deeply felt common purpose." George Bernard Shaw concurred. He praised the Italian dictator for being "a man of the people" who knew how to manipulate them.

Croly died in 1930 a spent force. His colleague and fellow TNR mystic Waldo Frank remembered him fondly as a man whose passion endowed "government commissions with ideals of knight-errantry." Croly "was a kind of saint," said literary critic Edmund Wilson. "In another age he might have become the founder of a religious order." George Soule, *The New Republic's* polemicist for economic planning, wrote that what was important in Croly's vision was that it elevated "the process of liberation of the personality, not mere achievement of honest city government, regulation of monopolies, or better conditions for labor." Soule explained that liberalism, as Croly intended it, was "a mental attitude, the faith in the pursuit of a new truth as the chief agency of human deliverance." Croly's vision was meant to transcend politics and take on the character of a spiritual mission.

During World War I, H.G. Wells told his American acolyte Sinclair Lewis: "Don't write me down a Bolshevik. I'm a Wilsonite. . . . For the first time in my life there is a man in the world I'm content to follow." Like his admirers at *The New Republic* (the very name of the then new magazine recalled the New Republicans of Wells's *A Modern Utopia*), Wells had been both an ardent anti-nationalist and a strong supporter of Woodrow Wilson's vision for the new post-war global harmony. But just as the ruthless efficiency of Prussian aristocracy had been defeated in World War I, so too were liberal dreams for the new world overcome by the terrible bloodshed. The American refusal to join the League of Nations was only one of many failures that left intact the romantic nationalism and militarism that had helped produce WWI.

The bewilderment and disillusion in the wake of the war created an extraordinary demand for answers. Why had all civilized standards broken down in the course of the first total war? Why had so much sacrifice come to so little? Why was war giving way to revolution? The "peacemakers" of Versailles were themselves racked by the fear that, in a metaphor they often used, they were standing on the rim of a volcano that would consume them.

Anyone who could offer "a clue, any clue, to the riddle" of why a war to protect the status quo ante had been so destabilizing "was assured a large and attentive audience," explained the prominent historian Carlton J. H. Hayes. Lenin, with the advantage of Marxism's ready-made answers, was the first off the mark. The Bolshevik leader, attributing all evil to the malign power of private property, ascribed the war to the cupidity of capitalism and offered Communist internationalism as the means to peace. For perplexed Americans struggling to make sense of America's new role in the world, it was Wells who provided an alternative answer.

The American intellectual world "has been, for a number of years, in the highest state of suggestibility toward Mr. Wells," noted Randolph Bourne in 1916. "His power of seeming to express for us the ideas and dilemmas which we feel spring out of our modernity" seems "magical." In 1920, Wells's massive *Outline of History*, which sought to make sense of modernity, brought him to the peak of his influence. It was the best-selling nonfiction book of the 1920s. Between 1920, when it was published, and 1932, it sold one and a half million copies. Described as both a 1,400-page pamphlet and a tour de force, it was intended by Wells and taken by many of his readers as a sort of secular Bible complete with a creation story—in this case Darwinian—and a promise of redemption. The world would be cleansed of the scourge of nationalism by the New Republicans/samurai that Wells had described in his earlier *Modern Utopia*. Utilizing advances in communication and relying on their higher intelligence, these elites would form a global, peace-loving government. All of humanity, he said, had a common origin that allowed for a shared path toward its goal: "to conceive a common purpose in relation to which all men may live happily, and to create and develop a common consciousness and a common stock of knowledge that may serve and illuminate that purpose." History was, in effect, "the common adventure of all mankind."

As with Marx, the past was important primarily as a prelude to what it promised for the future. Wells saw himself as writing for the entire world when he described the recent war was as "the product of an "educational breakdown" in which the retrograde ideals of nationalism and patriotism had been allowed to effloresce. "There can be no peace now . . . but a common peace in all the world; no prosperity but a general prosperity," Wells wrote. "But there can be no peace and prosperity without common historical ideas." The *Outline*'s aim was to establish a common heritage for all mankind so as to merge "the narrow globe of the individual experience" into a "wider being," a shared identity as a species searching for the higher evolutionary path. When in 1923 Wells spent some enjoyable time in the company of Carl Jung, he found that the psychoanalyst's concept of the "collective unconscious" was strikingly similar to his own suppositions about "the mind of the race."

· *Outline* promised, said Walter Lippmann, "recreation in the literal meaning of the word." He implored Americans to study it, saying: "To any one who promised to spend the winter reading this book, I should vote to give leave of absence for six months relief from . . . an immediate sense of responsibility for the upkeep of the human race." Lippmann further informed his *New Republic* readers, and there was no irony here, "You will probably set the book down with a vast sense of your own superiority." And from an American liberal point of view, there was a good deal to like. Wells, while mocking Christianity, saw the example of the diverse American colonists able to unite around a common cause in 1776 as a model for the world to come.

In the early 1920s, Wells, despite his political failures in England as a candidate for the Labor Party, was, in America, a giant to be reckoned with. When he came to New York in 1921 to cover the Washington Disarmament Conference for the *New York World* and the *London Daily Mail,* he was received as a "reporter-judge," noted Max Eastman. The widely shared sense of Wells as "a priest-like teacher," said Eastman, "carried him to his highest point at that momentous or meant to be momentous conference." At the disarmament talks, Wells, a power in his own right, was treated with more deference than the official delegates representing the major nations. While in New York, Wells visited bohemian art studios and made the acquaintance of the birth-control rebel Margaret Sanger, a beautiful woman who could have served as the heroine of one of his novels, Wells's biographers have noted. A banquet, "was tendered" to Wells, Eastman said, "at the Ritz-Carlton Hotel by Ralph Pulitzer, the proprietor of the *New York World*, and the outstanding dignitaries of the city—legal, political, financial, journalistic, literary—were invited to it."

In the course of the 1920s, Wells would meet with Presidents Harding and Hoover at the White House. But while Wells was still publically lionized, his intellectual influence, till then profound, was beginning to decline. Some liberals, disillusioned by the outcome of WWI and angered by the hysteria of the post-war Red Scare, saw in his optimism the simplicities of a "Fabian schoolmarm" stuck in the hopeful years before the war. Soviet sympathizers mocked him as "the last of the Great Parlor Socialists." Literary intellectuals found Wells "too rosy, too linear," notes historian Frederick Hoffman. They were drawn instead to the decadence of 1920s Paris and to Oswald Spengler's "darkly cynical *Decline of the West*," with its contempt for the very idea of progress.

In 1924, Wells wrote the essay "The Spirit of Fascism: Is There Any Good in It?" His answer was a resounding no. He compared the Italian Fascists to the Ku Klux Klan. The liberal in Wells argued: "Moscow and Rome are alike in this, that they embody the rule of a minority conceited enough to believe that they have a clue to the tangled incoherencies of human life, and need only sufficiently terrorize criticism and opposition to achieve a general happiness. . . . Neither recognizes the enormously tentative quality of human institutions, and the tangled and scarcely explored difficulties in the path of social reconstruction." He described both Fascists and Communists as "ignorant, immodest, impatient fools" who failed to see that "the owner of the future is the unconvenanted scientific man who works without hurry and delay, dissolving problem after problem in the solvent of clear knowledge, insisting on plain speech and free publication, refusing concealment, refusing to conspire and compel."

But liberal that he was, both Fascism and Communism were in their own way too democratic for him. They had both attained power, as he saw it, by an ill-advised appeal to the masses. For Wells, the underlying fact was that "the common uneducated man is a violent fool in social and public affairs."

In 1928, Wells laid out his alternative to Fascism and Communism in *The Open Conspiracy: Blue Prints for a World Revolution*. He revised and republished the work a few years later with a new title—*What Are We to Do with Our Lives?*—that pointed to the book's quasi-religious themes. Wells's acolytes championed *The Open Conspiracy* as a modern version of *The Communist Manifesto*, arguing that it "might be the most important book published in the twentieth century." But *The Open Conspiracy* was largely a rehash of Wells's already well-known, and among many liberals, widely accepted ideas about the importance of making "the freemasonry of the highly competent" into the new ruling class. This elite would, in the course of setting the world straight, give meaning to their own lives by subjecting society to "the great processes of social reconstruction." Here was the outlet that would allow the samurai to "escape from the distressful pettiness and mortality of the individual life."

There was even a hint of what was to come in the 1960s in Wells's suggestion that slaying the ghosts of superstition would pave the path to earthly Elysium. In this new world run by the Open Conspiracy elites, "man . . . from his birth will breathe sweetness and generosity and use his mind and hands cleanly and exactly," he wrote. "He will feel better, will be better, think better, see, taste, and hear better than men do now. His under-soul will no longer be a mutinous cavern of ill-treated suppressions and of impulses repressed without understanding." In short, golden youths would lead lives of deliciously complete sexual fulfillment.

There was no room for the proletariat in this new world. "We no longer want that breeding swarm of hefty sweaty bodies, without which the former civilizations could not have endured," he wrote. "We want watchful and understanding guardians and drivers of complex delicate machines, which can be mishandled and brutalized and spoilt all too easily." He would always be critical of Marxism, but he saw the Soviet experiment as proof of his foresight: "The idea of reorganizing the affairs of the world on quite a big scale, which was 'Utopian,' and so forth, in 1926 and 1927, and still 'bold' in 1928, has now spread about the world until nearly everybody has it. It has broken out all over the place, thanks largely to the mental stimulation of the Russian Five Year Plan." But drawing as he often did on Marx's "utopian" predecessors, he promised an anodyne adaptation of Soviet central planning shorn of police-state thuggery: "A great central organization of economic science would necessarily produce direction; it would indicate what had best be done here, there, and everywhere . . . It would not be an organization of will, imposing its directives upon a reluctant or recalcitrant race; it would be a direction, just as a map is a direction. . . . A map imposes no will on anyone, breaks no one in to its 'policy.' And yet we obey our maps."

The book fell flat. As one critic explained, "Wells is the mostly highly imaginative human being living, [but] his intellect can't keep pace with his imagination." Wells "arouses, he stimulates, but he can't deliver the architectural plans for a new world." But that didn't keep him from repeatedly trying. A 1918 critical review of Wells's novel *Joan and Peter: The Story of an Education* had foreseen his dilemma: "Even the magic of Mr. Wells's name may eventually lose its hypnotic effect. No novelist, not even one of Mr. Wells's repute, can survive the strain of such persistent repetition."

CHAPTER 6

★ ★ ★

Red Decade

For the American critics of mass culture, it was the good times of the 1920s, not the depression of the 1930s, that proved terrifying. "It wasn't the depression that got me," explained literary critic Malcolm Cowley, "it was the boom . . . the conventionality, artificiality . . . the organized stupidity" of America. While the exoskeleton of their critical constructs was rearranged in the national shift from Twenties prosperity to Thirties penury, "an imposing unity of internal sentiment," in the words of Bernard DeVoto, inspired the critics.

New Republic editor and mystic Waldo Frank, who had once played musical duets with Bourne, saw himself as the prophet's heir and, like Bourne and Croly, aimed to be the herald of a revolutionary spiritual awakening. Loathing the immigrant masses as he did, he placed his hopes in "the dynamic force" of revolution, in dying pre-modern cultures, and in "a small band of gallant writers." Referring to the "gallant writers," he explained: "We were all sworn foes of capitalism, not because we knew it would not work, but because we judged it, even in success, to be lethal to the human spirit."

The Depression offered hope for liberal intellectuals such as Waldo Frank and Edmund Wilson. The American expatriates in Paris, noted Harold Stearns, who had led the exodus in the 1920s, were drawn back home animated by the chance to transform America. "European and Russian yearners when they got back home," said Stearns, "they couldn't get on the Russian bandwagon fast enough."

In the early 1930s, Waldo Frank embraced Marx. "I accept him wholly," said the convert. Frank had found in the proletariat a class that was thoroughly modern, in Marxist terms, but it had "not been hopelessly corrupted by the . . . capitalistic order," notes historian Richard Ellis. The same people described as "philistine hordes" by Frank and other writers in the 1920s were redeemed, now that they had become suffering supplicants suitable for molding by their betters.

For Frank, Soviet workers were "like poets suddenly recalled into the surface of a prosaic world" where their happy labor sanctified their work because Stalin had given "industry a transcendent purpose." The New Soviet Man, argued the journalist Maurice Hindus, based on his travels in Russia, was achieving the cultural goals of the lyrical left, dispensing with fear of God, sex, family, and unemployment in pursuit of a cooperative future that unleashed man's inherent goodness. "The peasant, the unsophisticated toiler," explained Frank, has a self-knowledge that is "humble but authentic," which Western culture has buried in capitalist pathologies. And that is why "there is more hope in the uncultured workers of all races: more hope . . . because the finished products of modern rationalist-capitalist culture is hopeless."

By 1931, capitalism was seen as having failed the pragmatic test: It didn't work. In 1931 and 1932, destitute farmers raided grocery stores, threatened judges, and terrorized sheriffs and creditors, while veterans marched on Washington for better pensions and labor unrest mounted. Columbia University's influential and conservative president, Nicholas Murray Butler, warned the country that the "final test of capitalism" was at hand.

"To the writers and artists of my generation who had grown up in the shadow of the Big Business era and had always resented its barbarism, its crowding-out of everything they cared about, these depression years were not depressing but stimulating," Edmund Wilson later recalled. "One couldn't help being exhilarated at the sudden unexpected collapse of that stupid gigantic fraud," he wrote, referring to American capitalism. But what to make of the opportunity to overthrow America's business empire? The sense of crisis produced an intense interest in the Soviet Union. In

1931, almost as many books on the Soviet Union appeared as had been published in the prior thirteen years since the Bolshevik Revolution.

Lincoln Steffens, the most influential liberal journalist of the era, saw the Bolsheviks as the bohemians of a "holy Russia" who were nurturing the artistic imagination. After three brief pilgrimages to the Soviet Union, Steffens wrote in *The Nation* of a "new culture, an economic, scientific, not a moral, culture." The Bolsheviks and not the Americans, Steffens explained, were the true pragmatists; they were conducting a grand experiment by setting "up a dictatorship supported by a small trained minority, to make and maintain for generations a scientific arrangement of economic forces which would result in economic democracy first and political democracy last." It was in anticipation of one of his trips to the Soviet Union that he famously wrote, "I've been over into the future, and it works."

Lincoln Steffens's 1931 *Autobiography* has been described as "possibly the most influential book of the 1930s." Strictly speaking, it wasn't about the Soviet Union. Steffens didn't preach capital C Communism; rather, speaking to the generation of post-1919 liberals, he argued that all efforts at reform in America were hopeless. The business economy, or the "system," as he called it (anticipating 1960s radicals), was the source of all corruption. It had to be replaced root and branch. Here, thanks to Steffens, was an American brand of communism. For "younger people," explained literary critic Granville Hicks, "the *Autobiography* was the one true map of the American economic wilderness," and they "regarded his words as marching orders." For many people, Steffens seemed to make sense of the economic disaster.

Owing to the proselytizing of Steffens and others, the early 1930s saw mass conversions to Communism. Or, in the language of the time, people "went left." In the 1920s, these same artists, critics, professors, and ballet dancers, explained Eugene Lyons, had gone in for "dadaism, surrealism, symbolism, lost-generation antics, and what not...had defied the bourgeoisie with lower-case letters, stuttering sentences and chopped up female torsos scattered on canvas." But with the Depression, they went slumming, "trading in their prosperity bohemianism for proletarian bohemianism."

Policy-minded liberals, such as Stuart Chase and George Soule, developed what they called a "hard-boiled" critique of America's market economy. America's problem, they argued, was the "chaos of capitalism." They admired the Soviet Union and were inspired by the achievements of the Soviet Five-Year Plan, although they thought it an inexact model for the far more developed United States. They proposed centralized but not necessarily undemocratic planning as the alternative to the "unruliness of capitalism." "The productive professions," explained Soule as the New Deal was taking shape, "are just beginning to assume some of the political prerogatives which their actual place in a highly organized industrial society warrants, and to which their superior competence in matters of social theory entitles them." Dazzled by credulous visitors to the land of the future, American liberals, sure that planning was the answer, never questioned the doctored Soviet numbers on productivity.

Thanks in considerable measure to Chase and Soule, planning became the mantra of left-liberals throughout the Thirties, to the extent that even when FDR was at the height of his popularity, they viewed the New Deal as timid and inadequate. "Why should Russians have all the fun of remaking the world?" Chase asked. But even as Chase and Soule downgraded civil liberties and political participation to make way for an American statism, they were never able to explain how the regimentation essential for planning was compatible with even limited democracy.

The promise of planning was mere near beer for Edmund Wilson, who became the leader of the Henry Adams left. While planners and technocrats inspired by the War Industries Board of World War I and the Soviet Five-Year Plan saw a potentially shining future rising out of a dark, disordered bourgeois past, another strain of the movement saw that bleak past leading only to an even bleaker future. Edmund Wilson, who spoke of himself as a man of the nineteenth century (he was described by the poet E.E. Cummings as "the man in the iron necktie" walking the beaches of Wellfleet in a starched dress shirt) did Henry Adams one better: For a time, he became a Marxist.

In 1931, Wilson broke with the tradition Croly had established: "It seems to me impossible at the present time for people of Croly's general aims and convictions to continue to believe in the salvation of our society by the gradual and natural approximation to socialism which he himself generally called Progressivism, but which has generally come to be known as liberalism." Writing for *The New Republic* in 1932, where both he and Chase were editors, Wilson famously blasted Chase and others for being irremediably moderate, for praising the Soviet Union yet expressing reservations about Marxism. "Their political thinking is mediocre because their solidarity is middle-class," Wilson explained. "A genuine opposition must...openly confess that the Declaration of Independence and the Constitution are due to be supplanted by some new manifesto and some new bill of rights," Wilson wrote. "It must dissociate its economics completely from what is by this time a purely rhetorical ideal of American democracy...[which is] bound up in our minds with the capitalist system." And because the herd, in his view, could be sold on anything, he wanted the public-relations techniques that had come of age in the 1920s applied to the selling of Marxism. "I believe that if the American radicals and progressives who repudiate the Marxian dogma and the strategy of the Communist Party hope to accomplish anything valuable, they must take Communism away from the Communists...without ambiguity or reservation, asserting emphatically that their ultimate goal is the ownership of the means of production by the government and an industrial rather than regional representation."

Chase responded by noting that he had recently written a piece for *The Nation* entitled "If I Were Dictator," which paid scant deference to bourgeois freedoms and discussed his support for "the Russian dictatorship." His real sin, Chase said, was not that he was moderate. What ideologues such as Wilson couldn't accept, he argued, was that he refused to bind himself to what Karl Marx had said seventy years ago. Instead, Chase said, he was genuinely pragmatic because he wished to forge up-to-date, practical solutions to the economic crisis.

The exchange between a leading cultural critic and a leading planner represented the two streams of liberalism that emerged from World War I. Wilson's politics of sensibility and Chase's rationalist critique of capitalist disorder shared a common enemy: America's middle-class business civilization. What divided them was the question of solutions: Was a Marxist revolution the surefire answer, or would more tinkering suffice to produce compelling policies? What tied them together was the belief that they possessed a priestly knowledge—which entitled them, as it had the Bolsheviks, to govern the degraded masses. Both men were enthralled by the ideal of a new justly hierarchical and yet organic society in which despised middle-class ideals would be put in their proper place.

In the 1930s, both men dropped the critique of concentrated power that liberals had rightly directed at Woodrow Wilson a few years earlier. "The so-called liberals who today think that federalism was invented by the Liberty League and is defended only by hirelings of the DuPonts did not have the same appetite for centralized power when they ran afoul of it in war time and during the reign of the Anti-Saloon League," noted Walter Lippmann. These dispositions—anarchic when allies of the middle class are in power, authoritarian when their own allies are in power—recur time and again, down to the present, as the ongoing intellectual lineaments of the liberal sensibility.

The new class leadership implicit in the writings of Croly came into focus in a 1932 manifesto entitled "Culture and the Crisis," written on behalf of "the brainworkers" of America. Dismissing the liberals and the Socialists as merely American reformers, it caught the zenophiliac temper of the times by wholeheartedly embracing the USSR. Fifty-three writers, intellectuals, and artists signed it as an endorsement of the 1932 Communist Party presidential team of William Foster, a labor organizer and board member of the ACLU, and James Foster, the first African American to be part of a national ticket. Among the signees were such prominent writers as Lincoln Steffens, Erskine Caldwell, Sherwood Anderson, John Dos Passos, Countee Cullen, Waldo Frank, Edmund Wilson, Sidney Hook, and Langston Hughes. Most of its thirty-two pages were Communist boilerplate: exaltations of the USSR alongside denunciations of "immensely stupid businessmen." But there were points when the cultural critique of the 1920s flowed into the economic critique of the 1930s. Intellectuals, the manifesto said, were suffering "spiritual degradation" under capitalism. Like the "muscle workers," it complained, "we, too, the intellectuals workers, are of the oppressed." Only when capitalism is abolished, as in the Soviet Union, could professional workers express their true creativity. This, noted philosopher Sidney Hook, "was the first time in the history of American thought that an organized group of intellectuals had committed themselves to the support of a social philosophy totally at variance with the American democratic system." As such, it gave an enormous boost to the then tiny Communist Party that had been laboring on the margins of American culture.

★ ★ ★

Before he met FDR, H.G. Wells, with his claims on the future, had written an article entitled "The Place of Franklin Roosevelt in History" for the October 1933 issue of *Liberty* magazine. Wells predicted not only the failure of the New Deal but also the possibility that the new president would in effect be overthrown by the brainworkers of the bureaucracy and civil service. He soon changed his mind. After meeting FDR and his Brain Trust in 1934, Wells thought he had found his Western counterpart to Lenin.

"My impression of both him and Mrs. Roosevelt," Wells wrote, "is that they are unlimited people, entirely modern in the openness of their minds and the logic of their actions." Here, for a time at least, was a political hero he could identify with wholeheartedly: "He demonstrates that comprehensive new ideas can be taken up, tried out and made operative in general affairs without rigidity or dogma. He is continuously revolutionary in the new way without ever provoking a stark revolutionary crisis."

Wells met with Brain Trusters Raymond Moley, Felix Frankfurter, and Rex Tugwell. As young thinkers, some of the Brain Trusters had been reared on the ideas of the utopian Edward Bellamy, who had also influenced Wells, so it's no surprise that Wells found the Brain Trusters impressive. In them, he saw the nucleus of the new elite, the "competent receivers" of the "Open Conspiracy" who, even if FDR wasn't aware of it, were destined, in time, to take power. "I do not say that the President has these revolutionary ideas in so elaborate and comprehensive a form as they have come to me," wrote the ever self-assured Wells, but "unless I misjudge him, they will presently possess him altogether." In FDR he had found "the most effective transmitting instrument possible for the coming of the new world order." It was a judgment Wells retained even after his subsequent meeting with Stalin.

In 1934, four months after he met with FDR and his Brain Trust, the sixty-eight-year-old Wells, then the president of Poets, Essayists, and Novelists (P.E.N.), an international association dedicated to defense of freedom of speech, had an extended meeting with Stalin. Wells, noted Malcolm Cowley, the Stalin-sympathizing literary critic of *The New Republic*, was "not an official figure," but when he met with Stalin, "he spoke with the voice of Anglo-American liberalism." Seeking to outflank

Stalin, Wells told the Soviet dictator: “It seems to me that I am more to the Left than you. I think the old system is closer to the end than you think.” Wells asked an unimpressed Stalin to abandon the class struggle on the grounds that the future lay with the Royal Society, the leading British academy, which had called scientific planning the best path to the future. Stalin, echoing Lenin’s earlier reaction to Wells, responded with a lecture on the unavoidably bourgeois character of experts and the centrality of the class struggle.

Wells thought the loss of freedom for Soviet writers was but temporary and seemed to largely accept Stalin’s insistence that there was vigorous debate within the Communist Party. Despite Stalin’s impermeability, Wells concluded: “I have never met a man more candid, fair, and honest, and it is to these qualities and to nothing occult and sinister, that he owes his tremendous undisputed ascendancy in Russia. . . . He owes his position to the fact that no one is afraid of him and everyone trusts him.” Wells summed up the differences between Washington and Moscow: “‘The one is a receptive and coordinating brain center; the other is a concentrated and personal direction.” The desired goal, “a progressively more organized big-scale community,” was “precisely the same.” In other words, the U.S. and the USSR were converging ideologically. *The New Republic* and *The Nation* were churning out this and similar notions on a weekly basis.

In the 1920s, the leading Communist cultural figure Mike Gold had declared Mencken the nation’s “greatest influence.” In the 1930s, Mencken’s fall from grace was precipitous. Not only had Roosevelt repealed his favorite target, Prohibition, but the economic hardships imposed by the Depression also changed the tone of politics and the culture. Mencken’s “booboisie” had been redeemed as noble but suffering workers. “The heart and soul of our country was the heart and soul of the common man,” declared President Roosevelt. When Mencken, the “sage of Baltimore,” derided unions and Roosevelt’s government activism, he was left stranded and worse. His former acolytes sill hated the bourgeoisie, but many had become Communists. “You couldn’t throw a stone into a Communist Party mass meeting,” noted Lincoln Steffens in 1936, “without hitting someone who, one time in the past, heartily agreed with Mr. Mencken's bitter assault on everything that was typically bourgeois."

Mencken was marginalized, but George Bernard Shaw, his frequent ally in subjects and sensibility, and long an icon for American liberals, remained influential. Over the years, Mencken and Shaw often ended up on the same side of conflicts. Both were contemptuous of democracy, American culture, and Christian civilization, and both had a soft spot for the Kaiser and Hitler. Shaw had a soft spot as well for Mussolini and even wrote speeches for the would-be British Mussolini, Oswald Mosley. The worst Mencken could say of Hitler was that the German reminded him of a "vulgar Klansman." But Shaw was also enamored of Stalin, and it was there that the two men differed.

Like Mencken, Shaw was a great wit. As early as 1912, he was objecting to "the Americanization of the whole world." Shaw first visited America in 1933, having declined previous invitations on the ground that he "couldn't face" it. He crowed over the Wall Street crash and declared: "I'm a Communist. And tell that to your government." After two and a half hours in Hollywood, he quipped to a famed director, "The trouble is, Mr. Goldwyn, you are interested in art, whereas I am interested in money."

But as with Mencken, Shaw's gifts for ridicule were far more developed than his grasp of politics. "When my friends learned I was going to Russia, they loaded me with tinned food of all sorts," Shaw wrote. "They thought Russia was starving. But I threw all their food out of the window in Poland before I reached the Soviet frontier." This in the middle of a vast Soviet-induced famine that killed millions. The wit that had allowed Mencken and Shaw to seem so audacious fell flat in a time of depression and dictatorship.

In 1933, at the age of seventy-five, Shaw visited the USSR with Lady Astor. "The Astors suddenly took it into their heads to see for themselves whether Russia is really the earthly paradise I had declared it to be," he later wrote. "And they challenged me to go with them." The wealthy Lady Astor was the first woman in parliament and a devout Christian Scientist. She saw that Stalin and Hitler were "blood brothers and very bloody brothers at that." Shaw, the master of moral equivalence, countered that "nothing should be said about the concentration camps, because it was we [the British] who invented them during the Boer war." When Lady

Astor complained that there was no freedom of speech in the Soviet Union, Shaw replied that at least the Russians were "free from the illusions of democracy."

Faced with evidence of Soviet horrors, he quipped, in typical Shavian fashion, "Yes, I have seen all the 'terrors' & I was terribly pleased by them." As someone who had long seen "extermination of lesser beings as a worthwhile evolutionary effort," Shaw blithely argued that "our question is not to kill or not to kill, but how to select the right people to kill." He added, "The essential difference between the Russian liquidator with his pistol (or whatever his humane killer may be) and the British hangman is that they do not operate on the same sort of person." With these awkward stabs at irony, meant to express support for Stalin, not only did Shaw refuse to acknowledge the decencies of his own society, but he also exposed the ugly underside of his "advanced" liberal views. When he returned to the West, Shaw delivered a radio broadcast, delivered over the BBC in England and CBS in America, that had the Menckenesqe title "Look, You Boobs." In the address, the famous Irishman who had rejected vaccination, vivisection, and the germ theory of disease declared his authority on the realities of the Soviet Union. This was moral foolishness with enormous consequences.

The reality was that the Ukrainian terror-famine produced by Stalin's collectivization of agriculture killed millions of people in 1932 and 1933. The abolition of private farming enforced by the Soviet secret police turned the breadbasket of Europe into a charnel house. Had the reality of Soviet mass murder been widely reported in the West, it might have had an impact on the leftward leap in American liberal opinion. There were some relatively accurate reports of the suffering and cruelty, but they were overshadowed by apologies issuing from a man of strong liberal sensibilities, Walter Duranty, of the *New York Times.* While the Soviets simply denied that mass deaths were taking place, Duranty was more creative.

Like his fellow liberals, Duranty, who in part was a product of pre-WWI Greenwich Village, saw a focus on moral issues as a relic of Victorianism. "Right and wrong are evasive terms at best and I have never felt it was my problem—or that of any other reporter—to sit in moral judgment," he wrote. "What I want to know is whether a policy or a political lie or a regime will work or not, and I refuse to be sidetracked by moral issues." Duranty, who coined the term "Stalinism," acknowledged that there were casualties in the Soviet countryside, but he saw them as merely collateral damage on "the march toward progress." Russia had been so backward, he argued, that Stalin had needed to make war on his own people in order to force-march the country into the future. Duranty put it in stark terms in his poem "Red Square":

> Peter's bloody old Russia and Lenin's new devoted Russia. . . .
> They harmonize exactly, Kremlin tower and Lenin tomb.

Duranty admitted to the readers of the *New York Times* that the campaign to modernize Russia had sometimes been mismanaged and that there had been "serious food shortages throughout the country." But he went on to reassure them: "There is no actual starvation or death from starvation, but there is widespread mortality from diseases due to malnutrition. . . . These conditions are bad, but there is no famine." Duranty knew otherwise, but as he famously explained it in a slogan revived in the 1960s, "you can't make an omelet without breaking eggs."

In 1933, a banquet was given at the Waldorf-Astoria to celebrate the diplomatic recognition of the USSR by the United States. A list of names was read, each politely applauded by the guests, until Walter Duranty's name was reached; then, "the only really prolonged pandemonium was evoked," wrote Alexander Woollcott in *The New Yorker*. "Indeed, one got the impression that America, in a spasm of discernment, was recognizing both Russia and Walter Duranty." This scene at the Waldorf, notes the great historian of the Soviet terror Robert Conquest, was clearly a full-dress appearance of the liberal establishment whose ménage with Communism would thrive until the late 1940s.

It was from his superior perspective that Duranty explained, in the style of Mencken and Shaw, that the Russians and Americans who were angry about events in the USSR were to be dismissed. In his 1935 *Autobiography*, he approvingly quoted a friend:

> Don't forget . . . the majority of people . . . are nearly always wrong about everything . . . there are long odds in favor of your being right if you

> take the opposite view from the majority. All this talk of Democracy and the 'Sovereign Peepul' and the *vox populi* being *vox dei* is just a trick by cunning demagogues to kid the masses.

The people may not have gotten it wrong, but left-leaning intellectuals most certainly misunderstood what was happening in the both the USSR and America. While the *New York Times* explained away the reality of mass killing in the USSR, American liberals, rightly frightened by the rise of Nazi Germany, were caught up in the contrived fear of a right-wing takeover at home.

In the early 1930s, the success of Huey Long (the populist governor of Louisiana), Charles Coughlin (the demagogic anti-Semitic "radio priest"), and William Dudley Pelley and his wannabe Euro-fascists the Silver Shirts initiated a phenomenon that historian Leo Ribuffo has dubbed "the Brown Scare." Some of the Brown Scare consisted of mere boilerplate leftism, as when liberals quoted Lenin to the effect that "fascism was the last agonized stage of capitalism." Some of it was self-serving, as when the would-be central planner George Soule insisted in 1933 that the Brain Trust, "the thin red line of experts" with their ideas about central planning, was all that stood between the U.S. and "a capitalist dictatorship."

The charge that the American middle class was proto-fascist embedded itself deeply in liberal thinking. In their study of Muncie, Indiana, the pioneering sociologists Robert and Helen Lynd argued that in the town's conformity, "one glimpses...the possible seeds of an eventual coercive control which in Europe goes under the name of fascism." Similarly, independent leftist Alfred Bingham claimed in 1935 that "the American middle class are in fact ripe for fascism" imposed by big business, which would seize power in the name of curbing alien influences.

The incipient fascism of the middle class was taken up by novelists Nathanael West and Sinclair Lewis. West's *A Cool Million*, which parodied the Horatio Alger novels, took up all themes of 1920s literary Bolshevism, themes later incorporated into the misnamed "New Left." West, an upper-middle-class New Yorker whose nihilist impulses left him impervious to the attraction of Communism, was taken with idea of knocking America off its pedestal. His *Cool Million* described a skit called "The Pageant of

America, or, a Curse on Columbus," in which "Quakers were shown being branded, Indians brutalized and cheated, Negroes sold, children sweated to death." In West's novel, demagogue Shagpoke Whipple of Vermont, a former president modeled on Calvin Coolidge, hoped to lead the lower middle class in a fascist revolution so as to fend off the incursions of Communists and international Jewish Bankers.

West's attempt to catch the zeitgeist of literary liberalism and the Brown Scare fell flat, but Sinclair Lewis scored by directing the liberals' fear and contempt to the average Joe and Jill who belonged to the local Rotary or the Moose and Elks Lodges. Like his fellow liberals, Lewis had been repulsed by the intolerance during and after WWI. And like them, he paid little attention to the nature of the Kaiser's regime. When Hitler came along peddling a farrago of mysticism, militarism, romanticism, resentment, German legends about racial purity, and a version of eugenics popular among American liberals, Lewis, steeped in a loathing for Main Street, transliterated the Nazi iron heel into the meetings of the local Rotary Club. In a triumph of intellectual insularity, his still widely read 1935 novel, *It Can't Happen Here*, warned of the danger of a homespun American fascism driven by small-town conformity.

It Can't Happen Here was greeted with extraordinary praise. *The New Yorker* review by Clifton Fadiman described it as "one of the most important books ever produced in this country." "It is so crucial, so passionate," wrote Fadiman, "so honest, so vital that only dogmatists, schismatics, and reactionaries will care to pick flaws in it." Published at a time when the American population was but 127 million, the book quickly sold 320,000 copies. A theatrical version staged by the Federal Theater Project was similarly successful. Opening just prior to the 1936 presidential election, the production ran in eighteen cities, drawing 379,000 viewers in only four months.

Reissued periodically, *It Can't Happen Here* became part of every young intellectual's required reading and a national byword that persists down to the present. Readers of Phillip Roth's 2004 novel *The Plot Against America*, a fable of sorts in which Charles Lindbergh leads a fascist takeover of the United States in 1940, will be struck by the echoes of *It Can't Happen Here*. When New American Library recently brought out a new printing of *It Can't Happen Here*, newspaper columnists, bloggers, and pundits such as Paul Krugman and Anthony Lewis drew on the book's authority to warn against what they saw as the current slow-motion right-wing takeover of the United States by another down-home strongman, George W. Bush. For today's alarmists, as for Clifton Fadiman, the book, its implausible plot notwithstanding, is an unchallengeable revelation.

But the scenario in *It Can't Happen Here* bore what was at best a tortured relationship to the events at the time. The Nazi seizure of power in Germany, which Sinclair Lewis's wife Dorothy Thompson had reported on extensively, helped exacerbate fears of fascism in America. What Lewis provided was a scenario (then and now) for one of the many recurring sources of liberal hysteria. The premise of the novel, written before the assassination of the charismatic Louisiana populist Huey Long, was that Long and Father Coughlin, the anti-Semitic radio priest, along with other assorted demagogues would combine to win the 1936 election for the obscure Union Party. The creaky plot says little about FDR, who plays only a cameo role in the novel: At the Democratic Convention, he is brushed aside as the potential nominee because he is "far too lacking in circus tinsel and general clownishness to succeed at this critical hour of the nation's hysteria, when the electorate wanted a ringmaster-revolutionary."

Senator Berzelius "Buzz" Windrip, who with his amalgam of a Finnish name and Southern-populist style is meant to be a national version of Huey Long, wins the White House and then begins to seize power. Part of what makes the scenario implausible is that Long and Coughlin were influential only as long as the public saw them as working with FDR. When they opposed him, their popularity plummeted. Congressman William Lemke, a midwestern isolationist backed by Coughlin and by Long's anti-Semitic aide Gerald L.K. Smith, became the Union Party's presidential nominee in 1936. But Lemke drew only 2 percent of the vote, barely making a dent in Roosevelt's landslide victory.

The book's mix of seriousness and satire doesn't wear well. Lewis himself mocked the plaudits for what he knew was a poorly written book. "Boys, I love you all," he told a left-wing audience that was honoring him for *It Can't Happen Here*. "And a writer loves to have his latest book praised. But let me tell you, it isn't a very good book." He was right.

The characters, other than Lewis's alter ego, Vermont newspaper editor Doremus Jessup, are mere plot contrivances. Windrip, as his semi-satirical name implies, is a stock stage villain. He seems to be modeled in part on Elmer Gantry, the bogus but charismatic preacher in Lewis's earlier book of the same name, but he's a far less compelling figure. There's some drama as the novel approaches Windrip's takeover, but then Lewis seems to lose interest and the book plays out in an almost rote fashion with Windrip establishing a Mussolini-style corporate state only to be brought down by a heroic underground.

The feisty Jessup is an engaging character, a staunch Jeffersonian who has no use for overmighty corporations and who "doesn't like murder as a means of argument." Skeptical about the nostrums of both the left and right, he has little good to say about American Communists who had made Russia "their holy land." In one of the book's many set pieces, Jessup exclaims: "There is no Solution! There never will be a time when there won't be a large proportion of people who feel poor no matter how much they have, and envy their neighbors. . . . All the Utopias—Brook Farm, Robert Owen's sanctuary of chatter, Upton Sinclair's Helicon Hall—and their regulation end in scandal, feuds, poverty, griminess, disillusion." Doremus Jessup has been forgotten, but the novel, or at least the conceit that inspired it, endures because its lasting appeal lies elsewhere.

The book's success is based on an intellectual and imaginative failure. Lewis, who was never much interested in politics, doesn't take the trouble to think through what an American fascism would be like. He simply asserts that when it comes (as it must), it will be cloaked in the flag and patriotism while assuming the form of Mussolini's corporate state, and serving the interests of the fat cats pulling the strings behind the scenes. He makes some passing remarks about big businessmen as "pirates" but does little with this. He never establishes a plausible nexus between the failings of small-minded small-towners and the gigantic tentacles of Windrip's centralized police state.

The heart of *It Can't Happen Here* is laid out in the opening chapter, which presents the local Rotary Club, with its Veterans of Foreign Wars tub-thumping patriotism and prohibitionist moralism, as comparable, on a small scale, to the mass movements that brought Fascism to Europe. Later in the novel, he has a character explain, half-satirically and half-seriously, "This is Revolution in terms of Rotary." In other words, Lewis's imagined fascism is little more than *Main Street* writ political. When he wants to mock Windrip, he describes him as a "professional common man" who is "chummy with all waitresses at . . . lunch rooms." For Lewis, fascism is the product of backslapping Rotarians, Elks, and Masons, as well as various and sundry other versions of joiners that Tocqueville had once celebrated as the basis of American self-government. There is more than a hint of snobbery in all this. The book's local incarnation of evil is Jessup's shiftless, resentful handyman Shad Ledue, who was a member of the "Odd Fellows and the Ancient and Independent Order of Rams." Ledue uses Windrip's ascension to rise above himself and displace Jessup from his rightful place in the local hierarchy of power.

If the book were merely an indictment of red-state nativist intolerance, there would be little to distinguish it from numerous other novels and plays of the 1920s that were part of "the revolt against the village." Lewis was hardly the only writer of the period to, Mencken-like, describe the average American as a "boob" or "peasant." What made *It Can't Happen Here* compelling was that it showed the boobs working through a familiar institution, the local Rotary, to become a menace to the Republic.

When the Roosevelt administration got into rough waters over its court-packing schemes, Secretary of the Interior Ickes invoked *It Can't Happen Here* to brand FDR's critics as fascists. In a 1937 national speech broadcast over NBC radio, Ickes argued that the economy was controlled by a handful of plutocrats who were on a "sit-down strike" against the government. "It *is* happening here," he insisted, warning as Lewis's novel did about a fascist takeover of America. The nation, said Ickes, faced the specter of "big-business fascism."

The game of political misdirection succeeded brilliantly. At the height of Stalin's purges and the Moscow show trials that were part of the purge, the Popular Front that extended from the Roosevelt coalition leftward presented itself as the alternative to the dangers of homegrown fascism.

Soviet worship reached its peak between 1935 and 1939. Stalin tried to advance his geopolitical ambitions by proclaiming a national Communism for the Soviet Union, which led the Communist Party to take on the coloration of each nation in which it was lodged. "Communism," in the slogan of the day, became "twentieth-century Americanism." Clifford Odets, a leading playwright on Broadway, wrote middlebrow plays with leftist themes; leading novelists such as Hemingway and Steinbeck were in the

Communist orbit. Two-thousand-dollars-a-week Hollywood screenwriters could be both loyal Americans and fellow travelers.

During the Popular Front, liberals and Communists could join what they took to be an anti-Fascist alliance with the USSR. It was a time when there could be no enemies to the left. As historian Sam Tanenhaus notes, in these years, Alger Hiss and Laurence Duggan, both employed by the American State Department, could pass on confidential cables to the Soviets and still consider themselves faithful New Dealers. Others in the outer circle of Soviet supporters saw themselves as cooperating with Stalin on their own terms.

But the Soviet Union that they were cooperating with was a fiction, the literary creation of intellectuals whose illusions about the USSR were created out of whole cloth, as had been their theories about America in the 1920s. They saw in the Soviet Union what they were looking for rather than what was there. When American fellow travelers heard news of the Moscow trials, they had two primary strategies. Faced with the absurdity of Nazi-spy charges being brought against a Bolshevik hero such as Bukharin, they could simply assume that the accused was guilty, as did *The New Republic*'s Malcolm Cowley. To do otherwise would have forced them to question their faith in the promised Soviet paradise. The other strategy was to change the subject to a grievance, such as the imagined innocence of Sacco and Vanzetti or the genuine plight of miners toiling long hour for short wages.

In the mid-1920s, propagandist Willi Münzenberg had helped turn Sacco and Vanzetti into an international cause, as discussed in Chapter 4. His aim, he boasted, had been to "penetrate every conceivable milieu, get hold of artists and professors, make use of cinemas and theatres, and spread . . . the doctrine." He was the first, says historian Stephen Koch, to see that "social snobbery and high fashion" could be enlisted in the cause of Communism. In a preview of 1960s "radical chic," he drew support from "the most fantastic assortment of fellow travelers among the rich and socially elite," observed Eugene Lyons. Münzenberg saw that the support of actors and actresses could make a political opinion fashionable, and it would then spread of its own accord. He was prescient; by the mid-1930s, it had become "smart" to be "red." One front group would breed many more, in a pattern that Münzenberg referred to as "rabbit breeding." The "Cause" was taken up by "Penthouse Bolsheviks," "the swanky and well-to-do" who were flattered by "the sensation of being let in on a conspiracy." "Mink and ermine and starched shirt fronts became a matter of course at openings of plays endorsed by the [Marxist newspaper] *New Masses* and the New Theater," Lyons noted. "Limousines with liveried chauffeurs delivered earnest ladies to the picket lines" as they combined revolution with slumming. From the *Baltimore Evening Sun* of November 8, 1937: "Wearing a black ensemble with orchids at the shoulder, Mrs. William A. Becker, national president of the Daughters of the American Revolution, attended the reception at the Soviet Embassy last night to celebrate the twentieth anniversary of the Russian Revolution."

Some of the "Penthouse Bolsheviks" were hedging their bets. But others saw, if only implicitly, that socializing with the Communists could be a brilliant double move. They not only distinguished themselves from the ordinary rich by associating themselves, if only at a distance, with the downtrodden, but they were also creating a connection with the country that might come to rule the world. "They were descending among the lowly and ascending among the mighty in one simple operation and it was a thrilling feat," Lyons wrote. "It had charity teas beat a dozen ways. . . . A sentimental escape from their dilemma has been provided by the conviction, widely held among them, that aristocrats and proletarians have a natural bond of sympathy, and a common enemy on the middle and lower middle classes." At the same time, he added, "upper-class revolutionaries have usually preferred to equip their children with the old-school tie they denounced."

The theatrics of the "Penthouse Bolsheviks" fired the imagination of middle-class professionals aspiring to identify both upward and downward on the social scale. For every "cause cocktail party in a millionaire mansion, there were a hundred in middle-class apartments," Lyons said. "The society women who, in a less ideological year, might have taken up table-rapping or theosophy now took up the Friends of the Soviet Union or some equivalent excitement."

"It developed, strangely, that the American middle class had no strong objection to being attacked and torpedoed; it seemed willing to be sunk for the insurance that was paid in a strange new coin," wrote literary critic Lionel Trilling. "The middle class found that it consisted of two halves, bourgeoisie and booboisie." The bourgeois somehow saw the critique as true of others but not of themselves. By the mid-1930s, "many of the Babbits had taken note of the new cultural expectations and were joyfully attending Eugene O'Neill's plays," notes historian Michael Kimmage. "The middle class had split in two. There were those trapped in the vulgar mainstream culture and those attuned to the avant-garde's critique of the middle class."

The New Deal of the late 1930s unavoidably drew on the same circle of professors and professionals enamored of Moscow. A Communist connection, Edmund Wilson said, became a useful credential for a government job. We know from the unimpeachable Venona transcripts (intercepts of radio communications between the American Communist Party and the Kremlin) that by the late 1930s, there were Soviet sympathizers honeycombed throughout the federal government. But it was only after WWII that the ties between New Dealers, fellow travelers, and Soviet spies became political and emotional tinder.

At the apogee of their influence, the liberals rebranded as Progressives used their influence in government, Hollywood, the press, and the academy to do exactly what they had rightly criticized Woodrow Wilson for doing. Just as Wilson had tried to shut down criticism of America's involvement in WWI and its wartime conduct, the Progressives, smitten with their newfound power, cast critics of the Soviet Union on both left and right as fascist sympathizers. Lionel Trilling captured the currents of the time when he wrote:

> The progressive professional and middle class forces are framing a new culture, based on the old liberal-radical culture but designed now to hide the new anomaly by which they lead their intellectual and emotional lives. For they must believe, it seems, that imperialist arms advance proletarian revolution, that oppression by the right people brings liberty.

Repression turned out to be a matter of whose ox was gored.

Bernard DeVoto—who would win a Pulitzer Prize for *Across the Wide Missouri*, an account of the how the Mountain West was settled—was a shirtsleeve Democrat who challenged the aristocratic yearning of 1920s anti-Americanism and its continuation as Stalinism in the 1930s. DeVoto saw the irony of philo-Soviet liberalism. In the 1930s, "a ferment . . . induced many writers to make a violent assault on the freedom that had been so lately won for them," wrote DeVoto. "It will be sagacious to remember that this attempt to enforce a test oath on writers, this effort to impose on literature stated imperatives and a fixed orthodoxy, was made not by American society but by American writers." When the Dies Committee, later known as the House Committee on Un-American Activities, held hearings in 1938 on the dangers of radical professors and a Soviet takeover in America, Bernard DeVoto mocked the conspiracy nuts. But he also noted that the Communist Party wanted the Committee to investigate Trotskyites. DeVoto grasped the nature of the game. "To the liberal editors, the freedom of college teachers," he wrote, "is exactly like other liberties: something used to keep the opposing team offside."

DeVoto, horrified by the way that the elite literary culture of liberalism left America unprepared to face the Nazi threat, took aim at the author of *Main Street*, *Babbitt*, and *It Can't Happen Here*: He rebuked Lewis for writing from "the High Place" and producing novels that conveyed contempt for the middle class. DeVoto also brought Hemingway and the poet Robinson Jeffers into his critical sights. Referring to them, he observed that some of the literary coterie made a fetish of American inadequacy—businessmen, for instance, were depicted as impotent men, barely able to reproduce—while another strand of the literati saw the American masses as inferior to animals. "It is a short step," DeVoto argued, "from thinking of the mob to thinking of the wolf pack, from the praise of instinct to war against reason, from art's vision of man as contemptible to dictatorship's vision of men as slaves."

DeVoto, who could have been accused of what T.S. Eliot decried as "plainmanism," insisted on "the democratic view of life . . . that holds quite simply that the dignity of man is unalienable." The writers made famous by the 1920s, an angry DeVoto observed, not only "failed to safeguard our democracy between the two great wars . . . they gave aid and comfort to our enemies." DeVoto accurately discerned a striking correspondence between the Spenglerian view of America as a decadent, mechanized mass of festering foolishness—a view influential among European Fascists—and the description of America disseminated by the literary vanguard of the 1920s.

DeVoto noted that by 1941 some of the literary liberals, such as Van Wyck Brooks and Lewis Mumford, had changed their minds and come to enthusiastically support America in its war against Hitler. Brooks, who had done so much to inspire the 1920s coterie, later described himself and his friends as querulous "bats that have flown in the twilight between the two wars." Mumford, in a newfound ardor born of guilt for his early philo Germanism, wanted to suppress the free speech of the anti-interventionists. DeVoto wanted none of this. "I cannot believe," he wrote, "that ignorant love is more stable than ignorant contempt." He predicted that their embrace of America would be but a passing moment: "The literary man associating himself as with brothers of one heart with the democracy who were yesterday the boobs, the suckers, the fall guys, the Rotarians, the coarse-souled materialists of all the world. Well, maybe . . . but probably not for long." Soon enough, "one-eyed literary folk will once more be beholding the land of broken promises, inhabited only be inferior people who destroy individuality and break the Artist's heart." DeVoto died in 1955, so he never saw his fears realized in the 1960s when Mumford, returning to his Spenglerian roots, was once again hailed as a prophet for rejecting the very concept of progress.

DeVoto's indictment was never effectively answered.

CHAPTER 7

★ ★ ★

The Passing Glory of the Vital Center

"It's amazing in retrospect," wrote journalist Nicholas Lemann for *The Atlantic* in 1998, "that a long string of Presidents—from Truman all the way to Carter—felt a twinge of terror at the possibility of . . . incurring the disapproval of Arthur Schlesinger." Schlesinger, the Nestor of post–World War II liberalism, confidant of Adlai Stevenson, adviser to President Kennedy, aide to Robert Kennedy, historian of the New Deal and of John and Robert Kennedy, and perpetual fixture of Midtown Manhattan cocktail parties, brought together New York and Washington; he was a towering figure at the intersection of American intellectual and political life. Forever in thrall to the literary tropes of the 1920s, Schlesinger had no use for Jimmy Carter. He described the 1976 presidential election between Gerald Ford and Jimmy Carter as something out of "the works of Sinclair Lewis: Babbitt vs. Elmer Gantry."

As Harvard man Harold Stearns had defined the birth of liberalism in the wake of World War I, with his books *Liberalism in America* and *Civilization in the United States,* so did Arthur Schlesinger, the son of a Harvard history professor and himself a Harvard graduate, redefine liberalism, albeit temporarily, in the aftermath of WWII. Schlesinger's 1949 book, *The Vital Center: The Politics of Freedom*, "announced the spirit of an age to itself," one reviewer raved. For a brief period, liberalism genuinely embodied the characteristics of moderation, nuance, and complexity for which it has always applauded itself.

The Vital Center, by taking into account the horrors of Soviet and Nazi totalitarianism, broke with the utopian liberalism that preceded it. Schlesinger's liberalism in this era was, as he put it, empirical, pragmatic, and incremental. It was the product of the intersection between his personal history and the post-war events at home and abroad, which for a time made it almost impossible to ignore the realities of Stalinism.

The personal element was his education, in part, by his father's friend Bernard DeVoto. In 1940, the twenty-three-year-old Schlesinger accompanied the older man as they drove across the West researching what would become DeVoto's trilogy of prize-winning books on the settlement of the American West. "We lived divided lives," Schlesinger recounted in his memoir, *A Life in the Twentieth Century*, "half absorbed by thoughts of the mountain men . . . half absorbed by reports over the car radio of Nazi Panzer divisions striking at the heart of France." In the first book of the trilogy, *Year of Decision, 1846*, DeVoto drew parallels between the utopian experiments of the period, such as Brook Farm in 1840s Massachusetts, and the grand hopes of the westward-bound pioneers. Traveling with DeVoto appears to have provided the young Schlesinger with an insight into America's complexities that had been beyond the ken of the 1920s liberals whom DeVoto had chastised. After WWII, the two men would team up to criticize the attempts to romanticize the slave society of the old South and to mock McCarthyism.

In the late 1940s, what remained of 1930s utopianism temporarily sank under the news of Communist conquests in Eastern Europe and China, and revelations of Soviet espionage at home. Drawing on the trove of declassified American material and the sources made available by the fall of the USSR, historian Harvey Kleher notes that there is no doubt that the U.S. Departments of State, Treasury, and Justice, among others, had been thoroughly infiltrated by Americans spying for the Soviets. "There also is no longer any question about the fact that Julius and Ethel Rosenberg were Soviet spies (although Ethel played a very minor role)," Kleher writes. "Julius is identifiable in Venona transcripts under the code-name Liberal. No significant federal operation, including the Manhattan Project, was immune to Soviet espionage."

The Hiss–Chambers case brought the role of Communists in the federal government to a boil. With the Hiss affair in mind, Edmund Wilson in 1953 wrote a new introduction to his randy 1929 novel, *I Thought of Daisy*:

> Some time in the late 1930s at a time when [the Soviets were] . . . coming to seem respectable and Communism a passport to power in an impending international bureaucracy, I thought of doing a brief sequel to *Daisy*. In which . . . some Washington official . . . would be giving himself a sense of importance and enjoying a good deal of excitement through an underground connection with the Communists. . . . [Their] set would go on, drinking, playing bridge and making passes at one another's girls with the conviction that these activities had been given a new dignity by being used to cover up operations which would eventually prove world-shaking and land them somehow at the top of the heap. . . . [But] everybody has now heard about the people I was meaning to satirize."

Whittaker Chambers, an awkward, haunted man of Dostoyevskian suffering, tried to warn the Roosevelt administration and the FBI of Soviet espionage in 1939, but authorities ignored him. After the war, Chambers accused his former comrade in the Communist underground, Alger Hiss, of having served as a spy for the Soviet Union during the Roosevelt presidency. Chambers, who had broken with the Communists and for a time gone into hiding for his own protection, reluctantly implicated Hiss. Hiss had been a high-ranking State Department official who advised FDR at Yalta. He was guilty as charged, we now know beyond doubt, but he steadfastly and dramatically declared his innocence. That set up a courtroom confrontation between the two men that revealed to the country the inability of Roosevelt and the New Dealers to take Soviet infiltration seriously. Schlesinger, an FDR loyalist to his dying day, nonetheless saw Roosevelt's security policies as a "spectacular failure."

At the time, the man whom both "pink" Roosevelt haters and isolationists most loved to loathe—quite unfairly—was Dean Acheson, President Truman's secretary of state. Acheson appeared "the projection of all the hostilities of the midwestern mind at bay; his waxed mustache, his mincing accent, his personal loyalty to a traitor [Alger Hiss] who also belonged to the Harvard Club," wrote literary critic Leslie Fiedler. "One is never quite sure he wasn't invented by a cartoonist." It was as if Sinclair Lewis was posthumously writing a novel about midwestern boobs and their betters.

Had the Hiss case been the end of the matter, the civil war on the left between anti-Stalinists and Stalin's apologists might have produced a morally clarifying debate that pushed some liberals to come to grips with their own failings. But when Acheson, who was a great anti-Communist secretary of state, insisted that he would never turn his back on the Communist Alger Hiss, he opened the door to the demagogue Joe McCarthy.

Before McCarthy emerged on the scene in 1950 with his supposed list of spies—he had no information—anti-Communism had been handled not only by congressional yahoos on the House Un-American Activities Committee but also by anti-Stalinist and ex-Stalinist activists and intellectuals who had acquired knowledge of Communism in the course of close combat. But with McCarthy, a Republican senator from Wisconsin, the yahoos came to the fore.

McCarthy was a great and long-lasting gift to the American left. He allowed apologists for Stalin's murderous regime to present themselves as innocent victims of Main Street's prejudices. Even more important in the long run, McCarthyism meant that America's Communists were never required to explain themselves. This would become a matter of considerable import when a so-called New Left emerged in the 1960s.

In 1949, two landmark political books—the already mentioned *Vital Center*, by Schlesinger, and Peter Viereck's *Conservatism Revisited*—seemed to define the new post-war shape of American politics. The two books were beautifully wrought essays written by friends, both Harvard-educated historians of considerable depth and breadth. The thirty-two-year-old Schlesinger's book redefined liberalism for the generation that had fought its way through the Depression and World War II, while the thirty-three-year-old Viereck's work was hailed as the first account of the "the new conservatism." Both men, the children of politically committed parents, defined themselves in opposition to fascism and communism, "the twin evils of totalitarianism," even as they were unambiguous critics of what they saw as Senator McCarthy's vulgar populism.

Writing almost in parallel, Schlesinger and Viereck staked out philosophically conservative positions—based on a sense of man's fallen nature—from which to advocate a modulated political optimism grounded in prudent empiricism. Both Schlesinger and Viereck, at the time men of almost Erasmian balance, feared the impact on democracy of the "anxieties" induced by freedom. Writing in the wake of the mass movements that had convulsed Europe, they were disdainful of both laissez-faire capitalism and the Babbittry they associated with business leaders, even as they looked to elites to contain democracy's rawer tendencies. Unlike Schlesinger, Viereck saw that Babbittry wasn't confined to businesspeople but could take hold among liberals as well. He argued that the "progressive has made a professional new conformism out of non-conformism." Viereck, like Lionel Trilling, saw that McCarthyism would spur a backdoor revival of philo-communist thinking through the creation of an anti-anti-communism. Viereck's book is all but forgotten today, while *The Vital Center* continues to be a lodestar for liberals looking for direction.

What accounts for the eclipse of one and the continued allure of the other? We should attach some significance to the way they made their arguments. Neither man was sensitive to the ethnic and religious dimensions of American life. But in a short book, Viereck spent, as he later acknowledged, far too much time explicating the virtues of Klemens von Metternich, the Austrian architect of the long post-Napoleonic peace in Europe. It was true that America's post-war system of alliances as well as the United Nations were influenced by Metternich's attempt to contain the earlier ideological scourge of Jacobinism. But Americans had a hard time connecting with Metternich, an aristocrat who insisted on "deference" from his social inferiors. The political and class spectrum was then narrower in America than anywhere else in the West.

Schlesinger's heroes were far more accessible. He argued in *The Vital Center* that FDR was continuing the course embarked on by Andrew Jackson, who fought the privileged power of the Bank of the United States in the name of popular aspirations, the same way that Roosevelt championed the average American when he took on the "economic royalists" and "malefactors of wealth." This tactic grounded the New Deal's state-brokered compromises between free-market capitalism and the claims of "community" in homegrown traditions.

Schlesinger's critics, such as historian Marvin Myers, insisted that he had gotten Jackson all wrong. The Jacksonians, Myers argued with considerable skill and evidence, looked to free markets as a bulwark against the privileges they associated with political cronyism. But Meyers and other learned critics had little popular impact. Schlesinger succeeded in persuading most liberals that the New Deal was far more than merely a temporary bargain to meet the emergency of the Great Depression. Rather, liberals became (and many remain) convinced that the New Deal not only emerged from the ceaseless struggle between business and the people, but that it also provided the ultimate solution for all time of the class conflict that supposedly defined American history.

Viereck's Burkean gradualism was a partisan dead end. In 1952, much to the dismay of other conservatives, he supported the Democrat Adlai Stevenson for president. By the mid-1950s, he was bypassed as an alternative strand of conservatism gained ground, one that was more attuned to America's vigorously capitalist past and far less burdened by the fear of populism as a harbinger of totalitarianism. In his 1962 introduction for a new edition of *The New Conservatism*, an overwrought Viereck denounced the political populism of the William F. Buckley and Barry Goldwater brand of conservatism as a "a façade for either plutocratic profiteering or fascist-style thought-control nationalism." This "street corner" conservatism, as it came to be known in the cities, marked the beginning of a political break; no longer would conservatives focus on the madness of the 1930s, as Viereck did, or endorse the Republicans' residual stick-in-the-mud pre–New Deal politics.

Schlesinger's resolutely partisan approach to politics and policy endured. But, as Viereck noted in the early 1950s, "time is a taxidermist—he makes rebels stuffy." Liberalism, Viereck saw, was becoming increasingly small-C conservative in its defense of New Deal policies.

A great deal of ink has been wasted over whether Schlesinger got Communism and the Cold War right. He did. Writing before the publication of Orwell's *1984* or Hannah Arendt's *On Totalitarianism* or Jacob Talmon's far more substantial *Origins of Totalitarian Democracy*, he argued that "the totalitarian left and the totalitarian right meet at last . . . on the grounds of terror and tyranny." Schlesinger, who anticipated the Sino-Soviet split, argued that Communism was "if anything a passing stage," a "disease" that may afflict some "in the quest for modernity." The rebarbative attacks in the 1960s were wide of the mark, whether they issued from the New Left, which blamed Schlesinger for McCarthyism and Vietnam, or from the right, which calumnied him as a timid professor unwilling to confront evil in the world.

In retrospect, Schlesinger relied far too heavily on Eric Fromm's now forgotten, then fashionable, Frankfurt School ideas about the anxiety of individuality. But much of *The Vital Center* is a fount of common sense for liberals. He dismissed the left-wing hysterics who warned of an impending American fascism. He mocked the neurotic "wailers" who used "liberalism as an outlet for private grievances and frustrations," as compared with the "doers" who commit themselves to the "tedious study of detail" in order "to assume the burden of civic responsibility." And he was contemptuous of the "doughfaces," a term that originally applied to Northern men of Southern principles during the Civil War, but which he applied to Henry Wallace and the fellow travelers who were "democratic men with totalitarian principles." Although the term never caught on, the contemporary parallels are all too obvious.

For all its virtues, the misunderstandings of *The Vital Center* go to the heart of liberalism's failings. Schlesinger, as he would later admit, had vastly underestimated the dynamism of American capitalism, and he had almost nothing to say about the problems of state-brokered interest groups fostered by the New Deal. Eric Goldman's paean to the New Deal, *Rendezvous with Destiny: A History of Modern American Reform*, published three years later, in 1952, ends pessimistically but presciently, noting that "the process of the atomization of 'the people' into special interest groups" posed a threat to the viability of a moderate liberalism.

But the key problem at the emotional and political heart of *The Vital Center* has gone virtually unnoticed: The political and cultural snobbery that informs the book nearly proved, for a time, the undoing of American liberalism. Schlesinger's politics were driven less by a concern for the well-being of most Americans than by a burning hostility toward business, despite its crucial role in winning World War II. Writing about *The*

Vital Center in *A Life in the Twentieth Century*, his memoir published in 2000, Schlesinger acknowledged: "I was captivated by Schumpeter's aristocratic scorn for merchants, as I had been by [the proto-fascist] George Sorel's contempt for the cowardice of the bourgeoisie in his *Reflections on Violence*. . . . So, without predicting its demise, I underrated the vitality of capitalism."

The second, overlooked chapter of *The Vital Center*, "The Failure of the Right," reproduces in tone and content the warrior critique of business civilization adopted by Teddy Roosevelt, who disdained capitalists as people with the "ideals" of "pawnbrokers." Drawing on the resentful writing of the Adams brothers—Brooks, Charles, and Henry—Schlesinger described "the normal American businessman" in repugnant terms: "[He] is insecure and confused. . . . Tear away the veil of Rotarian self-congratulation or Marxist demonology, and you are likely to find the irresolute and hesitating figure of George F. Babbit." Schlesinger agreed thoroughly with Charles Adams's dismissal of the type: "I have known and tolerably well a good many 'successful' men—'big' financially—and a less interesting crowd I do not care to encounter." Even more telling, while he acknowledged the necessity of a leadership class even in a democracy, Schlesinger insisted that "timid" businesspeople were incapable of joining that governing stratum. "The capitalists," he wrote, quoting Henry Cabot Lodge, "have not been in the political sense an effective governing class." What we needed, he argued, referring to Churchill, was "the advantage of an intelligent aristocracy." But he never specified where that aristocracy was to come from, although he obviously thought that Harvard-educated men like himself should be at the heart of it.

Schlesinger's sentiments were supported by another anti-Stalinist, Ivy League liberal: the literary critic Lionel Trilling. Trilling, who failed to see the role of self-interest in liberal politics and culture, wanted a new clerisy to displace the public role of businessmen. He wanted to replace Marx with the great mid-nineteenth-century English literary critic Mathew Arnold, who was ambivalent at best about democracy but sure that businesspeople were unfit to govern. Like Schlesinger, Trilling saw a state staffed by university men as the beau ideal for the future. And like Schlesinger, he would hail first Adlai Stevenson and then JFK as the incarnation of that ideal.

Roosevelt temporarily reconciled elitism and majoritarianism. Most American believed that the New Deal's Brain Trust was acting on behalf of, in FDR's words, "the will of the great majority of the people as distinguished from the judgment of a small minority." New Deal liberalism had been erected on the understanding that it was the job of a self-effacing elite, employed by the government, to protect the virtuous people from rapacious business interests. But it was an unstable arrangement.

The Vital Center, written in the wake of Truman's come-from-behind victory in the 1948 election, seemed to be a vindication of the liberal politics Schlesinger approved. In the name of advancing the Fair Deal's extensions of the New Deal, Truman had triumphed over not only Republicans and business, but also Henry Wallace and the supporters of the Soviet Union on the left, and Strom Thurmond and the Dixiecrat segregationists on the right. But the new president "appeared to have stepped out of Sinclair Lewis's novel *Babbitt*," notes liberal journalist Eric Alterman. "Truman was a Mason and a Shriner, a member in good standing of the American Legion and the Veterans of Foreign Wars," and a small businessman whose hat shop had gone bankrupt. Schlesinger could barely bring himself to mention the Missouri haberdasher's name in *The Vital Center*. "Not only is he himself a man of mediocre and limited capacity," Schlesinger had once written of Truman, "but . . . he has managed to surround himself with his intellectual equals." Truman was so socially unacceptable that Schlesinger had briefly joined the movement to draft the stately Dwight Eisenhower for president in 1948, although he later admitted that he had no idea of the former general's political views. Truman reciprocated in kind. He quipped, "There should be a real liberal party in this country, and I don't mean a crackpot professional one."

By the late 1950s, Schlesinger had shifted his criticism of American business from economic concerns to moral and aesthetic ones, notes *First Things* editor James Nuechterlein. In his *Politics of Hope*, a collection of essay written largely in the 1950s, Schlesinger complained about America's "Eisenhower trance," in which a profusion of "gadgets and gimmicks" produced a "deep spiritual malaise." Schlesinger's solution to this condition was not so much heroic leadership as imitation: Governor

Adlai Stevenson of Illinois would in office re-create, Schlesinger hoped, the glorious style of Henry Adams.

The patrician Adlai Stevenson II, the grandson of Vice President Adlai Stevenson I (1893–1997), was the Democrats' nominee to run for president against General Eisenhower in 1952 and 1956. A Southerner in his racial sentiments, he chose an Alabama segregationist as his running mate in 1952. Yet, because liberalism was for many liberals essentially a matter of style, Stevenson came across to liberal intellectuals as one of them. Like other liberal intellectuals, for instance, Stevenson had supported Alger Hiss; indeed he had been a character witness at his trial. Stevenson became the model for the post-war party, although his support for Neal Deal policies was only lukewarm. "Liberalism," explained economist John Kenneth Galbraith, "came to mean support of Stevenson." When a follower told Stevenson that while he had lost the election, he had "educated the country," Stevenson sniffed, "Yes, but a lot of people flunked the exam."

Stevenson had a weak appeal to working-class voters. He "was the first leading Democratic politician to become a critic rather than a celebrator of middle-class American culture," notes political historian Michael Barone. In defeat, Stevenson's followers invoked the fallback trope of American liberals: Their nominee hadn't failed; American society had failed him, in voting twice for Eisenhower.

JFK's Camelot of the "best and the brightest" was able to temporarily reconcile the tension between enlightened elite leadership, as Schlesinger saw it, and popular sentiment. But in the wake of Vietnam and the urban riots of the 1960s, the New Politics liberals of the post-Kennedy era saw the people themselves and the American culture they embodied as the problem that demanded government action. By 1968, the Schlesinger who had once fetishized Jacksonian workingmen and 1930s American nationalists described Americans "as the most frightening people on this planet."

Schlesinger discerned a tension between "the educated few and the uneducated many," as when he warned that Eugene McCarthy's 1968 presidential campaign was turning the Democratic Party in to a "semiprecious rally of the illuminati." But by 1972, he had come to see blue-collar America as composed of "the most emotional and primitive champions of conservatism—who want to crack down on the 'niggers,' imprison the long-haired college kids, and bomb the hell out of the North Vietnamese." By 1972, Schlesinger was supporting George McGovern, the candidate of the New Politics.

In the new liberalism that emerged out of the political cauldron of the 1960s, professionals such as lawyers and social workers mobilized to protect victimized groups from a supposedly virulent majority. But too often professionals have a vested interest in inflating their own worth at the expense of those they look to instruct. "Uncertain . . . of the nature of their constituency, many liberals tend to cover their confusion with an intense if generally unfocused moralism," Nuechterlein wrote in 1977.

Schlesinger's "educated few" have today become a multitudinous tribe in their own right. In England they have their own party, the Liberal Democrats; in the U.S., they are stuck in an often uneasy cohabitation with representatives of the unwashed. No longer self-effacing servants of working America, as in the '30s, or of victims' groups, as in the '70s and '80s, they are increasingly looking for power in their own right.

Arthur Schlesinger, a Bourbon liberal who proudly stated in his journals that he had the same views at the end of his life as when he wrote *The Vital Center* in 1949, had little to say about this dilemma. But the attitudes he advanced in *The Vital Center* live on in the aristocratic aping of professional liberals who expect, given their putative expertise, to be obeyed. Impotent in the face of a disobedient public, as in the Reagan years, they express the same disdain for Middle America that Schlesinger once reserved for businessmen.

CHAPTER 8

★ ★ ★

How Highbrows Killed Culture and Paved the Path to the 1960s

One of the foundational myths of contemporary liberalism is the idea that American culture in the 1950s was not only a stifling swamp of banality but also a subtle form of fascism that constituted a danger to the Republic. Whatever the excesses of the Sixties might have been, so the argument goes, that decade represented the necessary struggle to free America's brain-damaged automatons from their captivity at the hands of the Lords of Kitsch and Conformity. And yet, from a remove of more than a half century, we can see that the 1950s were in fact a high point for American culture—a period when many in the vast middle class aspired to elevate their tastes and acquired the means and opportunity to do so.

The wildly successful attack on American popular culture of the 1950s was an outgrowth of noxious ideas that consumed the intellectual classes of the West in the first five decades of the twentieth century—ideas so vague and so general that they were not discredited by the unprecedented flowering of popular art in the United States in the years after World War II. And, in the most savage of ironies, rather than changing popular culture for the better, that attack has instead led to a popular culture so debased as to obviate parody.

Throughout the opening decades of the twentieth century, American liberals engaged in a spirited critique of Americanism, a condition they understood as the mass pursuit of prosperity by an energetic but crude, grasping people chasing their private ambitions without the benefit of a clerisy to guide them. In thrall to their futile quest for material well-being, and numbed by the popular entertainments that appealed to the lowest common denominator in a nation of immigrants, Americans were supposedly incapable of recognizing the superiority of European culture as defined by its literary achievements. This critique gave rise to the "anything goes" ferment of the Jazz Age, as young writers looked to break free from the conventions of mainstream Protestant America.

The concept of mass culture as a deadening danger took on a new power and coherence with the publication in 1932 of two major works, José Ortega y Gasset's *Revolt of the Masses* and Aldous Huxley's *Brave New World*. Both books, which became required reading for a half century of college students in the wake of World War II, came to be seen as prophecies of 1950s American conformism. Their warnings about the dangers of a consumerist dystopia have long been integrated into the American liberal worldview.

Ortega's extended essay and Huxley's novel were written at a dark time for democracy. In the course of the 1920s, first Portugal, then Spain, Italy, Greece, Japan, Poland, and Czechoslovakia, followed by Austria, Hungary, Yugoslavia, and a host of Latin American countries had turned to dictatorship. As both *The Revolt of the Masses* and *Brave New World* were being composed, Fascism was in the saddle in Italy and the Nazis were threatening to seize power in Germany—yet Ortega and Huxley saw American culture as the greatest threat to the future.

Ortega mocked common sense and empiricism as the "idiot," "plebeian," and "demagogic" "criteriology of Sancho Panza." They were, he said, the tradition of the mob. Like Huxley, he had a literary sense of reality that drew heavily on rhetorical flourishes. He saw no irony in first publishing *The Revolt of the Masses*, a book denouncing popular culture, in a popularly circulated Spanish newspaper. Obsessed with the danger of overpopulation, Ortega set himself squarely against admitting the upwardly mobile into civilization. Ortega's assertions about the resentful, barely literate mob were built in part on Martin Heidegger's *Being and Time* (1927), which decried the inauthentic life led by mass man. Both Heidegger and Ortega wrote in the tradition of imperial Germany, arguing that World War I was in part a struggle to defend the Teutonic soul from the debased modernity of modern machinery and mass production represented by America.

The Revolt of the Masses, which has been described as a *Communist Manifesto* in reverse, was a bestseller in 1930s Germany. Such success with the mass book-buying public of the Third Reich should have unnerved Ortega, but it didn't. When he added a prologue in 1937, he neglected to mention the Nazis as he lamented the "stifling monotony" mass man had imposed on Europe, converting it into a vast anthill. Congratulating himself on the anti-Americanism of his text, Ortega scoffed at the idea that America, that "paradise of the masses," could ever defend European civilization.

Huxley's *Brave New World* was heavily influenced by Mencken. Unlike the other great totalitarian dystopias, Huxley's World State is ordered on the wants of the governed rather than the governors. The only potentially dissatisfied people in Huxley's dystopia are a handful of Alphas—or what we would today call "the creative class"—who, unlike the bovine masses, aren't satisfied with a steady diet of sex and drugs.

Mencken and Huxley shared an aristocratic ideal based on an idyllic past. They romanticized a time before the age of machinery and mass production, when the lower orders lived in happy subordination and intellectual eccentricity was encouraged among the elites. In this beautiful world, alienation was as unknown as bearbaiting and cockfighting, "and those who wanted to amuse themselves were," in Huxley's words, "compelled, in their humble way, to be artists."

Both writers considered the egalitarianism of American democracy a degraded form of government that, in Ortega's words, discouraged "respect or esteem for superior individuals." Intellectuals, they complained, weren't given their due by the human detritus of this new world. Huxley, a member of the Eugenics Society, saw mass literacy, mass education, and popular newspapers as having "created an immense class of what I may call the New Stupid." He proposed that the British government raise the price of newsprint ten or twentyfold because the New Stupid, manipulated by newspaper plutocrats, were imposing a soul-crushing conformity on humanity. The masses, so his argument went, needed to be curtailed for their own good and for the greater good of high culture.

Huxley, writing in a 1927 issue of *Harper's*, called for an aristocracy of intellect, and in a slim volume entitled *Proper Studies*, published the same year, he called for culling the masses through negative eugenics. "The active and intelligent oligarchies of the ideal state do not yet exist," he told *Harper's* readers, "but the Fascist party in Italy, the Communist party in Russia, the Kuomintang in China are still their inadequate precursors." In the future, he insisted, "political democracy as now practiced will be unknown; our descendants will want a more efficient and rational form of government." He warned Americans that while they were wedded to "the old-fashioned democratic and humanitarian ideas of the eighteenth century . . . the force of circumstances will be too powerful for them" and they, too, would come to be governed by a new aristocracy of spirituality and intellect.

In 1931, as Huxley was composing *Brave New World*, he wrote newspaper articles arguing that "we must abandon democracy and allow ourselves to be ruled dictatorially by men who will compel us to do and suffer what a rational foresight demands." It was Huxley's view that "dictatorship and scientific propaganda may provide the only means of saving humanity from the misery of anarchy." Many of the elements in the "brave new world" that contemporary readers find jarring actually appealed to Huxley. The sorting of individuals by type, eugenic breeding, and hierarchic leadership were policies for which he had proselytized. The problem with the dystopia he created in *Brave New World*, as he saw it, was the lack of spiritual insight and spiritual greatness in its leaders.

The "brave new world" is America, to some extent, or rather Huxley's bleak view of America, which he once described as "a land where there is probably less personal freedom than in any other country in the world with the possible exception of Bolshevik Russia." In this Americanized *Brave New World,* workers are mass-produced, Henry Ford–style, and they live in a mindless drug-induced state of happiness little different from the drug-like state induced by the American popular culture Huxley so loathed. In the "brave new world," as in America, the lack of freedom isn't externally imposed—it is, rather, an expression of a culture and polity organized around the wishes of the masses. America's failing, Huxley insisted, was its "lack of an intellectual aristocracy . . . secure in its position and authority" so that it could constrain people from "thinking and acting . . . like the characters in a novel by Sinclair Lewis."

This potent critique of mass culture was suddenly muted in the 1930s by the rise of the Communist Party in the United States, which required of the intellectuals who flocked to it a sentimental reconsideration of the masses. And it seemed as though it had been discredited to some degree by World War II. The middle-class "hollow men (as in T.S. Eliot's poem of the same name), whom liberal intellectuals had been taught to despise, proved their mettle by defeating the Nazis and saving Western civilization itself.

But writing in 1944, Bernard DeVoto anticipated that the surcease of scorn would be only temporary: "The squares, boobs, Babbitts, and Rotarians despised by literary liberals would soon again become targets for their betters. America would once again become the land where the masses were organized to crush an artist's hopes."

When World War II ended in 1945, the New York intellectual Delmore Schwartz kept repeating, "It's 1919 over again." The philosopher William Barrett, a friend of his, explained Schwartz's excitement: "Our generation had been brought up on the remembrance of the 1920s as the great golden age of the avant-garde. . . . We expected history to repeat itself."

And in some ways it did. An incessant flow of talk and writing about "mass society" and "mass culture" was the amniotic fluid from which young liberals emerged in the 1950s and 1960s. In her 2001 memoir, the critic Nora Sayre described the climate of opinion in that era: The Hollywood writers and New York leftists around whom she grew up in the 1950s shared Mencken's scabrous view of the booboisie and his loathing of Main Street; these were "the values and tropisms," she said, that were "very much alive in our living room." Literary critic Richard Chase concurred. Writing in the 1950s, he argued that "radicalism today in America means (with certain differences) what it meant to Randolph Bourne in 1917."

With each new advance in American prosperity, the reactionary vision of Huxley and Ortega gained ground even as its targets shifted. In the 1950s version of the mass-culture critique, the men and women of America were said to have become alienated from their authentic selves not by the conformist Babbitts but by a pervasive popular culture that kept them in a state of vegetative torpor. Everything from women's magazines to radio to comic books was implicated in this scheme, driven by the need of American capitalists to keep people in a perpetual state of false consciousness.

Mass Culture: The Popular Arts in America, a 1956 collection of essays co-edited by Bernard Rosenberg, a contributing editor of the Socialist magazine *Dissent*, explained the dangers at hand. "Contemporary man finds that his life has been emptied of meaning, that it has been trivialized," Rosenberg wrote. "He is alienated from his past, from his work, his community, and possibly from himself—although this 'self' is hard to locate. At the same time he has an unprecedented amount of time on his hands which he must kill . . . lest it kill him."

The evidence for this epidemic of inauthenticity was 561 pages of articles on such pressing concerns as "The Problem of the Paper-Backs," "Card-playing as Mass Culture," and "Television and the Patterns of Mass Culture." One short article by Irving Howe, a co-founder of *Dissent* who would go on to become a distinguished literary critic, contained the following passage:

> On the surface the Donald Duck and Mickey Mouse cartoons seem merely pleasant little fictions but they are actually over laden with the most aggressive, competitive, and sadistic themes. On the verge of hysteria, Donald Duck is a frustrated little monster who has something of the SS man in him and whom we, also having something of the SS man in us, naturally find quite charming.

Howe would eventually distance himself from such effusions and mock "the endless chatter about 'conformity' that has swept the country." But fanciful fears of advertising, "suburban fascism," dangerously stable families, backyard barbecues, white bread, and tail fins came to seem all too real to those influenced by the exiled German academics and philosophers who enjoyed an enormous (and often undeserved) intellectual prestige. Their writing always seemed to carry the intimidating rumble of profundity, which, we later learned, was largely a matter of misdirection intended to obscure their own relationship with the German traditions that had led to the horrors of WWII.

★ ★ ★

The Frankfurt School, led by Theodor Adorno and Max Horkheimer, theorized that the rough beast of popular fascism would rear up at last in bourgeois America. Relying on an unholy blend of Freud and early Marx, the Frankfurt School writers averred that private life had ceased to be private since it had been colonized by the forces of industrialized leisure—movies, radio, TV, and comic books. These amusements were, they argued, the modern equivalent of the "bread and circuses" used to contain Rome's plebeians as the empire descended into decadence. With their formidable rhetorical skills, they had the intellectual dexterity to argue past the lack of evidence and insist that the jackboots were coming. They held that the underlying reality of American life, dominated by hectoring fathers à la Freud, was intrinsically fascist; American-style fascists therefore had no need for an overt movement of the sort represented by the Nazis. Rather, apple-pie fascism was a slow but inexorable process.

The Frankfurt School represented a new kind of left. It did not accept the notion that man was progressing inevitably to a higher state of consciousness. The elimination of poverty and the reduction of backbreaking work through machinery—once seen as great achievements that would help the workingman achieve his mastery of the bourgeoisie—were, in fact, the enslavement of man by mere technology.

"In the over-developed countries," wrote Herbert Marcuse, who became the most famous Frankfurt School theoretician of the 1960s, "an ever-larger part of the population becomes one huge captive audience—captured not by a total regime, but by the liberties of the citizens whose media of amusement and elevation compels the Other to partake of their sounds, sights, and smells." He was arguing, in effect, for greater social segregation between the elite and the hoi polloi.

Dwight Macdonald, the most influential American critic of mass culture in the late 1950s, concurred with the Frankfurt School. Writing in crackling prose redolent of Mencken's, he too argued that bourgeois prosperity was creating a cultural wasteland: "The work week has shrunk, real wages have risen, and never in history have so many people attained such a high standard of living as in this country since 1945," Macdonald complained. "Money, leisure, and knowledge," he went on, "the prerequisites for culture, are more plentiful and more evenly distributed than ever before." And that was the problem. Educated at Phillips Exeter Academy and Yale and associated with the anti-Stalinist leftists at *Partisan Review*, Macdonald couldn't bring himself to support the United States against the Nazis in World War II, on the grounds that "Europe has its Hitlers, but we have our Rotarians."

Macdonald made himself the chief critic of the cultural category he dubbed the "middlebrow." The great danger to America, he argued in his most famous essay, "Masscult and Midcult," was the effort by the masses to elevate themselves culturally. Because of the middlebrow impulse, book clubs had spread across the country like so much "ooze." The result, he believed, could only be the pollution of high culture and its degradation in becoming popular culture. "Two cultures have developed in this country," insisted Macdonald, and "it is to the national interest to keep them separate." His words were vicious. "Already we have far too much of this insipidity—masses of people who are half breeds" daring to partake of "the American culture of the cheap newspaper, the movies, the popular song, the ubiquitous automobile" and creating "hordes of men and women without a spiritual country . . . without taste, without standards but those of the mob."

The toxic intermixing of high and low was nearly unstoppable. The hordes were at the gate: "The masses are not people, they are not The Man in the Street or The Average Man, they are not even that figment of liberal condescension, The Common Man. The masses are, rather, man as non-man." He approvingly quoted author Roger Fry's misanthropic notion: "Humans have lost the power to be individuals. They have become social insects like bees and ants." But for Macdonald, this was a particularly American pathology.

And what were these insects up to? They were sampling the greatest works of Western civilization for the first time. "Twenty years ago, you couldn't sell Beethoven out of New York," a salesman enthused in *Mass Culture: The Popular Arts in America*. "Today we sell Palestrina, Monteverdi, Gabrieli, and Renaissance and Baroque music in large quantities." The public's expanding taste and increased income produced a 250 percent growth in the number of local symphony orchestras between 1940 and 1955. In that same year, 1955, 15 million people paid to attend major-league baseball games, while 35 million paid to attend classical-music concerts. The New York Metropolitan Opera's Saturday-afternoon radio broadcast drew a listenership of 15 million out of an overall population of 165 million.

The overwhelming new medium of television was particularly decried by critics of mass culture. But, as the sociologist David White, co-editor with Rosenberg of *Mass Culture*, noted, NBC spent $500,000 in 1956 to present a three-hour version of Shakespeare's *Richard III* starring Laurence Olivier. The broadcast drew 50 million viewers; as many as 25 million watched all three hours. White went on to note that "on March 16, 1956, a Sunday chosen at random," the viewer could have seen a discussion of the life and times of Toulouse-Lautrec by three prominent art critics, an interview with theologian Paul Tillich, an adaptation of Walter Van Tilburg Clark's *Hook*, a documentary on mental illness with Dr. William Menninger, and a ninety-minute performance of *The Taming of the Shrew*.

At the same time, book sales doubled. Saul Bellow's *The Adventures of Augie March*, a National Book Award winner, had only modest sales when it was first published in 1953. But it went on to sell a million copies in paperback—the softcover book having been introduced on a grand scale after the war. Anthropologist Ruth Benedict's *Patterns of Culture*, published in 1934, sold modestly until the advent of the paperback. By the mid-'50s this assault by Benedict on Victorian moral absolutes in the name of cultural tolerance had sold a half million copies.

In 1947, notes Alex Beam in his 2009 book *A Great Idea at the Time*, Robert Hutchins, then president of the University of Chicago, and the autodidact philosopher Mortimer Adler launched an effort to bring the great books of Western Civilization to the people. In 1948, Hutchins and Adler drew 2,500 people to a Chicago auditorium to hear them lead a discussion of the trial of Socrates. By 1951, there were 2,500 Great Books discussion groups, with roughly 25,000 members meeting "all over the country, in public libraries, in church basements, Chamber of Commerce offices, corporate conference rooms at IBM and Grumman Aircraft, in private homes, on army bases," and even in prisons. At the peak of the Great Books boom, Beam writes, 50,000 Americans a year were buying collections of the writings of Plato, Aristotle, the Founding Fathers, and Hegel at prices that "started at $298 and topped out at $1,175, the equivalent of $2,500 to $9,800 today."

This was the danger against which critics of mass culture, inflamed with indignation, arrayed themselves in righteous opposition.

But with the advent of the youth movement of the 1960s, the elite attack took a new and odd turn. The shift in sensibility was first announced by the 31-year-old Susan Sontag, in a 1964 *Partisan Review* essay entitled "Notes on Camp." The essay, which sent Sontag's shares soaring on the intellectual stock exchange, dissolved the boundaries between high culture and mass culture in favor of a new sensibility she described as "camp." Camp is playful, a rebuke of sorts to the cultural mandarins. More precisely, camp involves a new, more complex relation to what she called "the serious." It allowed people to "be serious about the frivolous, frivolous about the serious." Sontag was saying it was all right for serious people to enjoy the kitsch of popular culture as long as they did it with the correct—superior and ironic—attitude.

Sontag, who thought of herself as a displaced European suffering among philistine Americans, echoed Randolph Bourne in asserting that "intelligence" was "really a kind of taste: taste in ideas." And the "new aristocrats of taste" were those led by homosexual men who saw that comic books, popular art, and pornography, viewed with the right spirit of irony and mischief, were an extension of the new sensibility that saw "life as theater." In this victory of style over content and aesthetics over morality, Sontag defined the emerging ethos of the '60s. The middlebrow menace was banished to the sidelines.

By the late 1970s, the aim of camp to "dethrone the serious" had all but succeeded. And once the last remnants of bourgeois morality largely melted away, there was little to make even mock cultural rebellion meaningful. The "serious" was replaced by a cheerful mindlessness, and the cultural striving of middlebrow Americans came to a quiet end. Why should the well-meaning Middle American labor to read a complex novel by an intellectual or try to work his way through a Great Book if the cultural poohbahs first mocked his efforts and then said they were pointless anyway because what mattered was living "life as theater"? Today, if there were a T.S. Eliot, *Time* Magazine would no more put him on the cover than it would sing the praises of George W. Bush. *Time*'s literary critic writes children's fantasy novels and chose a book about fairies as one of the crowning cultural achievements of 2012. Since the highbrow have permission to view the "frivolous as the serious," why shouldn't everybody else do the same?

Dwight Macdonald, who spat on the ambitions of the "midcult" man, took an interesting journey himself in the 1960s. He became a movie critic and later a contributor to television's *Today* show. When student radicals took over buildings on the campus of Columbia University, Macdonald celebrated them and responded mildly when members of the Students for a Democratic Society (which gave birth to the terrorist Weathermen) literally set fire to the manuscript of a professor. The man who had denounced the barbarism of the American middle class saw true barbarism in practice and found it wonderfully stimulating.

"You know how sympathetic in general I am to the Young, they're the best generation I've known in this country, the cleverest and the most serious and decent," Macdonald said, of the 1960s rebels. And then, speaking words that would mark the disgraceful epitaph of the successful assault on the remarkable American cultural moment of the 1950s, he said, wistfully, "I wish they'd read a little."

CHAPTER 9

★ ★ ★

Not a New Left but a New Class

Substantively, as opposed to stylistically, there was no *New* Left. The old left's delusions about the USSR were replaced by new delusions about Third World dictators such as Castro, Nkrumah, and Nasser. The underlying utopian tropes of the old left were refurbished not replaced. Utopian fantasies about eliminating private property were supplemented with utopian fantasies about free love and polymorphic perversity.

It was a matter of old wine in new bottles. The battle against Babbitry, carried out in the 1950s through the assault on mass culture, grew more intense. Liberals still searched for the authenticity and energy denied them by the artificiality of capitalism and democracy. And like the lyrical leftists of the period between 1900 and 1917, liberals sought energy and authenticity in the promise of sexual fulfillment. Waldo Frank, the anti-capitalist literary leftist of the 1920s who had become a Communist in the '30s, reemerged in the late '50s, still searching for the fount of vitality, as a chair of the Fair Play for Cuba Committee, a front group for Castro. Liberals, trapped in the left–right dichotomy of the 1930s, still saw themselves as fending off the impending arrival of fascism, this time borne by Cold War anti-Communism.

William Phillips, an editor of *Partisan Review*, which anti-Stalinists had founded in the 1930s, noted that "suddenly the intellectual mood became a radical one again" in the late 1950s and early '60s. "It looked as though we were back in the '30s again." Writing in the early 1980s, philosopher William Barrett saw it similarly: "Immured in the '30s, we failed the decades that were to come. As the attitude of a liberal Marxism, vague enough to begin with, became even vaguer and more vaporous, it infected the whole of American Liberalism, and was to erupt again as the infantile Leftism of the 1960s." The nuanced, empirical, and anti-Communist liberalism of the 1950s was but a brief passing phase in the long-term ideological realignment of American politics begun by President Roosevelt in the 1930s.

The first federal equal-rights legislation for women passed in 1962, the year that saw the first hint of the electoral politics to come. MIT historian H. Stuart Hughes drew rousing crowds as a peace candidate in the Massachusetts Democratic senatorial primary that was won by Ted Kennedy, who would soon adopt much of Hughes's program. The campaign, which aimed at eliminating nuclear weapons, produced a mass mobilization of students and "of educated prosperous suburbia." "As I came to understand my followers better," wrote Hughes, a self-described Socialist,

> I began to understand that for years they had been waiting for this sort of campaign. They longed to challenge the consensus, to question the basic assumptions by which their fellow citizens lived. Through the 1950s, they had quietly gone about their business, behaving as their neighbors did, swallowing down their anger and their fear for their children. For a whole decade the tension of self-contained protest had been building up. . . . The result was an emotional explosion.

This was before Vietnam and racial violence had heated up.

The early 1960s resembled the pre–World War I period of the lyrical left, when utopian expectations ran high. In the early 1960s, the expectations were for more than just a new Camelot. The achievements of Martin Luther King and the civil rights movement promised a new era of racial harmony; the development of the birth control pill promised a new age of sexual freedom; automation promised an end to drudgery; and the economic boom of the 1960s promised a new level of shared well-being.

National income doubled in the course of the '60s. The poverty rate was cut in half as unemployment dropped to only 3.5 percent and inflation-adjusted personal income grew by nearly 40 percent. Home ownership reached record highs that have been difficult to surpass.

The unadulterated euphoria ended with Kennedy's assassination, but utopian dreams were kept alive by the apparent promise of mind-altering drugs. The seeming debacle of the 1964 Goldwater presidential campaign further stoked liberal optimism. In the wake of LBJ's 1964 landslide, liberals dominated all the branches of federal government, which were gushing with revenues thanks to an economy that had grown 25 percent in just four years.

Inspired by this bounty, at the signing ceremony for the War on Poverty legislation in August 1964, Johnson promised, "The days of the dole in this country are numbered." The "conquest of poverty," the 1964 Economic Report of the President explained, was "well within our power." "About $11 billion a year," the report claimed, would bring all poor families up to the $3,000 income level that had been defined as the minimum for a decent life. The next year, notes anti-poverty activist Peter Cove, "the government allocated even more than the report had called for—$14.7 billion—to transfer payments" designed to lift the poor out of poverty. At the 1964 Christmas-tree lighting, President Johnson declared, "These are the most hopeful times in all the years since Christ was born in Bethlehem."

Johnson was seconded by futurists and utopians for whom a society of spontaneous pleasure seemed at hand. But the rise in crime, the eruption of racial riots, and the escalation of the war in Vietnam soured the country on first Lyndon Johnson and then Richard Nixon, who, with their old-hat New Deal policies, were both depicted by liberals as the second coming of the Third Reich. For a decade, from the mid-'60s to the mid-'70s, public life was roiled by the intersection of millenarian reveries and apocalyptic fears. The promise and pretense of an all-encompassing expertise capable of conquering poverty clashed with the dystopian realities of cities caught in the violent grip of an increasingly feral underclass. The clash kept the country continually off-balance.

In the 1960s, American society, thanks to automation, was reconfigured from a mass-manufacturing to a post-industrial and increasingly knowledge-based economy. The number of Americans between ages twenty-five and twenty-nine who had a college degree nearly tripled from 1950 to 1970, growing from 7.7 to 20.7 percent of the population. In the late nineteenth century, William James famously argued that college graduates would have to do for democracy what dukes and earls had done for monarchy—they would have to become an aristocracy of sorts.

Before WWI, Randolph Bourne had envisioned an army of youth who would transform the land:

> It could have for its aim the improvement of the quality of our living. . . . I have a picture of a host of eager young missionaries swarming over the land spreading the health knowledge, the knowledge of domestic science, of gardening, of tastefulness, that they have learned in school. . . . Food inspection, factory inspection, organized relief, the care of dependents, playground service, nursing in hospitals—all this would be a field for such an educational service.

The "army of youth" Bourne envisioned was the advanced brigade of what emerged as a "New Class." The political generation that came of age in the turmoil of the 1960s tended to divide between those with bohemian temperaments and those with a bureaucratic bent. Both were disdainful of the torpid ways of Middle America, which they would come to blame for racism at home, imperialism in Vietnam, and sexual repression in the bedroom. The bohemian-libertarian strain rebelled against what Paul Goodman called "the social machine" that "processed" people. But while the bohemians were far more colorful—each year on the anniversary of Woodstock, we still have TV specials to celebrate its sheer wonderfulness—it was the future bureaucrats who, as part of the New Class, reshaped the Democratic Party and liberalism.

The technocratic strain of American thinking pioneered by Thorstein Veblen and advanced by New Dealers Adolph Berle, George Soule, Stuart Chase, and Thurman Arnold, as well as their heir the liberal economist John Kenneth Galbraith, argued that control of economic life was passing from the owners of capital to the professional managers who actually ran the country's production facilities. In his best-selling 1958 book *The Affluent Society*, Galbraith argued that managers and technicians and scientists uncorrupted by the entrepreneurs' excessive self-interest worked for the inherent pleasure of their endeavors. Capitalism would be transformed from within, he contended. Rather than maximizing profits, the vanguard of university-trained managers would reshape the American economy according to the Wellsian values they had studied in college.

Galbraith's influence among liberals derived from his snobbish wit, as when he constructed straw men whom he could mock as captives of "the conventional wisdom." Galbraith, more than any other liberal, was able to meld two of the central strands of 1920s liberalism: a Menckenesqe contempt for the burghers and an undue regard for technocrats who cloaked their prejudices in the language of social science.

In the early 1960s, the New York intellectual David Bazelon suggested that education had become to the new economy what capital had been to the old one, such that "trained thought is becoming the value that commands other values." Galbraith saw in the Kennedy administration and its new Brain Trust the merger of reason and power that led him to pronounce: "The question [of the elimination] of poverty is less one of feasibility than will. Educational deficiencies can be overcome. Mental deficiencies can be treated." Few listened to Daniel Patrick Moynihan's warning that the Kennedy Brain Trust had engaged in "a serious misreading of the Eisenhower years," when "it had *seemed* that men of vigor and purpose could not but do infinitely better than such a crowd of Rotarians and press agents."

In January of 1963, *Time* chose fifteen American scientists as its Men of the Year. "Statesman and savants, builders and even priests are their servants," intoned Time. "Science is at the apogee of its power." The sciences, including social science, made people almost giddy with expectation. The moon race, heart transplants, the polio vaccine, miracle wheat, super pesticides, think tanks, anti-poverty programs, systems analysis, computers—all were potentially world-changing. "The land" said journalist Ward Elliot, "rang with calls for more Ph.D.s to win all the wars that we were fighting with a grand mobilization of expertise." He continued:

> The hippy strain aside, both flanks of what became the left-liberal civil war between New Deal social democrats and New Leftists shared the belief in the power of trained intelligence. The founding document of SDS [Students for a Democratic Society], the 1962 Port Huron statement, criticized liberalism for its timidity. Liberals, they insisted,

possessed the knowledge to transform the world but were too cowardly to actually see the job through, so that the young radicals would have to step forth and finish the work. As an example of the new knowledge, the Port Huron statement endorsed the development of nuclear power.

Thick with "red diaper" babies, some of whom celebrated the dashing Tom Hayden as "the next Lenin," SDS was inspired by the Freedom Riders. Referring to the courage of African-American students who engaged in sit-ins, Hayden admiringly noted that they were "miles ahead of us" white students. They already understood, argued Hayden, "the sterility of liberals." There was a smooth transition from militant liberalism to what was dubbed New Leftism.

During his presidency, Kennedy had repeatedly criticized the irrationalism of far-right-wing anti-Communists and their segregationist cousins. In April 1963, the police in Birmingham, Alabama, had set dogs upon peaceful civil rights marchers, and in June, segregationists in Mississippi assassinated NAACP leader Medgar Evers. In October, protesters in Dallas had harassed Adlai Stevenson, Kennedy's United Nations ambassador. Dallas was a notoriously segregated city, and the John Birch Society (whose members thought President Eisenhower had been under Communist sway) was a part of the city's political culture. The society's Dallas leader was General Edwin Walker, whom Lee Harvey Oswald had tried to kill in April of 1963 by shooting at him through a window in his home. (Oswald just missed.)

Thus, when Kennedy was shot on November 22, 1963, it was widely assumed that his killer was the kind of hate-filled reactionary who believed that Kennedy was selling out America to Soviet Communism and showing too little resistance to the civil rights movement. Such an assumption was buttressed by the great liberal intellectuals of the 1950s, such as Richard Hofstadter and Daniel Bell, whose writings had attempted to show that segregationists and the followers of Joe McCarthy—with their "paranoid style" of politics, in Hofstadter's phrase—were insecure, backward-looking extremists who threatened America's bright future.

In the minds of liberals, then, Kennedy's killer should have been a right-wing fanatic. But he wasn't. Oswald was a left-wing autodidact who had defected to the Soviet Union. When he found the USSR too bureaucratic, he returned to America and began proselytizing for Fidel Castro and his supposedly new brand of Third World revolution. Nor was Oswald an irrational, discontented Dostoyevskian loner, as some depicted him. He was in fact a joiner of movements and something of a self-defined intellectual who thought that his mixture of Marxism and anarchism made him smarter and more sophisticated than his frivolous peers. More problematic was the argument of James Reston, the influential *New York Times* columnist who, just after the assassination, argued in a column called "A Portion of Guilt for All" that Kennedy had been crucified on the altar of American violence. Brushing aside the evidence, Reston held that "all of us had a part in the slaying of the president." This claim was but a step from what became the standard-issue 1960s argument that American was a "sick society."

But Reston was the soul of reason compared with the conspiracy theorists who laid the assassination at the feet of a shadowy business cabal or the CIA—or even President Johnson. It turned out that the paranoid style described by Hofstadter was equally a property of the left and right. Liberals were becoming unhinged. But at the same time that liberals were losing their grip on reality, Lyndon Johnson's landslide defeat of Barry Goldwater in the 1964 election amped up both utopian expectations and attacks on Johnson by anti-Vietnam-war intellectuals who compared Johnson to Hitler. Their motives were mixed. They had reason to be appalled by Vietnam, but also, as Paul Potter of SDS put it directly: "The intellectuals want power."

Bill Moyers, a young aide to Lyndon Johnson, made no bones about it: "Johnson has a talent for power," and "power these days is brains, and he goes for it." The prominent journalist Theodore White agreed. In 1967, he grandly pronounced that there is a "new power-system in American life—and the new priesthood . . . of American action-intellectuals."

Half of Johnson's cabinet was composed not of businessmen and politicians but academics. The secretary of Health, Education, and Welfare, John Gardner, had a slip of the tongue that captured the moment: "When the faculty gets together—I mean, when the *Cabinet* gets together. . ." The politics of Sinclair Lewis's *Main Street*, Teddy White asserted, were at an end, as were the old limited-government ideas that had sprung from it. By contrast, he concluded, "[for] intellectuals, now is a Golden Age."

But the Golden Age was short lived. It was already over by the time White wrote. "The elite intelligentsia," said Daniel Patrick Moynihan in response to the brutal attacks he suffered for acknowledging the breakdown of the black family, "are turning against the country—in science, in politics, in the foundations of patriotism."

Enhanced education brought with it claims to a superior social status. Princeton professor and historian of liberalism Eric Goldman, a key LBJ adviser, saw that a new power group was abroad in the land. He called the members of this new highly literate formation "metromericans." He described them as the self-conscious junior executive, the lawyer, the accountant and his wife in the suburbs of New York, Chicago, or San Francisco who "derived a sense of status from reading Saul Bellow's *Herzog*, John Kenneth Galbraith's *Affluent Society*, and David Reisman's *Lonely Crowd*." The metromericans tended sincerely to react to public figures and public issues in a way similar to these intellectuals, and they "cared about political leaders who cared about men like Bellow, Galbraith and Riesman."

Goldman's "metromericans" were reinforced by the emerging New Class of young highly educated professionals. The young professionals in-training had been told time and again that they were, in the words of one of their chroniclers, *Village Voice* columnist Jack Newfield, "the brightest and most sensitive members of their generation." They were a "prophetic minority," said Newfield, "the best young this nation will produce for generations." They were taught that they needed to plan for others who were less capable and less worthy than they were. Herbert Croly's 1909 book *The Promise of American Life*, the Ur-text of early liberalism, became the political Baedeker for the would-be clerisy of the 1960s. In 1965 alone, *The Promise* was reprinted by three major publishers, each featuring a new introduction by a prominent liberal historian (in one case, Arthur Schlesinger).

In these days of the Great Society, teachers at the best schools taught their students to read *The Promise* not only as the founding document of modern American liberalism—and a prophesy of the New Deal—but also as a charter empowering them to become the country's future political and cultural leaders. Their influence would, David Bazelon argued presciently, explode when they achieved "an awareness of themselves as a class." That self-awareness, their sense of self-consciousness as a group, was borne into public life by the great conflicts in the 1960s over race and war. Endowed with the moral authority that came from their ethically justified opposition to racism and the ill-conceived war in Vietnam, they came to see themselves as a new governing class, and they looked to other dissident elements of society to serve as their cat's-paws. Blacks, youth, and later women all entered their imagination as possible prosthetic-proletariats who might overthrow the existing order.

The influential left-wing academic Christopher Lasch, at the time a neo-Marxist, argued that the dissatisfaction of the New Class made it part of "the emerging anti-bourgeois movement" in America. "The immediate constituency for a radical movement, it is clear," he wrote, "lies in the professions, in sections of suburbia, in the ghetto, and above all in the university, which more than any other institution has become a center of radicalism." Nationally, the coalition of liberals and radicals that Lasch envisioned was first visible in the 1968 Democratic Party primaries when what Michael Harrington dubbed "the constituency of conscience" rallied behind the insurgent candidacy of Eugene McCarthy and pushed President Lyndon Johnson out of the 1968 Democratic Party primaries. By 1968, liberals largely shared the New Left's moral outrage at Johnson's presidency and the war in Vietnam. Because they shared so much of the New Left's disdain for middle-class morality, and its suspicions of capitalism as predatory, liberals found it hard to defend themselves from the radicals' assaults.

Liberalism of the 1950s had not only been anti-Communist, but it had also feared that fascism in the form of a soul-sapping mass culture was an imminent danger to America. As discussed in Chapter 8, the work of Ortega, Huxley, and the Frankfurt School philosophers gave voice to this fear of homegrown fascism. By the 1960s, this fear had only grown: The '60s New Left discerned a new and even more pressing fascist threat, coming from what it called "corporate liberalism," which was in effect synonymous with the expansion of government power at home and abroad under the aegis of the Great Society. The idea that liberalism was a disguised form of fascism became an article of faith for many in the New Left. The literal truth of the claim of fascism wasn't at issue. In the wake of the Kennedy assassination, "the paranoid sense that American liberalism was Fascism in disguise," explained New Leftist Evan Stark, "defined an oppositional project which broke decisively with the boring machinations of Communists and Trots as well as Social Democratic gradualism, a total opposition pushed to creativity by its very unpredictability." In ordinary times, such excess would have been written off as crankiness, but with race riots at home and a bloody war abroad, political life became caught up in what the French call *surenchère*—political one-upsmanship—in which the contestants tried to surpass each other in denouncing the evils of the society.

Subtly, two substantial changes occurred in liberal thinking. Imbued with the promise of an earthly paradise of sexual freedom, the emerging left-liberalism promoted both the privatization of virtue and vice as well as the politicization of the personal. In the new dispensation, repression of individual libidinal desire was equated with the kind of political oppression associated with police states. A merely liberal society, argued SDS leader Tom Hayden, stifles human creativity, leaving men "impotent" and unable to achieve either orgasmic or social fulfillment. "In SDS," explained an associate of Hayden's, "fucking is a statement of community" and a cure for alienation. This emphasis on the intensity of experience as the measure of value made possible arguments that gained wide currency, even though such arguments not only resisted facts, they tried to transcend them

Edgar Z. Friedenberg, frequent contributor to *The New York Review of Books* in the 1960s, noted approvingly that "elitism is the great and distinctive contribution students are making to American society." But Jack Newfield, who had praised the campus New Left extensively in the pages of the *Village Voice*, saw an underside to its success. "In the future, it is possible that the new occupational structure will provide the basis of a two-class society of educated technocrats and janitors," he wrote. "If this were to happen, then the emergence of an unprecedented number of college graduates . . . would have the most reactionary consequences."

Eric Hoffer, the longshoreman philosopher who watched as the San Francisco docks automated in the 1950s and '60s, saw the underside of liberalism and how it reinforced the changes that were occurring in the economy. Hoffer celebrated the American exceptionalism that liberals had been bemoaning ever since the 1920s, and he feared that with the coming of the post-industrial age, America would "no longer be the common man's continent." "The masses are on their way out," he wrote. "[The] elites are finally catching up with us. We can hear the swish of leather as saddles are heaved on our backs. The intellectuals and the young, booted and spurred, feel themselves born to ride us." Hoffer foresaw that the New Class would try to govern the working people much as colonial officials governed the natives. They are, he wrote, an "army of scribes clamoring for a society in which planning, regulation, and supervision are paramount and the prerogative of the educated." And although the California State University system in which there is now one bureaucrat for every professor was well in the future, he anticipated that "since the tempo of the production of the literate is continually increasing, the prospect is of ever swelling bureaucracies."

CHAPTER 10

★ ★ ★

From Jim Crow to Crow Jim

As liberals Whigishly recount the story of the 1960s to themselves, the movement for racial equality is rightly credited with a ripple effect whereby a widening circle of outsiders—women, Hispanics, gays, and the disabled—were finally drawn into the sacred circle of full citizenship. It was, said liberal author Peter Clecak, "a stunning success evidenced in the widening and deepening of personhood" and "the enlargement of cultural space." Clecak was both right and radically incomplete.

The left-liberalism that emerged from the 1960s was simultaneously statist and libertarian. As in the civil rights movement, the state became the instrument for freeing individuals from social oppression by liberating them from stifling norms, including the imperatives to work and marry. The upshot was a country in which liberal lawyers, acting as the advanced guard of a reforming bureaucracy, were pitted against the wider society so that mutuality gave way to competing loyalties.

LBJ worried that the civil rights laws would cost the Democrats the South politically. What he didn't see was that nationally, it cost liberalism its aura of representing the average American. Some of the tensions were unavoidable, but as victories over adversity hardened into bureaucratic impositions on Middle America, the liberal propensity for searching out ever more marginal instances of racial or gender inequity undermined the ideal of self-government while polarizing the polity.

In the 1960s and '70s, the American "can-do" spirit crashed against the barriers of seemingly unbridgeable racial hostility at home and an implacable North Vietnamese foe abroad. The time between the Watts race riots of 1965 and American withdrawal from Vietnam in the aftermath of Watergate were, for many American liberals and their children, a period of impending apocalypse. For them, America had lost the founding birthright that had endowed the country with a sense of its own inherent goodness and invincibility. The concurrent crises of foreign policy, race, and culture subjected the nation's institutions to an intense criticism that sometimes revealed the ugly disparity between professed principles and actual practices.

As in the period during WWI, liberals saw their hopes betrayed not by the right but by a president they had initially thought of as one of their own. The sequence of events was different, but the similarities were nonetheless striking. Vietnam stirred the same sort of sentiments about the supposedly inherently evil nature of America as had WWI and the Depression. The WWI-era writings of Randolph Bourne were reissued to a wide readership in liberal policy circles and on college campuses. As in WWI, when many liberals overlooked the evils of the Kaiserreich, the Stalinists of North Vietnam were largely given a moral free pass. And as in the 1930s, the call for a new kind of freedom at home was joined by a love affair with tyrannical regimes abroad.

Under the very best of circumstances, the belated and imposed entry of African Americans into the mainstream of American life would have been a wrenching affair. World War II produced a heightened concern with tolerance and racial injustice as Catholics and Jews were more fully accepted as part of the nation's fabric; but even so, American democracy wasn't up to the task of seamlessly integrating African Americans. In the wake of the *Brown v. Board of Education* decision, it took what Tocqueville described as a "tutelary power"—the Supreme Court, a bevy of Republican judges holding court in Southern jurisdictions, and Martin Luther King and the Freedom Riders—to begin dismantling segregation in the South. Making amends for America's original sin was bound to deflate democracy.

The sins of segregation were bound, when finally confronted, to present a forceful challenge to America's sense of itself as a self-governing people. A century and a quarter earlier, Alexis de Tocqueville saw that because an entire people cannot "rise above itself" only a "despot" could free African Americans from the shackles of legalized prejudice. That "despot" was the federal courts.

In 1938, in the midst of the New Deal (which depended on white Southern votes), Judge Harlan Stone saw that judicial power, though it had for good reason been regarded as undemocratic, could actually promote democracy when used on behalf of "discrete and insular minorities" cut off from "those political processes ordinarily to be relied upon to protect minorities." This was the thinking that led to *Brown v. Board of Education*. "What Brown had begot," noted Judge J. Harvie Wilkerson in 1979, "was a union of the mightiest and lowliest in America, a mystical passionate union bound by the pained depths of the black man's cry for justice and the moral authority, unique to the Court, to see that justice realized."

The great misfortune of the 1950s, a time of unprecedented African-American upward mobility, was that neither of the two leading political figures of the period— neither President Eisenhower nor his Democratic challenger in 1952 and 1956, Adlai Stevenson—was committed to racial integration. Eisenhower temporized and only hesitantly enforced desegregation decrees when challenged by obdurate Southerners. Southerners resisting desegregation were "not bad people," Eisenhower told his appointee Chief Justice Earl Warren. "All they are concerned about is to see that their sweet little girls are not required to sit in school alongside some big overgrown Negroes." In private conversation, Stevenson saw the gradualism of "moderate minded" Southerners as the "only Negro hope."

It was the very alienation of liberals from the mainstream of American life that made them far more sensitive to the injustices of racism and segregation than other Americans were. The successes of the civil rights movement were made possible by an alliance between Martin Luther King and integrationist liberals who rightly insisted on a common citizenship for all Americans. Their achievements were the high point of twentieth-century American liberalism. A deserved glow of virtue accompanied the efforts to desegregate America; it faded, however, in the pall cast by urban riots and the dead ends of black nationalism and multiculturalism.

The period in which whites, as represented by the national political leadership, and African Americans agreed on the need to create a colorblind country was unfortunately very brief. Both the formal equality of full citizenship and equality of income promised little in the short run for the vast majority of the black population. By the mid-1960s, black demands had shifted from color blindness to color consciousness. Black nationalism and calls for redemptive violence overshadowed the earlier acclaim for integration efforts, a shift widely attributed to the fact that blacks now confronted the subtle forms of discrimination in the North rather than the open segregation of the South. This explanation, while partly true, obscures the growth of an ideology from which liberalism has drawn political sustenance, purchased at a considerable price.

While American political leaders equivocated, anticolonial struggles in Africa, the development of the Marxist and neofascist ideology of Third Worldism, and the buildup of frustrations in the big cities set the stage for the revolutionary rhetoric and riots of the 1960s and an Africa-American politics built on a soft version of separatism. "The 1950s and early 1960s," notes journalist Michael Tomasky, "saw the left embracing not just Third World independence movements, but wholesale repudiation of the principles on which the First World had been built."

In 1903, the great black intellectual W.E.B. Du Bois wrote, "The problem of the twentieth century is the problem of the color line—the relation of the darker to the lighter races of men in Asia and Africa, in America and the islands of the sea." His words were given geopolitical meaning during World War I by the German general Colmar von der Goltz, who saw the discontent of native people, dominated by British and French colonialism, as the weak spot of the West. "The hallmark of the twentieth century," he argued, "must be the revolution of the colored races against the colonial imperialism of Europe." In the wake of WWI, the German baton was taken up the USSR, which organized the Congress of the Peoples of the East, held in Baku, Azerbaijan, in 1920. But the Soviet effort to deploy the Third World against the West came to fruition only after WWII, when decolonization opened up new possibilities.

The 1955 Bandung Conference, in Indonesia, of twenty-nine Asian and African states, many created by decolonization, announced the emergence of the Third World as a player in world affairs. It in turn engendered a new ideology, Third Worldism, which thrilled African-American intellectuals by promising to redefine American blacks not as a national minority but as part of a new international majority.

Representative Adam Clayton Powell, a Democrat from Harlem, saw the emerging countries as uniting "colored" humanity against Western oppression. The French philosopher Jean-Paul Sartre similarly argued that the West would be "liberated" from capitalism, with its fetishes of democracy, pluralism, and voting. Sartre influenced Frantz Fanon, a psychiatrist from the French colony of Martinique, who would become the most important voice of Third Worldism among young black activists and intellectuals. Fanon seemed to supply the means to restore the black man's collective dignity: The purifying power of collective violence, he said, would heal the psychological damage done by colonial oppression and white culture. He insisted that anyone who was not at least partly black had a "Hitler hidden in him."

Fanon's most influential book, *The Wretched of the Earth*, published in America shortly before the 1965 Watts riots, rejected acculturation to Western ways and argued that collective action was the only curative for the psychic wounds of colonialism and racism. "Violence alone, violence committed by the people, violence organized and educated by its leaders," he wrote, "makes it possible for the masses to understand social truths" and frees them from "despair and inaction."*

The Wretched of the Earth became required reading for 1960s radicals. It reinforced the views of the preeminent street preacher of the time, Malcolm Little, known as a Malcolm X. A bisexual hustler and small-time hoodlum, Malcolm X found strength in the black nationalism preached by the Nation of Islam, an idiosyncratic American break-off from orthodox Islam. Elijah Muhammad, the leader of the Nation of Islam spoke of the "home country" as a locale where blacks and Muslims ruled, and where the white man was despised as a devil, a snake who alone accounted for all black ills.

---

* The Cuban revolution of 1959 took the most prosperous island in the Caribbean and sent it backward. Its leader Fidel Castro had been an admirer of Francisco Franco, but he and his knight errant Che Guevara became icons among America liberals. They represented the hope embraced by black militants and critics of mass culture that the Third World, unspoiled by the depredations of capitalist prosperity, could be the future of humanity. Fanon's writing on race and the Algerian Revolution, dramatized in the film *The Battle of Algiers*, resonated with many African Americans, who felt similarly bitter.

The charismatic Malcolm X took Elijah Muhammad's message and gave it a far broader currency, seeking not so much justice as revenge. He drew on the history of black oppression in American and roused crowds with his searing accounts of slavery and humiliations piled upon humiliations by the white man who had stripped Africans of their very names and identity. "We didn't land on Plymouth rock," he declaimed. "My brothers and sisters, Plymouth Rock landed on us."

Malcolm X's instrument of revenge would be the colored and Islamic masses: In the course of reclaiming a black identity, their hatred would reshape the globe. When he heard that President Kennedy had been assassinated, he responded that it was a case of "chickens coming home to roost." And justice would require the death of far more than one white president. He dreamed of an A-bomb being dropped on New York, and he inspired his followers to imagine a race war in the U.S. This great battle would free the Vietnamese of the American presence and also overthrow white power at home. Malcolm X, who had become an orthodox Muslim, was murdered by gunmen connected to the Nation of Islam.

"There is not a Negro alive," wrote black novelist James Baldwin, "who does not have this rage in his blood." Like Malcolm X, Baldwin argued against integration into American society on the grounds that it would strip blacks of their true, racially generated, identity. The price of acculturation was "self-hatred," he said. And, in any case, he asked, why should blacks want to become part of "the white man's world"? "Intellectually, morally, and spiritually, [it] has the meaningless ring of a hollow drum and the odor of slow death," he said, adopting the arguments of the mass-culture critics. "Who has not dreamed of violence? That fantastical violence which will drown in blood, wash away in blood, not only generation upon generation of horror, but will also release the individual horror, carried everywhere in the heart?" Acculturation to white norms was nothing less than acquiescence in colonialism. "Black has *become* a beautiful color," Baldwin proclaimed, "not because it is loved but because it is feared." By that measure, the street toughs of the lumpen-proletariat were a revolutionary force. "What the Negro *has* discovered, and on an international level, is the power to intimidate."

In 1965, the future was acted out on stage at the St. Marks Theater in Manhattan's East Village. The theater presented *The Slave* in a double bill with *The Toilet*, both by LeRoi Jones (later Amiri Baraka), who presented himself as a "would be black Nechayev" out to crush the "blue-eyed white devils." In *The Slave*, a neutered white Jewish liberal is beaten and shot and his wife raped as a prelude to the revolutionary destruction of the universities and the cities. Increasingly, anti-white hatred was cloaked in the garb of a race-oriented Marxism in which injustices such as unemployment were understood as capitalist violence, justifying black revolutionary counter-violence. Fanon-like, the dispossessed would liberate themselves by killing their tormentors.

On August 5, 1965, President Lyndon Johnson pushed through the landmark Voting Rights Act, opening a new era of black participation in American politics. A hopeful President Johnson declared that the law meant that the "American Negro" had now obtained the "freedom to enter the mainstream of American life." In just two years, black voter registration in Mississippi would leap from 7 to 70 percent. The Act was a moment of glory. It seemed to herald a bright future. But just six days later, on August 11, the Watts riots, sometimes better characterized as a "rebellion," broke out in Los Angeles, leaving thirty-four dead.

The rioting in the South Los Angeles section of Watts shook the hopes that African Americans might, with considerable additional aid, follow a path similar to one that earlier rural migrants to the city had taken. Watts seemed an improbable locale for mass violence. As early as the 1930s, it had the highest rate of black home ownership in the country. And blacks benefited from the WWII boom when Japanese internment and Mexican deportation created a demand for low-wage African-American labor. By 1964, the year prior to the Watts riots, an Urban League "statistical portrait" rated L.A. the best of sixty-eight cities for black employment, housing, and income. "In a Third World setting," said the travel writer Paul Theroux, "Watts would be upper middle class because its drug dealers would have been long since executed."

The rioting, set off in part by the heavy-handed tactics of the storied LAPD, led to 34 deaths, 1,032 injured, and 3,438 arrested. Due to the seriousness of the riots, the city declared martial law. Sergeant Ben Dunn of the LAPD said: "The streets of Watts resembled an all-out war zone in some far-off foreign country. It bore no resemblance to the United States of America." Black militants, infused with Third Worldism, put a positive spin on the violence in which an estimated 75,000 had participated.

Where officials spoke of rioting, they spoke of rebellion and even revolution. H. Rap Brown, the leader of the formerly nonviolent Student Nonviolent Coordinating Committee, described the onset of the rioting as the Independence Day of the internal colony. It was on that day that "the blacks of Watts picked up their guns to fight for their freedom," he said. "That was our Declaration of Independence, and we signed it with Molotov cocktails and rifles."

Watts signaled a secession of sorts from middle-class and white norms. The institutions such as the schools, the civil service, and the health department—so important to immigrant mobility—were redefined as dehumanizing instruments of white domination. Black power was to be a struggle not so much for self-sustaining freedom as for the self-satisfaction that comes from humbling one's oppressor. Its resentful aim was more retaliation than redress.

On the last day of rioting, August 17, 1965, "The Moynihan Report" on the breakdown of the black family was issued. It met a firestorm of verbal violence. Characterized as political "dynamite" by President Johnson's secretary of labor, Willard Wirtz, "The Moynihan Report" was an account of the black family based on statistical and African-American sources. The author, Daniel Patrick Moynihan, then an obscure assistant secretary of labor, eschewed cultural explanations for the collapse and placed blame on the legacy of slavery and economic discrimination that left black men unable to provide for their families. "The richest inheritance any child can have is a stable, loving, disciplined family," Moynihan wrote.

Moynihan's solution, largely lost in the controversy the report generated, was "to bring the structure of the Negro family in line with the rest of our society" by providing work for black men. To provide that work, the charming Moynihan—a man of many tensions, who feared that upper-middle-class liberals were driving white ethnics from the Democratic Party—called for both racial quotas and European-style family allowances.

It was among the more conceptually and financially radical proposals ever submitted to a president—and it is even more fascinating, in retrospect, to think that its author would be considered only a few years later as one of the founding members of the group of thinkers known as the neoconservatives. The defining quality of the neoconservatives when it came to domestic policy was a newly rueful skepticism about the efficacy of massive government programs exactly like the one Moynihan had proposed.

"The Moynihan Report" produced an avalanche of hatred that can be rightly described as the closing of the liberal mind. In 1965, writing to Gunnar Myrdal, the pioneering student of American race relations, a staggered Moynihan told the Swede that he had been violently "anathematized as a racist, a fascist, an authoritarian, a bourgeois, and so across the spectrum of epithets." "Everybody," recounted a black feminist, "wanted to cut Daniel Moynihan's heart out and feed it to the dogs." The new "liberalism," noted an agonized Moynihan, "couldn't cope with the truth." The truth was just as he had diagnosed it: For the next three decades, the ongoing agonies of the black family were accompanied by the death throes of a formerly triumphant liberalism.

The liberal flight from evidence and empiricism was reflected in the politics of America's most political city (D.C. aside), New York. Rather than deal with the crime swamping their city, liberals followed the prescriptions of their matinee-idol mayor, John Lindsay, and initiated, in the midst of an economic boom, a massive increase in the welfare rolls. As Lindsay and his supporters saw it, welfare was reparation for the injustices imposed on African Americans.

G.W. Plunkitt, the late-nineteenth-century wit of Tammany Hall, once quipped: "Have you ever thought what would become of the country if the bosses were put out of business, and their places were taken by a lot of cart-tail orators and college graduates? It would mean chaos." Seer that he was, Plunkitt anticipated the sort of mischief and misfortune that New York's first true post-Tammany mayoralty would produce under John Lindsay. Lindsay's reign of the best and brightest sparked a Kulturkampf between black and whites, blacks and Jews, unions and back nationalists, the ethnic heirs of the New Deal and the heirs to the civil rights movement. All these tensions crystallized around the Ocean Hill–Brownsville school-decentralization strife in Brooklyn, a conflict so intense that it was described in apocalyptic terms at the time. Even today, if you ask older New Yorkers "which side were you on," you'll see the embers of their anger burning brightly.

The singular emphasis on white racism as the sole source of African-American poverty was exemplified by the "Kerner Commission Report" on the 1964–67 northern urban riots. It became holy writ for both white liberals and black nationalists. The key sections, written by Mayor Lindsay, accurately noted that the persecution suffered by African Americans far exceeded the discrimination suffered by immigrants to the big cities. But Lindsay downplayed the many similarities between illiterate immigrants from dirt-poor semi-feudal southern Italy and blacks arriving from the Mississippi Delta. All the new arrivals from backward rural areas suffered the dislocation of migration and the need to adapt to an urban industrial setting. Lindsay, like Malcolm X, reduced everything to white racism.

When Lindsay ran for reelection in 1969, he pioneered the top-bottom political coalition that would increasingly come to define liberalism. Lindsay's two opponents in the campaign both attracted white lower-middle-class and middle-class supporters who were enraged by the mayor, whom they mocked as a "limousine liberal." Faced with this, Lindsay cleverly jettisoned the intermediate stratum of society for a political alliance of the black and Puerto Rican poor on the one hand and wealthy white liberals on the other.

Lindsay's top-bottom electoral coalition had an au courant cultural correlate: swanky parties that uptown New Yorkers threw for the Black Panthers and their Puerto Rican imitators, the Young Lords. In the 1930s, the "Penthouse Bolsheviks" not only lived large but also elevated themselves morally above the ordinary folk in their support of left-wing causes. In the late 1960s and early 1970s, liberal New Yorkers, yearning for the thrills of the "white negro" once removed, rediscovered a new version of that double game.

In the most celebrated version of this era's radical chic, the enormously talented composer Leonard Bernstein, who came of age politically during the Comintern's Popular Front policy of the 1930s, held a party for handsome, leather-clad, Afro-plumed, Oakland street toughs who had made themselves heroes of the New Left. The Black Panthers presented a hard, thrilling version of black power. They spoke of rebuilding the inner cities as cooperative post-bourgeois societies of the sort supposedly created by the Cubans and the North Vietnamese. As a Panther leader explained it:

> To decentralize...implement probably on just the community level—socialism. And that's probably too Marxist-Leninist for those

> motherfuckers to understand, but we think that Stalin was very clear in this concept, that socialism could be implemented in one country; we say it can be implemented in one community.

The Panther spokesman in Bernstein's luxuriously appointed living room—with celebrities such as Barbara Walters, Eddy Duchin, and Frank Stanton listening raptly as waiters passed hors d'oeuvres—explained that the United States was "the most oppressive country in the world, maybe in the history of the world." Of the ninety or so present, only one person, the movie producer Otto Preminger, a refugee from Nazi Germany, voiced an objection. The party for "the beautiful people," explained Tom Wolfe in his memorable account of the event, was a "radical chic" means for the guests to certify their superiority over the hated middle class, the little people who had voted for John Lindsay's opponents because they feared crime.

The effect of the 1960s riots and the rise of radical chic was that African Americans were invited to enter into the larger society on their own terms. The schools, which had once helped set white-skinned peasants on the path to success, ceased incorporating dark-skinned peasants from the backward South into mainstream culture. Discipline as a prerequisite for adult success was displaced by the authentic self-expression of the ill-educated. The newcomers, it was said, were not culturally deprived; they were "differently abled," more spontaneous and expressive. And after all, should a society guilty of Vietnam and racism be allowed to impose its values on innocent victims of its depredation? Like devout Christians getting right with Jesus, liberals struggled to get right with racism. They wanted to help blacks in the worst way, and that's just what they did.

The white liberal idealization of the black hipster, seen as the incarnation of authentic experience, produced considerable collateral damage. In the 1920s, the first generation of liberals looked to Mexican peasants and East European mystics for inspiration when they sought to cleanse themselves of the emotional impurities imposed by middle-class mores. During the 1930s, as Whittaker Chambers recounted in his moving memoir, *Witness*, liberals saw "the working class as a source of unspoiled energy which may salvage the crumbling West." In the 1950s, the anthropologist Margaret Mead depicted the islanders on Samoa—who had been freed from slavery, cannibalism, and human sacrifice by an alliance of natives and Christian missionaries—as people free of the Western foibles of sexual inhibition and jealousy. The naive Mead, like her successors in the 1960s, had been played for a fool by the locals.

By the end of the '60s, liberals who at first had been troubled by the rising violence of the decade were now—having been tutored by black hipsters such as LeRoi Jones—exhilarated by its possibilities. The hipsters who specialized in "knowing the score" knew that anything that angered the "squares" as much as random violence did must surely be cathartic. The riots were celebrated as a collective version of the apocalyptic orgasm.

The New York Review of Books, perhaps the premium organ of radical chic, placed a Molotov cocktail on its cover. *The New Republic*'s Richard Gilman, anticipating full-blown multiculturalism, argued that blacks have chosen to live by a separate set of myths that are not "subject" to the "scrutiny" of Western tradition. Only authentic blacks had a right to evaluate the political choice made by the toughs, argued Tom Wicker of the *New York Times*. For Wicker, the young street actors not only promised a release from inauthentic middle-class mores; they laid the ground for a new revolutionary class that would be capable, in alliance with the student radicals of the New Class, of overthrowing the old order.

In the words of one New York militant, the economy had to adjust to African Americans rather than the other way around. The Irish partly excepted, immigrants had traditionally had to climb the job ladder. In place of those rungs, liberals and black nationalists introduced a framework of state-sponsored mobility produced by creating whole new layers of government in the form of anti-poverty, anti-discrimination, housing, and social-services agencies. The bureaucracies provided middle-class jobs for educated African Americans and also a political outlet for white radicals looking for leverage against the larger society they had deemed hopelessly racist. The result was that the gains of the 1950s slowed as African Americans took the Irish path to the middle class: political power. It was a path all too visibly sabotaged, however, by black mayors such as Marion Barry, Coleman Young, and Richard Hatcher. Presenting themselves as radicals who were hip to the fraud of American society, these black-power mayors undermined their cities and Africa-American prospects in the name of the authenticity achieved by angering whites.

One of the leading spokesmen for black power in these years was Stokely Carmichael. He had once been a leader of the Student Nonviolent Coordinating Committee but shifted his allegiance to the street-tough Black Panthers. "Integration is a subterfuge for the maintenance of white supremacy," he asserted. "Can whites, particularly liberal whites, condemn themselves? Can they stop blaming us, and blame their own system? Are they capable of the shame that might become a revolutionary emotion?" His answer to all these questions was yes. In the ensuing years, white liberals such as the *Times*'s Tom Wicker abased themselves before the demands of black power. They excused each and every violation of norms formerly assumed to be transracial; black actions, the logic went, could be judged only by fellow blacks in light of what they needed to advance black power.

By Wicker's standards, and they were widely shared by liberals in this dawn of the age of political correctness, if black leaders described the violence sweeping the cities as part of a "rebellion" against white colonialism, then that's the description that was apt. And any talk about a "white flight" from criminality was evidence of racism. And because racism had rightly become taboo, whites who were genuinely consumed by guilt and fear and unable to discuss crime without being denounced accelerated their flight from the cities.

The proponents of black power found much to admire in Africa's "big men," such as Kenya's Jomo Kenyatta, who wrecked both the Kenyan economy and the career of Barack Obama's father. In some cases, black-power adherents sought to emulate the much-admired Kwame Nkrumah of Ghana. "Seek ye first the political kingdom," argued Nkrumah, "and all else shall be added unto you." In other words: Seize political power and from it wealth will follow. Nkrumah left Ghana in ruins.

America's "little big men," such as Coleman Young of Detroit and Marion Barry of Washington, D.C., seized power in their "chocolate cities." Young came to power in the long political wake of the 1967 Detroit riots, in which the National Guard and the 82nd Airborne were called in to quell five days of rioting; during the uproar, 40 people were killed, 1,000 injured, and 7,000 arrested. Hewing to black-nationalist principles, Mayor Young all but formally invited whites to leave the city. What remained after the riot, wrote the *Detroit News* in 1987, was "something worse than a slum." The remains of the downtown had become "inscrutable megaliths in a wilderness of rubble so desolate that you can stand in the middle of Woodward St., the heart of the riot, at midday and not see a single auto for miles in any direction."

Young was an innovator of sorts. His victorious fight to extend the city's income tax to commuters was part of a signal shift in liberal politics. When he was unable to wring more revenue from the auto companies that were beginning to decamp for less unionized states, Young and his progressive allies moved to extract more from the private economy by expanding the power of public-sector unions.

Marion Barry, who had become a force in the Student Nonviolent Coordinating Committee, feared that the politicized lumpens might threaten the social order of the nation's capital, and he offered himself as the intermediary between the "the streets and the suites." Barry presented himself as a hipster Marxist of sorts, as did Richard Hatcher in Gary, Indiana, and Sharpe James in Newark. These black leaders deprofessionalized their work forces and redistributed jobs and money to their political retainers and the public-sector unionists. They created unbeatable political machines in the name of the poor, who became increasingly impoverished. They left their cities, overrun by the rolling riots of a seemingly never-ending crime wave, in ruins.

In the segregated post–World War II world, Shelby Steele's striving, African-American father was accused of "getting above himself." "Responsibility," Steele writes, "made fools of us," because society quite literally labored to defeat his father's ambition, even as it left him entirely responsible for his life and family. In the wake of the 1960s, Steele explains, when segregation ended, a culture of responsibility without rights was replaced by a framework of rights without responsibilities. In this reversal, segregation was succeeded not by the responsibility that comes with freedom, but by the destructive assumption that African Americans are not accountable for their actions.

"One has to be grateful to white guilt," Steele notes, "for bringing about possibly the greatest social transformation in American history." But the guilt overshot its mark. The same tide that swept away segregation also took away the institutions and attitudes essential to thriving in freedom. Through "disassociation," as Steele terms it, whites strived to separate themselves from the stigma of racial bias. But in doing penance for the sins of racism, too many were more concerned with demonstrating their moral purity than with the actual results their policies produced. Good intentions were supposed to be enough.

What followed under the guise of eliminating "institutional racism" was the "redistribution of responsibility." Under this new dispensation, blacks as a group were considered no more the agents of their own destiny than they had been under slavery. What was different was that their suffering could be converted into political capital and social spending. Failure would serve only as further proof of black victimization, because race, several generations of academics and journalists explained, "was not a mere barrier but the all-determining reality" in which blacks lived And the answer to failed social spending was always more social spending.

Steele recalls listening to a 1967 speech by the comedian Dick Gregory, who called on his black audience to "get hip" and raise their consciousness. Thinking back, Steele notes that he was witnessing the birth of "hipster Marxism." The hipster knows the game is rigged but tries to subvert it to his own advantage. Here was an opportunity that most tricksters could only dream of, a chance, Steele explains, "for working over the master for the rube that he is." Like mayors selling poverty for dollars from Washington, "the black leadership sold black weakness" to guilty whites looking to buy redemption. The race hustlers claimed that there were separate "black ways of knowing," and "fad after fad like Ebonics" was an attempt to circumvent the hard work necessary for upward mobility. The idea of free will, Steele says, was derided by university sophisticates as "largely a delusion of the common man, a kitschy individualism that Americans like to flatter themselves with." But the determinism was always a game on both sides, because the sophisticates saw it as applying only to others.

Since racist America has been "responsible for our suffering, why not for our uplift?" black leaders asked. But logically that made no sense. How can you rest your hopes on whites after having insisted that they are all bred-to-the-bone racists? The answer, Steele suggests, is that the black leadership sold forgiveness to guilty whites, who turned a blind eye even as black leaders were bilking their own people.

Mayor Ed Koch of New York, who described himself as a "liberal with sanity," saw at first hand the corrosive effects of liberal social policy. Koch visited private and publicly constructed apartments and asked, "What kind of message is the city sending when people who do their best to work and make it on their own don't get to live as well as those whose failings and plight entitle them to free housing?" The upshot, as Koch explained it, was that while equality was professed in public, it was understood in private that minorities couldn't be held to the standards of the larger society. "The result is to do with kind words what was once done with racial segregation . . . to isolate minorities from full participation in American society."

CHAPTER 11

★ ★ ★

McGovernized

The events of 1968 came forty years after the publication of H.G. Wells's *The Open Conspiracy: Blue Prints for a World Revolution*, which was reissued in 1931 with the new title *What Are We to Do with Our Lives?* Well's worldview, as I looked at in Chapter 5, was suffused with disdain for the ill-educated masses. His dreams of utopian renewal rested on the Nietzschean assumption that a "declaration of war on the masses by the higher men is needed." Referring to blue-collar workers, he dismissed "the facile assumption that the people at a disadvantage will be stirred to anything more than chaotic and destructive expressions of resentment." But, added Wells in *Open Conspiracy*, "If . . . we lose the delusive comfort of belief in that magic giant, the Proletariat . . . we clear the way for the recognition of an élite of intelligent, creative-minded people." Foreshadowing the '60s, he insisted that they were the ones who should make "an organized effort to recast the world." Wells was rhapsodic about the possibilities:

> Within the peace and freedom that the Open Conspiracy is winning for us, all these good things that escape us now may be ensured. A graver humanity, stronger, more lovely, longer lived, will learn and develop the ever-enlarging possibilities of its destiny. For the first time, the full

> beauty of this world will be revealed to its unhurried eyes. . . . And all the best of us will be living on in that ampler life.

Could any of the gurus of the '60s, from Marcuse to Roszak, have said it any better?

The '68ers who despised the ticky-tacky suburban houses and all the petty people without "proud dreams" and "proud lusts"—"all those damn little clerks"—who lived in them were the heirs to Wells's vision. For the nearly fifty years that have passed since the heyday of Haight-Ashbury, the '68ers have carried the idealized image of that time, their own "Open Conspiracy" against the masses. For many, the image is as vivid as ever. Their only glimpse of utopia till they espied Barack Obama, it stands in their mind like a sand castle that has never been eroded by the tides of history.

After Richard Nixon's election in 1968, liberalism expressed itself in sharply contradictory terms. The old New Deal rhetoric, still sometimes useful, was trotted out to justify expanding government in the name of *shared* interests. But a second increasingly ascendant strain saw the need to expand government on behalf of separate and sometimes competing groups, women and all those minorities—blacks, Latinos, Indians, gays, the handicapped, the transgendered, etc.—whose rights or interests had been trampled by white males in particular and the white majority more generally. What both strands concurred on, post-'60s, was the need for a fundamental transformation.

The line between left-liberals and radicals was increasingly blurred. "If one examines the official positions of Americans for Democratic Action or the New Democratic Coalition's statement of principles in 1972, they are seen to be socialist in all respects save one—they do not mention socialism," noted Socialist Michael Harrington, commenting on two leading liberal organizations. "They are for the redistribution of wealth, government intervention on behalf of the poor, minorities, and working people, and for the extension of public ownership."

The New Class was deeply sympathetic to a cultural liberalism that placed a heightened individual consciousness at the center of life. What they sought was not only the reformation of the economy but, even more important, an aestheticization of day-to-day life, very much in the mode of Herbert Croly. The path to a life of sexual pleasure and social harmony could come by way of liberating the passions and harnessing the economy to public purposes. This meld of moral deregulation with economic and health regulation was an argument for a self-correcting free market in morals and a state-run economy.

Many left-liberals didn't see the need to overthrow outright America's inherently fascistic system. Instead, they advocated transforming the system from within. According to Galbraith, the intellectual and scientific community, working through the universities and the state, should demand that corporations (given that they are already public bodies in effect) be treated "as a detached and autonomous arm of the state." State control would ensure efficient production but also make corporations "responsive to the larger purposes of the society." Meanwhile, the members of the corporate "technostructure," as Galbraith termed it, having absorbed the liberalizing influence of the universities where they were trained, and no longer concerned in their jobs with maximizing profits, would come to see the corporation in the same way: "as an essentially technical arrangement for providing convenient goods and services in adequate volume." The industrial system would thus be corrupted from within at the same time that it was subjected to increasing control from without.

In 1972, McGovernism presented itself as the political path to America's redemption. In that year's Democratic National Convention, the "new politics" of an anti-anti-Communism triumphed over the old anti-Communist social-democratic tradition lodged in the private-sector labor unions. It was a campaign in which silk-stocking Republicans moved into the Democratic column while blue-collar ethnic Democrats began to exit their ancestral home. This later shift was symbolized by the convention's refusal to seat the Illinois delegation led by Mayor Richard Daley. Instead, it recognized the contingent headed by Jesse Jackson. The Democratic Party allied itself with both the New Class McGovernites and the public-sector unions, and lost its grip on the ethnic middle class. It was on its way to becoming a top-bottom party.

The Democrats' simultaneous shift up the income scale and to the left was reflected in a televised 1972 confrontation between John Kerry, of the Vietnam Veterans Against the War, and his fellow naval officer John O'Neill, a supporter of the war. The men would face off again thirty-two years later, in 2004, when Kerry was the Democrat's presidential nominee. In his book *The Rise of the Unmeltable Ethnics*, Michael Novak saw the underlying class dynamic that only intensified in the following years:

> Comparison was immediately drawn between Kerry's Yale pedigree, good looks, smooth speech, powerful connections, and the limited resources, plainness of manner, ordinariness of O'Neill. The two personified the class resentments that were building.

Richard Nixon rode those resentments to a landslide victory in 1972.

Great Society "social science" fared quite well under the Nixon presidency. Nearly half of Nixon's cabinet members were social "scientists." In 1969, for the first time since the National Science Foundation was created in 1950, social "science" was given an equal place at the grant-giving table with the hard sciences. Also in 1969, the Swedish Academy saw fit to endow for the first time a Nobel Prize in economics, proof positive that social "science" had made it. Between 1970 and 1975, government spending on social "science," which had increased rapidly through the '60s, was almost doubled under Republican presidents.

But within a few years, the seemingly magnificent edifice of social science was in shambles, its reach having far exceeded its grasp. The field's technocratic authority was dramatically weakened by criticism from both blue-collar America and from the new liberals, relying more and more on moral authoritarianism, who saw social science as a threat to their aims. In the wake of the 1960s riots and the rolling riot of crime that followed, lower-middle-class whites discovered that the costs of racial integration were to be placed squarely on their shoulders by preachy liberals who were insulated from the effects of their own policies. These blue-collar whites developed an angry disdain for the social-science theories that justified the forced-busing policies requiring their kids to leave their neighborhood schools for more dangerous locales. What was worse, even as busing failed to produce integration but instead accelerated white flight, its proponents insisted on simply expanding its ambit so fewer could escape.

At the same time, liberal policymakers faced a rebellion from within as it became clear that social science was a good deal less authoritative than many liberals had once assumed. "We want to eliminate poverty, crime, and drug addiction," said the Social Science Research Council, "but we don't know how." When asked what had gone wrong, Daniel Patrick Moynihan replied that the real disaster was social science. It was time, he said, for social scientists to assert their absence of knowledge "with respect to many of the urgent issues." Social science, as the emerging neoconservative movement liked to point out, was far better at showing why policies failed than how they could succeed.

Liberals did not abandon their interest in social science when it could be used to buttress their positions. But they were more than willing to scupper it when it endangered their interests. Abortion, for instance, had been framed as a matter of social-scientific predictions about the eugenic dangers of overpopulation. But the danger had been oversold. With *Roe v. Wade*, abortion was recast as a matter of rights. Rights talk, trading on the moral authority of the civil rights movement, became the new language of liberalism.

Poised between fears of Nixon's "silent majority" and George Wallace's populist "fascism" on the one hand, and the promise of liberation from majority rule on the other, the 1972 Democratic Party platform, written by McGovern's supporters, referred fifty-nine times to various rights, most of them newly minted. These included, for everyone, "the right to quality, accessibility, and sufficient quantity in tax-supported services and amenities." Various groups warranted their own subcategory: "the rights of children," "the rights of youth," "the rights of servicemen and servicewomen," etc. Mocked in light of McGovern's landslide defeat as "the longest suicide note ever written," the platform was "an attempt," in the words of Yale law professor Own Fiss, "to construct a new social reality."

The platform promised full employment by making "economic security a matter of right." Everyone was entitled to "a decent job and adequate income with dignity." Perhaps to this end, and with a tip of the hat toward racial sensitivities, the party promised to oppose "arbitrarily high standards for entry to jobs." Among the services that were to be furnished as a matter of right were "educational opportunity, health care, housing, and transportation." At the same time, should someone choose not to exercise his right to a good job, the platform decreed that "welfare-rights organizations must be recognized as representatives of welfare recipients."

Here was the traditional program of European Socialist parties rewritten in the language of rights. But the platform went further than the Europeans did. Rights in American had traditionally functioned to protect the individual from arbitrary state power. In the new dispensation, blacks were to be protected from whites, women from men, students from teachers, children from parents and family, and nature from predatory humans. An all-encompassing yet benevolently centralized state would be organized into flying squadrons of rights-protectors dispensed to oversee most human interactions. This new arrangement proved a challenge to both majoritarian politics and the ideal of limited government. Trial lawyers, notes historian Donald Critchlow, "emerged as leaders, strategists, and key advisers to militant environmentalists and consumer advocates, public-interest organizations, progressive unions, feminists and pro-choice activists, and advocates for single-payer health care in America."

McGovern had won only 25 percent of primary votes in 1972, but he won the nomination because he masterfully manipulated the delegate-selection rules—setting a pattern for the future of liberalism. In the words of a chant by the New Leftists at the convention: "The Streets of '68 are the aisles of '72." Full-bore McGovernism triumphed in the form of a government that expanded vastly in order to redress ever more numerous grievances against society. The state grew on three fronts as state and federal rule-making produced a bevy of local bureaucracies.

The iron triangle of interest groups, congressional committees, and the interest groups' allies in the press was particularly effective in promoting environmental scares; federal regulatory agencies such as the Equal Employment Opportunity Commission inserted themselves into institutional hiring decisions to ensure racial balance; and the courts reshaped schools, mental hospitals, and other institutions, usually for the worse, by way of class-action lawsuits. Government became not just larger but far more pervasive.

Senator Edmund Muskie of Maine, at one point the leading contender for the Democratic nomination in 1976, saw the danger ahead. In the wake of the enormous majorities delivered to the Democrats after the Watergate scandals, Muskie sent a blunt message to his fellow liberals: To preserve progressive governance, they had to reform liberalism. He threw down the gauntlet:

> Why can't liberals start raising hell about government so big, so complex, so expansive, and so unresponsive that it's dragging down every good program we've worked for? . . . Our challenge this decade is to restore the faith of Americans in the basic competence and purposes of government. . . . We must recognize that an efficient government—well-managed, cost-effective, equitable, and responsible—is in itself a social good. . . . The first priority of efficient government is not a retreat from social goals, but simply a realization that without it, those goals are meaningless.

There was another less visible but closely related transformation also occurring: the political rise of the public-sector unions, which had played a key role in the McGovern campaign. American unionism, explained labor historian and activist Gus Tyler, went through three stages in the twentieth century. First there was the Gompers era of craft unionism, then the rise of industrial unions in the middle third of the century, and finally, beginning with President Kennedy's 1962 executive order permitting the unionization of federal employees, public-sector unions came to the fore. Public-sector unionism shifted the labor movement's focus from enhancing labor's share of *business* profits to extracting more from taxpayers by expanding the size and cost of government.

Federal employees weren't allowed to strike, but between 1966 and 1968, a time of intense racial conflict, there were nearly 600 strikes by state and local public-sector unions. Self-described militant Jerry Wurf, the leader of the American Federation of State, County, and Municipal Employees (AFSCME) was a close ally of Martin Luther King's, and it was at a rally to support an AFSCME sanitation strike that King was assassinated in 1968.

In the 1970s, the public-sector unions became a political venue for New Leftist, feminist, and black activists hoping to carry on in the militant spirit of the 1960s. Bitter strikes erupted in San Francisco, where the mayor's house was bombed and water mains sabotaged. In New York, union members dumped raw sewage into the rivers, and in Pennsylvania, the AFSCME leader led his members with the charge "Let's go out and close down this goddamned state." But despite the disruptions and the spectacle of New York City driven to the edge of bankruptcy by the unions' relentless demand for more, public-sector unionism continued to thrive. Between 1960 and 1980, public-sector jobs grew at twice the rate of private-sector work.

The result in the blue states was that unionized government employees increasingly gained the power to tell voters how an expanding government would spend their money, rather than the other way around. With the old urban machines in terminal decay, the public-sector unions gradually became the Democratic Party's most formidable electoral machinery.

In the left-liberal political-intellectual world of the 1970s and early 1980s—the world that produced the McGovern platform, the world Obama would join—it was capitalism not communism that was on its last legs. The one-two punch of the 1970s oil shock soon followed by Watergate empowered liberal journalists and academics to proclaim a crisis of "legitimacy." And that was before the steep 1974–75 recession, the near-bankruptcy of New York (the capital of capitalism), and the stagflation of the late 1970s sent the stock market tumbling down on President Carter, who responded with his historic "malaise speech." In preparation for the speech, Carter told his guests at the Camp David presidential retreat:

> I think it's inevitable that there will be a lower standard of living than what everybody had always anticipated . . . I think there's going to have to be a reorientation of what people value in their lives. I believe that there has to be a more equitable sharing of what we have. . . . The only trend is downward.

Within this newly constricted horizon, liberalism's redistributionist impulse, never far below the surface, metastasized into a zero-sum approach—a strictly competitive game in which one person's gain must entail someone else's loss. Richard Barnet, of the left-wing Institute for Policy Studies, captured the new mood by embracing the virtues of scarcity. The West, said Barnet, is on a collision course with nature, and the entire world suffers from the West's pathologically ceaseless desire to better itself. But progress cannot help, he argued, because progress is merely creative "plunder." Regulation and managed economies are best because they force us to succumb to the "rediscovery of limits." Barnet drew a contrast between the happy past and the apocalyptic future:

> In a traditional society where nothing changes, most people accept their place with a certain grace. . . . But when the principle of mobility is introduced into a society and envy is stimulated to induce people to work harder and to consume more, the pain of deprivation becomes more intense and gaps begin to matter. . . . It is the monumental social problem of the planet, the cause of mass starvation, repression, and crime, petty and cosmic.

Barnet represented a powerful new current, one that Marx in his day had dismissed as "feudal socialism."

The Seventies, notes British journalist Andrew Anthony, were "a period of radical possibilities, the last time educated people could speak of 'revolution' without joking." It was in this context that the British historian Geoffrey Barraclough, writing in *The New York Review of Books*, saw the inevitability of "a coming depression," and economist Robert Lekachman saw a return of the 1930s and asked, "Is the system finished?" Economist Robert Heilbroner saw the end of capitalism at hand, while world historian Arnold Toynbee predicted a "stockade society" and a "siege economy" overseen by "ruthless authoritarian governments" as a consequence of the downturn. Even so thoughtful an observer as Daniel Patrick Moynihan, in 1975, foresaw radical changes ahead: "Liberal Democracy . . . [is] a holdover form of government . . . which has simply no relevance for the future. It is where the world was, not where it is going."

While the Western welfare state was said to be suffering from a "legitimation crisis," the promise of Euro-Communism blossomed in Italy and also in France, where an alliance of Mitterand's Socialists and pro-Moscow Marxists seemed poised to capture the 1977 election, bringing Communists into a Western European government for the first time since WWII. With the long-awaited crisis of capitalism at hand, the moldering decay of Brezhnev's USSR barely registered with many Western observers, such as John Kenneth Galbraith, who continued in the '70s to marvel at the strength of the Soviet system. Like H.G. Wells in the 1930s, Galbraith saw the United States and the Soviet Union converging, with the U.S. becoming more statist and socialist and the USSR more democratic.

Galbraith's views seem fanciful today, but they didn't in that era, when economic planning was still accorded considerable respect. The Nixon administration, though reviled by liberals, carried on the expansion of state power begun in the Great Society. And when Nixon's fall in the Watergate scandal produced landslide Democratic and liberal victories in the 1974 off-year elections, spending surged all the more as power shifted for a time from the executive to the legislative branch.

The 1970s surge in the government's regulatory power, overshadowed by the great events of the era, went largely unnoted, but it was nonetheless profound. Before the 1960s, government regulation was aimed at specific industries. But with the creation of the Equal Employment Opportunity Commission (1964), the Environmental Protection Agency (1970), the Consumer Products Safety Commission (1972), and the vast expansion of the Federal Trade Commission, government asserted its influence over the entire economy. As David Vogel put it in his 1989 book *Fluctuating Fortunes*: "No other capitalist nation ha[d] established such extensive controls over business decisions affecting environmental and consumer protection, equal employment opportunity, and occupational health and safety."

The conflict between the capitalists and their critics, which in Europe meant a battle about socialism, identified as such, became, in America, a clash between competing and hostile elites: Ivy League–trained public-interest lawyers against their corporate counterparts. In the 1970s, the public, though agitated about issues such as inflation and forced busing, mobilized on neither side and largely observed the battle from the sidelines. The U.S. was heading toward the creation of an American version of European statism.

In August of 1976, America's leading conservative, William F. Buckley, looked upon the upcoming elections with foreboding; the GOP, he said, was "moribund." Gary Wills, a conservative convert to liberalism, asked hopefully whether the Republicans might not be on the verge of disappearing. "If [Ford is] defeated," said Kevin Phillips, the man who had foreseen the Nixon victories of '68 and '72, "the GOP may crumble."

The 1976 elections brought one-party rule back to Washington as the Democrats rolled up huge majorities in both the House and Senate while maintaining their dominance in thirty-six of the fifty statehouses. Although the new president, Jimmy Carter, had defeated incumbent Gerald Ford only narrowly after dissipating a 35-point lead in the polls, the forty-six new congressional Democrats who came in with him promised the party a new start: Democrats had regained congressional majorities as large as those they enjoyed during the New Deal and Great Society years. Summing up the meaning of the election four months into the Carter administration, the Democratic Forum, a neoliberal ginger group, noted that their party controlled more than 80 percent of the mayoralties in the nation's larger cities and almost 75 percent of all the elected offices in the nation. The result: "The Democratic Party now stands in a position of national dominance."

There was little coherent opposition to this liberal surge. John Sears, Ronald Reagan's campaign manager in his unsuccessful 1976 bid to unseat Gerald Ford, announced that the much-heralded New Right, which had seemed a force on the rise, was simply "dead." Similarly, writing in *Commentary*, the flagship journal of neoconservatism, Jeane Kirkpatrick, later Reagan's first ambassador to the U.N. but still a Democrat at the time, pronounced the New Right a failure.

But the Carter administration never jelled. Carter was the first Democratic president since Grover Cleveland who proved unable to characterize his administration with an overarching slogan. Wilson had the New Freedom; Truman, the Fair Deal; Kennedy, the New Frontier; Johnson, the Great Society. But Carter inherited the shards of a once cohesive party blown into quarrelsome fragments. Carter tried to speak for the people as a whole but brought into his administration the Naderites and other so-called public-interest lawyers, who sued small townships, school districts, and scout troops in the name of social justice.

Carter was a disappointment to liberals, as expressed by one of Carter's many critics, the left-libertarian columnist Nicholas von Hoffman: "It is not that Carter is ignoring today's dramatic and necessary ideas. There aren't any." Liberal Democrats were suffering, said *Washington Post* columnist David Broder, from "intellectual anemia."

Within two years, by the time of the 1978 midterm elections, the expectations of 1976 had been confounded and very nearly reversed. Republican conservatives were gaining new strength while liberal Democrats suffered from a lack of direction, except for that supplied by the rights-based interest groups and the public-sector unions whose shared slogans always called for more government and more, always more, spending.

Western governments, confident in their expertise during the 1960s, thought they could use an aggressive Keynesian fiscal policy to drive and direct the economy. "By the proper choice of monetary and fiscal policy, we as the artists, mixing the colors of our palette, can have the capital formation and rate of current consumption that we desire," explained the preeminent liberal economist Paul Samuelson. The full potential of the economy and therefore full employment would be achieved by Galbraith's "best and brightest," who would masterfully manage aggregate demand in the name of the collective interest of the country. If all went well, argued an enthusiastic Galbraith, the de-Stalinized Soviet Union and the West, which was making fuller use of the state, would "converge" in a common model of industrial governance.

President Carter's high-profile ambassador to the U.N., fellow Georgian Andrew Young, agreed. Writing in *Commentary* in 1978, foreign-policy analyst Carl Gershman noted that Young, a celebrated veteran of the civil rights movement, was eager "in drawing comparisons between [that] movement and the current dissident movement in the Soviet Union." He quoted Young as saying, "As the Soviet Union becomes more prosperous, as more and more people are exposed to any kind of art and culture,"—especially through the medium of television, Gershman added—"t[here will be a] human rights explosion that will not be unlike our civil rights movement." Young wanted to put the U.S. on the "right side of the moral issues in this world." Young and the McGovernites had little to say about the unhappy consequences of America's departure from Vietnam— a million-plus Vietnamese "boat people" and genocidal slaughter in Cambodia—because, as they saw it, the United States was deeply complicit in evil. "We unfortunately have been very reluctant to accept the concept of economic responsibility for all of our citizens," Young explained. The Soviet Union repressed its dissidents, he conceded, but "many of our own students were shot down on their own campuses."

In the 1960s, economists claimed to have conquered the business cycle. The biggest problem, in their view, was how to spend the tax money generated by Keynesian stimuli. Between 1960 and 1979, government outlays in Western industrialized countries rose from 37 to 49 percent of the gross national product. But in the '70s, the Keynesian priesthood was baffled by the simultaneous rise in unemployment and inflation. Keynesians had long embraced the Phillips Curve, which predicted that as inflation grew, unemployment would decline. Instead, in the late '70s, both rose together. Carter's treasury secretary, W. Michael Blumenthal, himself an economist (one of four in the Carter cabinet), spoke of a Keynesian-dominated "economics profession that is close to bankruptcy."

With Keynesianism discredited, the country seemed faced with the choice of moving left, toward further technocratic and state control, or right, toward the revival of entrepreneurialism. The left was cheered by the 1978 Humphrey-Hawkins Full Employment Act, which, on paper, empowered the government to create a "reservoir of public employment" should the private economy falter. Passed at a time when unemployment was 6.3 percent, the bill nominally guaranteed a federal job to the unemployed if Congress and the Federal Reserve couldn't reduce unemployment to 3 percent by 1982. In keeping with the "legalitarian" spirit of the day, the bill's first draft allowed citizens to sue the federal government if it didn't provide them with a job once unemployment was 4 percent or above. Financier Felix Rohatyn, credited with the corporatist arrangements that pulled New York City out of bankruptcy, saw Humphrey-Hawkins as "the first step toward state planning of the economy."

At the same time, Michael Harrington, of the Democratic Socialist Organizing Committee, established a major presence within the Democratic Party, serving as a bridge between the New Politics/New Leftists and the more militant social democrats. Harrington had the support of unions such as the United Auto Workers, AFSCME, and the Machinists. The unions' willingness to work closely with Harrington led *Business Week* to report that "socialism" was "no longer a dirty word to labor." Harrington had developed a strong political friendship with Ted Kennedy and used the occasion of the 1978 midterm Democratic Convention (since abolished) to rebuff Carter and pave the way for the Massachusetts senator to challenge the incumbent in 1980. The stage seemed set for a Kennedy restoration. On a rhetorical level, Ted Kennedy presented himself as the man who could keep alive the hopes invested in John and Bobby, and advance the 1960s ideals of social justice. On a practical political level, Ted Kennedy was the candidate of the rights-based interest groups and the public-sector unions that both aimed to expand the power of government.

President Carter faced "the war of the parts against the whole," in the words of John Gardner, who had been a member of LBJ's cabinet. On one hand, Carter was confronted with the rights-based claims of the special-interest groups looking to governmentalize American life; on the other, he wished to speak for the country as a whole, a country that largely looked askance at the efforts to politicize American life. It was an impossible task.

Ted Kennedy, who was relieved to win reelection in 1976 after he backed the unpopular measure to bus low-income African Americans into the low-income Irish neighborhoods of South Boston, had become the leading spokesman for interest groups entrenched by the McGovern campaign. Kennedy "took little cognizance of the roaring inflation, high interest rates, and ballooning federal deficit . . . and pushed instead for a huge domestic spending package," Carter aide Stuart Eizenstat accurately observed.

The Kennedy challenge to Carter was the high point of the leftward surge of the late '70s, but the consequences of Carter's defeat at the hands of Reagan were slow to sink in. Liberals attributed Reagan's victory to Carter's clumsy political personality and tended to shrug it off as a passing matter. They focused instead on Harold Washington's 1983 triumph in winning the Chicago mayoralty, which they read as a sign that the left was still on the rise.

The impetus for expanding the state came most strongly from three overlapping sectors: African Americans in the big cities, academics, and public-sector unions. In the academy, which produced more graduate students between 1965 and 1975 than it had in the previous sixty-five years, a cultural Marxism took hold that has yet to surrender its grip. Senator Moynihan's son John, a student at Wesleyan, captured the mood: He described Wesleyan, which would move into the vanguard of campus multiculturalism, as "an overgrown playground where Westchester Marxists drove Daddy's car to the protest and conversation focused on feminism and boycotting Nestlé."

At the 1980 Democratic Convention, 39 percent of the delegates had postgraduate degrees, compared with 4 percent of the adult population; at the same time, more than half the delegates to the convention were public-sector employees. In the fiscal sphere, the growing demands of rights-based groups and public-sector unions led even the *New York Times* in 1980 to warn that the rising cost of government was triggering a fiscal crisis. The booming stock market of the '80s lasted twenty-five years, forestalling a denouement, but the woes of the late '70s would return.

Daniel Patrick Moynihan, who represented the waning social-democratic strand of liberalism, was a man known for his prescience. Moynihan saw into the future when, in 1980, he described the presidential contest between incumbent Jimmy Carter and challenger Ronald Reagan: "Psychologists call it role reversal. As a Democrat I call it terrifying. . . . Not by chance but by dint of substance and often complex argument, there is a movement to turn Republicans into Populists, a party of the people arrayed against a Democratic Party of the State."

In 1980, *The New Republic,* in an anticipatory pre-election postmortem, spoke of the country's dissatisfaction with a government that had grown ever larger and ever more intrusive and yet was, as the old warhorse Hubert Humphrey complained, staffed by people worth "zilch":

> Give these Democrats their way and paralysis would be the permanent public policy: every decision of executive agencies litigated endlessly in

> the courts, every difference of opinion elevated into a natural and constitutional right, skin color guarantee[ing] special rights, independent of duties and not available to others; reporters have rights specifically denied to others; the biggest right of all is that there be no public good, with a right to expect anything from anyone. This is the narcissism of individuals and groups swollen into ideological authoritarianism

The increasingly liberal Democrats had distanced themselves "from the idea of representative government," the consultant Robert Squier observed. We "did not go left, we went up the social scale." And while the leaders were going up, the voters were going out. The disparity between utopian rhetoric about a world where more rights meant more for all, because there was a free market of sorts in morals, clashed with the dystopian realities of cratered cities. Intellectually impoverished and unable to think through their failings, liberals responded to Reagan largely with contempt and vitriol.

Faced with the danger of the unthinkable, a Reagan victory, novelist and *Nation*-magazine stalwart E.L. Doctorow played the Sinclair Lewis card. Reagan, he noted, had grown up in "just the sorts of places responsible for one of the raging themes of American literature, the soul-murdering complacency of our provinces." Referring to the small towns in Illinois where Reagan had spent his youth, he mocked, "The best and brightest fled all our Galesburgs and Dixons, if they could, but the candidate was not among them." Reagan was, he added, a "third-rate student at a fifth-rate college."

When Reagan graduated Eureka College, one of the first institutions of higher learning in the U.S. to admit men and women on an equal basis, he became a radio announcer in Des Moines. The future president then used his local fame "giving talks to fraternal lodges, boys' clubs and the like, telling sports stories and deriving from them Y.M.C.A. sorts of morals." For Doctorow, evidently, the story of Reagan was *It Could Happen Here.*

The disdain for Reagan freed liberals from the need to rethink their policies. Besides, Reagan's victory, shock that it was, left the interest-group structure of congressional government intact. Intertwined with congressional committees and the media, liberal interest groups thrived by "parceling out to private parties the power to make public policy," explained political scientist Theodore Lowi. Liberal interests never reexamined their assumptions, even when faced with social and political failure. They never asked why, despite the vast sums expended, poverty had become worse rather than better. Instead, they pointed to shards of success and, more significantly, in the hopes of maintaining their grip, redefined the problem. Great Society social programs originally designed to reduce if not eliminate poverty were now justified in terms of rights, racial justice, or diversity. And then there was fallback to the fallback: the insistence on good intentions rather than outcomes. This now hoary claim received its classic formulation in FDR's 1936 "Rendezvous with Destiny" speech to the Democratic National Convention. "Divine justice weighs the sins of the cold-blooded and the sins of the warm-hearted on different scales," FDR claimed. "Better the occasional faults of a government that lives in a spirit of charity than the consistent omissions of a government frozen in the ice of its own indifference."

Susan Sontag had paved the way for arguing that what distinguished people, what defined them, was not the art they embraced but rather the manner in which they embraced it. And just as an ironic smugness came to connote cultural virtue, so too the claim that the public sector embraced public virtue, as compared with the small-time self-interest of businesspeople, meant that nonprofit ventures were by definition valuable, no matter how ineffective their job-training or anti-poverty efforts. In both the cultural and economic spheres, it was attitude and intentions—not outcomes—that mattered to liberals. Their claim to moral superiority rested more on self-image than real-world results.

Over time, however, benevolent pretensions morphed into political patronage. Peter Cove, of America Works, the for-profit group that has had great success in helping welfare recipients find jobs, saw that under the veneer of benevolence, varieties of self-interest were busy at work. Before the welfare reform of the 1990s, the more people there were on welfare, the more people would be employed and the more resources deployed on behalf of serving the people supposedly "serving" the poor. After the welfare reform in 1996, Cove had a conversation with a prominent member of the New York State Assembly from Brooklyn. The assemblywoman praised America Works as "perhaps the best welfare-to-work program I have seen." But when asked if she would support it in the legislature, she said no. When a startled Cove asked her why not, she replied:

"There is a Y.W.C.A. down the street from my campaign office. They run a welfare-to-work program. It is smaller than yours and not as good, but on Election Day, they bring out the votes." Over time, patronage replaced the pretense of benevolent policy as the basis for social-welfare programs.

CHAPTER 12

★ ★ ★

Progressives Against Progress: The Rise of Gentry Liberalism

For roughly the first two-thirds of the twentieth century, American liberals appeared to distinguish themselves from conservatives by what Lionel Trilling called "a spiritual orthodoxy of belief in progress." What Trilling mistakenly saw as the main stem of liberalism placed its hopes in human perfectibility. Regarding human nature as essentially both beneficent and malleable, liberals, like their socialist cousins, argued that with the aid of science and given the proper social and economic conditions, humanity could free itself from its cramped carapace of greed and distrust and enter a realm of true freedom and happiness. Conservatives, by contrast, generally clung to a tragic sense of man's inherent limitations. While acknowledging the benefits of science, they argued that it could never fundamentally reform, let alone transcend, the human condition. Conservatives maintained that many problems don't have a solution; rather than attempting Promethean feats, man would do best to find a balanced place in the world.

In the late 1960s, liberals appeared to have the better of the argument. Something approaching the realm of freedom seemed to have arrived. American workers, white and black, achieved hitherto unimagined levels of prosperity. In the nineteenth century, only utopian socialists had imagined that ordinary workers could achieve a degree of leisure; in the 1930s, radicals had insisted that prosperity was unattainable under American capitalism; yet these seemingly unreachable goals were achieved in the two decades after World War II.

Why, then, did American liberalism, starting in the early 1970s, undergo what seemed to be a historic metanoia, dismissing the idea of progress just as progress was being won? Multiple political and economic forces paved liberalism's path away from its mid century optimism and toward an aristocratic outlook reminiscent of the Tory Radicals of nineteenth-century Britain and the Southern Agrarians of the 1930s, who both saw industrialism as a threat to a refined, stable, and fulfilling life. Denouncing the "gospel of progress" as an "unrelenting war on nature," the Southern Agrarian poet John Crowe Ransom offered Southern gentility, with its traditional social stratification, as an alternative to both the pioneer ethic and industrialism, which he saw as brothers under the skin.

In the 1960s, the spirit of the Southern Agrarians was reborn in the modern environmental movement, complete with its recurrent hysterias. The first of those hysterias came from Rachel Carson's *The Silent Spring* (1962), which depicted a world shorn of birds by the effects of DDT. Like Sinclair Lewis's *Main Street* published in the wake of WWI, *The Silent Spring* was set against the backdrop of war—in this case, atomic testing.

Environmentalism also drew on the earlier Malthusian liberalism of H.G. Wells and Margaret Sanger, both proponents of population control and eugenics. At a time when prosperity seemed assured, environmentalism brought these different strands of liberalism together in a single, powerful movement. It attracted not only the neo-Malthusian organizations convinced that Lifeboat Earth was about to capsize from overpopulation but also the nuclear-freeze advocates and the back-to-the-earth dreamers who were yearning for the simple life.

But this was Malthusianism with a difference. Traditionally, the Malthusian argument had been directed at the hapless poor, presumed to be immured in a traditional baby-breeding way of life. But in America, the new version was, by way of the neo-Marxist critique of mass culture and mass consumption, directed at the materialist middle class. It promised an exit from the endless rat race, a way to step off the workaday treadmill and leave status anxiety behind. Environmentalism offered a grand stage for both government action and personal journeys of "authentic" self-discovery. Prosperity can produce win-win situations. But the competitive quest for exhibitions of green authenticity, of necessity a zero-sum game of status, offered an ideal stage for displays of environmental one-upsmanship in everything from cars to vacations to roofing.

If one were to pick a point at which liberalism's reversal took hold, it might be the celebration of the first Earth Day, in April 1970. Some 20 million Americans at 2,000 college campuses and 10,000 elementary and secondary schools took part in what was the largest nationwide demonstration ever held in the United States. The event gathered disparate New Left, conservationist, anti-war, anti-nuclear, and back-to-the-land groups into what became the church of environmentalism, complete with warnings of hellfire and damnation. Senator Gaylord Nelson of Wisconsin, the founder of Earth Day, invoked "responsible scientists" to give authority to his apocalyptic warning: "Accelerating rates of air pollution could become so serious by the 1980s that many people may be forced on the worst days to wear breathing helmets to survive outdoors. It has also been predicted that in twenty years man will live in domed cities."

Thanks in part to Earth Day's minions, progress, as liberals had once understood the term, came to be reviled as reactionary. In its place, Nature became the totem of authenticity, a sacred realm where technology and affluence had not bleached man's true essence out of existence. It was only by rolling in the mud of primitive practices that modern man could remove the stain of sinful science and materialism. In the words of Joni Mitchell's celebrated song "Woodstock": "We are stardust / We are golden / And we've got to get ourselves back to the garden."

In his 1973 book *The Death of Progress,* Bernard James laid out an argument already popularized in such bestsellers as Charles Reich's *The Greening of America* and William Irwin Thompson's *At the Edge of History.* "Progress seems to have become a lethal idée fixe, irreversibly destroying the very planet it depends upon to survive," James wrote. Like Reich, James criticized both the "George Babbitt" and "John Dewey" versions of "progress culture"—that is, visions of progress based on rising material attainment or on educational opportunities and upward mobility. "Progress ideology," he insisted, "whether preached by New Deal Liberals, conservative Western industrialists, or Soviet Zealots," always led in the same direction: environmental apocalypse. Liberalism, which had once viewed men and women as capable of shaping their own destinies, now saw humanity in the grip of vast forces that could be tamed only by extreme measures if man was to reverse the damage that industrial capitalism had inflicted on Mother Earth. It had become progressive to reject progress.

Rejected as well was the science that led to progress. In 1970, the Franco-American environmentalist René Dubos described what was quickly becoming a liberal consensus: "Most would agree that science and technology are responsible for some of our worst nightmares and have made our societies so complex as to be almost unmanageable." The same distrust of science was one reason that British author Francis Wheen described the 1970s as "the golden age of paranoia." Where American consumers had once felt confidence in food and drug laws that protected them from dirt and germs, a series of food scares involving additives made many view science, not nature, as the real threat to public health. Similarly, the sensational impact of the feminist book *Our Bodies, Ourselves*—which depicted doctors as a danger to women's well-being, while arguing, without qualifications, for natural childbirth—obscured the extraordinary safety gains that had made death during childbirth a rarity in developed nations.

Crankery, in short, became respectable. In 1972, Sir John Maddox, editor of the British journal *Nature*, noted that the kooks one used to see wearing sandwich boards to proclaim the imminent end of the Earth had been replaced by a growing number of frenzied activists and politicized scientists making precisely the same claim. In the years since then, liberalism has seen recurring waves of such end-of-days hysteria. These waves have shared not only a common pattern but often the same cast of characters. Strangely, the promised despoilations are most likely to be presented as imminent when Republicans are in the White House. In each case, liberals have argued that the threat of catastrophe can be averted only through drastic actions in which the ordinary political mechanisms of democracy are suspended and power is turned over to a body of experts. Wellsian supermen, no doubt Democrats, could rescue us.

Back in the early 1970s, it was overpopulation that was about to destroy the Earth. In his 1968 book *The Population Bomb*, Paul Ehrlich, who has been involved in all three recent end-of-times waves, warned that "the battle to feed all of humanity is over" on our crowded planet. He predicted mass starvation and called for compulsory sterilization to curb population growth, even comparing unplanned births to cancer: "A cancer is an uncontrolled multiplication of cells; the population explosion is an uncontrolled multiplication of people." An advocate of abortion on demand, Ehrlich wanted to ban photos of large, happy families from newspapers and magazines, and he called for new, heavy taxes on baby carriages and the like. He proposed a federal Department of Population and Environment that would regulate both procreation and the economy. But the population bomb, fear of which peaked during Richard Nixon's presidency, never detonated. Population in much of the world actually declined in the 1970s, and the green revolution, based on biologically modified foods, produced a sharp increase in crop productivity.

In the 1980s, the prophets of doom found another theme: the imminent danger of nuclear winter, the potential end of life on Earth resulting from a Soviet–American nuclear war. Even a limited nuclear exchange, argued politicized scientists such as Ehrlich and Carl Sagan, would release enough soot and dust into the atmosphere to block the sun's warming rays, producing drastic drops in temperature. Skeptics, such as Russell Seitz, acknowledged that even with the new, smaller warheads, a nuclear exchange would have fearsome consequences, but they argued effectively that the dangers were dramatically exaggerated. The nuke scare nevertheless received major backing from the liberal press. Nuclear-winter doomsayers placed their hopes, variously, in an unverifiable nuclear-weapons "freeze," American unilateral disarmament, or assigning control of nuclear weapons to international bodies. Back in the real world, nuclear fears eventually faded with Ronald Reagan's Cold War successes.

The third wave, which has been building for decades, is the campaign against global warming. The global-warming argument relied on the claim, effectively promoted by former vice president Al Gore, that the rapid growth of carbon dioxide in the atmosphere was producing an unprecedented rise in temperatures. This rise was summarized in the now notorious "hockey stick" graph, which supposedly showed that temperatures had been steady from roughly a.d. 1000 to 1900 but had sharply increased from 1900 on, thanks to industrialization. Brandishing the graph, the U.N.'s Intergovernmental Panel on Climate Change predicted that the first decade of the twenty-first century would be even warmer.

As it turned out, temperatures were essentially flat, and the entire global-warming argument came under increasing scrutiny. Skeptics pointed out that temperatures had repeatedly risen and fallen since a.d. 1000, describing, for instance, a "little ice age" between 1500 and 1850. The global-warming panic cooled further after a series of emails from the East Anglia University's Climatic Research Unit, the hub of global-warming claims, were leaked. They showed apparent collusion among scientists to exaggerate warming data and repress contradictory information.

As with the previous waves, politicized science played on liberal fears of progress: For Gore and his allies at the U.N., only a global command-and-control economy that kept growth in check could stave off imminent catastrophe. The anti-progress mind-set was by then familiar ground for liberals. Back in the 1970s, environmentalist E.J. Mishan had proposed dramatic solutions to the growth dilemma. He suggested banning all international air travel so that only those with the time and money could get to the choice spots—thus reintroducing, in effect, the class system. Should this prove too radical, Mishan proposed banning air travel "to a wide variety of mountain, lake, and coastal resorts, and to a selection of some islands from the many scattered about the globe; and within such areas also to abolish all motorised traffic." Echoing John Stuart Mill's mid-nineteenth-century call for a "stationary state" without economic growth, Mishan argued that "regions may be set aside for the true nature lover who is willing to make his pilgrimage by boat and willing leisurely to explore islands, valleys, bays, woodlands, on foot or on horseback."

As such proposals indicate, American liberalism has remarkably come to resemble nineteenth-century British Tory Radicalism, which, in aristocratic fashion, combined strong support for centralized monarchical power with a paternalistic concern for the poor. Liberalism's enemies were the middle classes and the aesthetic ugliness it associated with an industrial economy powered by bourgeois energies. For instance, John Ruskin, a leading nineteenth-century Tory Radical and a proponent of handicrafts, declaimed against "ilth," a negative version of the wealth produced by manufacturing.

Like the Tory Radicals, today's liberal gentry see the untamed middle classes as the true enemy. "Environmentalism offered the extraordinary opportunity to combine the qualities of virtue and selfishness," wrote William Tucker in a groundbreaking 1977 *Harper's* article on the opposition to construction of the Storm King power plant along New York's Hudson River. Tucker described the remarkable sight of a fleet of yachts—including one piloted by the old Stalinist singer Pete Seeger—sailing up and down the Hudson in protest. What Tucker tellingly described as the environmentalists' "aristocratic" vision called for a stratified, terraced society in which the knowing ones would order society for the rest of us. Touring American campuses in the mid 1970s, Norman Macrae of *The Economist* was shocked "to hear so many supposedly left-wing young Americans who still thought they were expressing an entirely new and progressive philosophy as they mouthed the same prejudices as Trollope's nineteenth-century Tory squires: attacking any further expansion of industry and commerce as impossibly vulgar, because ecologically unfair to their pheasants and wild ducks."

Neither the failure of the environmental apocalypse to arrive nor the steady improvement in environmental conditions over the last forty years has dampened the ardor of those eager to make hair shirts for others to wear. The call for political coercion as a path back to Ruskin's and Mishan's small-is-beautiful world is still with us. The radical environmentalists' Tory disdain for democracy and the mores of their inferiors remains undiminished. True to its late-1960s origins, political environmentalism in America gravitates toward both bureaucrats and hippies: toward a global, big-brother government that will keep the middle classes in line *and* toward a back-to-the-earth, peasant-like localism, imposed on others but presenting no threat to the elites' comfortable lives. Gentry liberals—progressives against progress—turn out to resemble nothing so much as nineteenth-century conservatives.

CHAPTER 13

★ ★ ★

"The Philosophical Crisis of American Liberalism"?

In the wake of George McGovern's defeat in the 1972 presidential election, Naderite Simon Lazarus wrote about what he called "the philosophical crisis of American liberalism." The New Deal, as Lazarus and his New Class allies understood it, had been taken down by the New Left. They believed that a rights-based politics based in post-materialist moralism had superseded the New Deal's materialist pro-growth politics. Lazarus saw a "philosophical crisis" in the inability of the victors in the 1972 Democratic Primary to create a new unifying paradigm for liberals, who were increasingly divided along race, class, and gender lines, and hypnotized by the drive for an environmentally themed authenticity. Forty years later, hamstrung by their refusal to compromise either their authenticity or their rights-based claims, liberals have achieved presidential success thanks to the vast expansion of new versions of old-fashioned government patronage. But they still lack a unifying framework.

The New Deal had initially been erected on the understanding that it was the job of government to protect the virtuous common man from

rapacious special interests. But after his landslide 1936 reelection, FDR began to remake the Democratic Party by sharply reducing the power of the two groups, Southern segregationist landowners and Tammany Hall tavern keepers, who had long been the party's dominant players. In their stead, FDR sought to build something new. He developed the concept of collective and economic rights, as represented first by the Wagner Act (1935), which gave organized labor an enormous boost, and then by his "Second Bill of Rights" speech (1944), which asserted claims against society for material benefits without listing any corresponding obligations. The assertion of economic rights began the process of displacing a constitutional order that since the Founding had been organized around individuals endowed with natural rights. In its place would be a new social order reorganized around groups making claims against the society, claims that would greatly multiply in the 1960s and '70s. In the emerging order, the growth of government paved the way for newly minted rights and entitlements, which in turn expanded government.

The difference between the Democratic Party's old and new clients was considerable. The party of saloonkeepers and segregationists hoped to win political majorities. Clientism and political majoritarianism were not inherently at odds. But the new rights-based client groups that came of age with McGovernism looked to courts and bureaucracies to deliver their demands. They were, at times, defiantly anti-majoritarian. Abortion, racial quotas, and environmental overreach were delivered not primarily by presidential or congressional majorities but by class-action lawsuits and by the iron triangle of interest groups, congressional subcommittees, and the liberal media. The new clients, fortified by their claims to rights new and old and insistent on upholding the claims of their identities, had little interest in the compromises needed for successful Democratic presidential administrations—of which there has been just one over the last sixty years.

While liberals worked on perfecting their rights regime, the private-sector middle class was subject to rising crime rates, collapsing cities, family breakdown, global and immigrant competition, and stagnant incomes. Violent crime rose sharply in the 1960s and kept rising till the 1990s. Thanks to the American Civil Liberties Union, the group founded by the first liberals in the wake of World War I, the growth in street violence was accompanied by a series of Supreme Court decisions, most notably *Mapp v. Ohio* and *Miranda v. Arizona*, that made it harder to effectively prosecute criminals.

Procedural reforms were overdue and a necessary accompaniment to the civil rights movement. Crime had long been kept under control, noted speechwriter Clark Whelton, by the illegitimate assumption that black faces didn't belong in white neighborhoods—penalty was meted out as "street justice." But when the Supreme Court reduced cases involving violent criminals into a game of punctilious proceduralism, public outrage ensued. Joe Califano, Carter's former secretary of Health, Education, and Welfare, warned his fellow liberals: "We have persisted in the dogged incantation of procedural and legalistic technicalities about protecting the rights of accused criminals without expressing comparable concern for those who have been mugged, robbed, raped, and burglarized."

In a classic example of power moving upscale, the Supreme Court encouraged lower federal and state courts to act as the supervisors of the day-to-day operation of police departments. The public, notes author J.R. Dunn, saw this as little more than a get-out-of-jail pass for lowlifes. With fewer and fewer career criminals being sent to prison, the courts, consumed with their own priestly righteousness, showed little interest in striking a reasonable balance between maintaining civil rights and keeping neighborhoods safe.

Liberals did their best to deflect the subject. Sometimes they decried mere talk of crime as coded racism, which it sometimes was. At other times, deploying the logic of eugenics, they, like Clarence Darrow, redefined criminals as the true victims, casualties of social circumstance and limited economic opportunity. None of this went over very well with the broader public, even though the citizens most harmed by rolling riots of crime tended to be the dwellers of the inner city.

In 1981, Warren Burger, the chief justice of the Supreme Court, told the American Bar Association: "Crime and the fear of crime have permeated the fabric of American life . . . Like it or not, today, we are approaching the status of an impotent society, whose capability of maintaining elementary security in the streets, in schools, and for the homes of the people is in doubt."

In his influential 1983 essay, "A Neoliberal's Manifesto," *Washington Monthly* editor Charles Peters, who had grown up in West Virginia on a steady diet of Democratic Party nostrums, tried to break out of "the automatic responses" that left liberals unable to cope with reality. "If neoconservatives are liberals who took a critical look at liberalism and decided to become conservatives, we are liberals who took the same look and decided to retain our goals but to abandon some of our prejudices," he wrote. Peters had no time for liberals who wanted more jobs but were hostile to business. "Our hero," he explained, "is the risk-taking entrepreneur who creates new jobs and better products." Nor did he approve of liberal lawyers "concocting exotic legal strategies" to help criminals "escape punishment" on the grounds that they were victims of society. He had no patience with a "fat, sloppy, and smug bureaucracy." "We want," he said, "a Government that can fire people who can't or won't do the job." Similarly, he wanted to have government programs means-tested on the grounds that far too much public spending went to the already well-off. Peters was among the first liberals to see that the government had become its own interest group. Like FDR, he feared that public-sector unions would diminish not only public services but society more generally.

Peters's insights were lost on the Democrats of 1984. Walter Mondale, Carter's vice president, won the Democratic nomination as the candidate of the National Organization for Women, the AFL-CIO, the civil rights establishment, and the teachers' unions. The feminist organizations imposed the less-than-prepossessing Representative Geraldine Ferraro on Mondale as his running mate, making her the first female on a major national ticket. The problem, explained Mondale adviser Richard Moe, was that "people simply don't want their president to by wholly owned by any group of special interests."

But, after the off-year elections of 1986 when the Democrats gained eight senatorial seats and retook control of the Senate, liberals were reinvigorated without having reformed themselves. Riding on the tailwinds produced by the election and a Reagan administration mired in the Iran-Contra scandal, they were convinced that the Republican era was over and a new era of liberalism was on the horizon. Surveying the scene, the 1960s liberal Richard Goodwin exulted, "Today for the first time since our defeat in Vietnam, one senses large numbers of Americans emerging from an almost willed sleep."

The Americans of 1988 had more rights than ever. Yet by and large, they felt more politically powerless. The 1988 presidential election was our first and so far only national race in which virtually all the central issues of the campaign—criminal rights, abortion rights, capital punishment, the required recital (by teachers) of the Pledge of Allegiance—were judicially generated.

The American Civil Liberties Union had been created after WWI to protest the Wilson administration's gross violations of First Amendment rights. In the 1930s, the ACLU's hostility to middle-class mores brought it into the orbit of Stalinism and the American Communist Party, and it was only too willing to subvert civil liberties in the name of "economic rights." Since the 1960s, the ACLU has looked upon criminals as an oppressed minority whose primitive vitality was being crushed by the ogre of bourgeois morality.

The ACLU came to exemplify a special ideological interest group with excessive power. The Democratic candidate for president in 1988, Michael Dukakis, and his campaign manager Susan Estrich were both Harvard-trained lawyers who, in the words of the Massachusetts governor, were "card-carrying members of the ACLU." As governor, Dukakis had issued a statement proclaiming the innocence of Sacco and Vanzetti. He began the 1988 campaign with a large lead over George Bush, the Republican vice president. Bush, a Yalie and every inch the American patrician, played off Dukakis's identification with the group disparagingly known as "the criminal-rights lobby." He told the public, stiffly: "I am not a card-carrying member of the ACLU. I am for the people." At a time when all of 15 percent of the population defined themselves as "liberal" and the very term had become a swear word of sorts, causing members of the faith to relabel themselves as "progressives," this was a winning move by the vice president. The more the public learned of Dukakis, the more he lost support.

Politics in a democracy ideally revolve around the compromises needed to secure widespread consent for government actions. In a well-functioning representative government, one that encourages citizen participation, the losers in a political contest at least retain the feeling that they had the chance to air their views and that the public heard their case. But a judicialized politics tries to bypass public consent. Profoundly anti-democratic when it goes beyond vindicating the fundamental rights of citizenship, judicial politics alienates voters by placing public policy in the private hands of lawyers and litigants. And because rights are absolute, it polarizes by producing winner-take-all outcomes, in which the losers tend to feel embittered. The politics of rights displaces the Bill of Rights and subverts the constitutional design for self-government. In effective democratic politics, opponents must rely upon a public process of persuasion and deliberation; the politics of rights replaced that process with a judiciary whose swollen powers brought disrepute to the essential notion of rights even as it undermined public trust in government. Abraham Lincoln anticipated the plight of the 1988 voters in his first inaugural address: "If the policy of the government, upon vital questions, affecting the whole people, is to be irrevocably fixed by decisions of the Supreme Court, the instant they are made, in ordinary litigation . . . the people will have ceased to be their own rulers."

The 1988 Dukakis defeat was a shock. What had put the country back to sleep, so to speak? How was it possible that a new-model liberal, a neoliberal technocrat such as Dukakis who was in favor of economic growth and economic justice, could have gone down to defeat? Dukakis was hurt by the Willie Horton issue. Horton, a convicted murderer serving a life sentence without parole, had been the beneficiary of a Dukakis-supported program to provide weekend furloughs for long-term prisoners. While he was out on just such a furlough. Horton committed rape and armed robbery. The Horton case was first brought to public attention by candidate Al Gore during the Democratic Party presidential primaries. Revived by the Bush campaign in the general election, it became a symbol for Dukakis and the ACLU on crime more generally. The attacks on the ACLU were, Democrats cried, little better than racist dirty tricks.

But grousing aside, liberal interest groups did little in the way of reevaluation. Instead, they doubled down on their bets: The fear of crime was still raging, but Ted Kennedy introduced a bill to require quotas in carrying out death sentences; in academic performance, female students were surging ahead of their male counterparts, but gender-equity experts patrolled the land to make sure that female "lateral thinking" shared equal billing with male "vertical thinking"; meanwhile, gay militants denounced "the AIDs pandemic" as "the fault of white middle-class-male majority."

A year after Dukakis went down to defeat, Virginia elected Douglas Wilder as its chief executive. He was the nation's first African-American governor since Reconstruction. Wilder, a moderate Democrat, won on a tough-on-crime and back-to-basics message that earned him votes in rural white Virginia. Wilder ran 10 points better among whites than had Dukakis. As Hastings Wyman of the *Southern Political Report* summed it up: "Being a liberal was more of a handicap than being black in Virginia.

Compelled to explain away the role that crime and family breakdown was playing in the collapse of the inner cities, liberalism moved away from social science and toward a French-influenced romantic irrationalism that came to be known as postmodernism. Postmodern academics saw themselves as a clerisy, keepers of priestly truths much beyond the ken of the general public. Reality, as many academics understood it, was a socially constructed expression of power relations. Paul Goodman's quip at the dawn of the Aquarian Age, in 1967, about the New Leftists now applied to the postmodernists as well: "[To them] there was no knowledge, only the sociology of knowledge."

Like the Fascist writers of the 1930s from whom their teachers had drawn their ideas, the postmodernists were both engaged in politics, as they understood it, and deeply cynical about democracy, which they saw as a game manipulated by nefarious right-wing forces. As they saw it, there was little to argue; the only question was, "Which side are you on?" "Truths are illusions we have forgotten are illusions," argued Nietzscheans such as Yale professor Paul de Man, one of the preeminent postmodernists. There were no objective truths, so the argument went, only the truth-effects created by the workings of power and the instabilities of language. And it was power that had come to dominate the humanities and that created the illusion of truth. Oppression was ubiquitous whether people recognized it or not. And because the capillary power of oppression makes a mockery of "freedom," so the logic went, why not use government to break through the invisible web of coercion spun by everyday fascism? The conception of truth as illusory may've had particular resonance for De Man: As a young man in WWII Belgium, he had published anti-Semitic essays in a pro-Nazi newspaper—a fact that caused an academic scandal when it became public knowledge only after his death.

Students who had imbibed postmodernism left college with the sense that while they had been enlightened, the workaday middle class was drowning in illusions. Worse yet, they found it difficult to credit the average Joe and Jill with a sincere but different point of view, because they had learned, after much study, that alternative opinions were merely masks for racism, sexism, and homophobia. Mocking cultural relativism, philosopher Ernest Gellner quipped that "because all knowledge is dubious, being theory-saturated/ethnocentric/paradigm-dominated/interest-linked (please choose your own preferred variant . . .), the anguish-ridden author . . . can put forward whatever he pleases." Epistemological hypochondria might have led to an intellectual and political modesty, as illustrated by the aphorism, "when the candles are away, all cats are gray." But it didn't.

The result was a double game. Epistemological nihilism, sometimes known as deconstruction, was linked to political certainty. The argument for the impossibility of objective judgments was awkwardly yoked to the unshakable judgment that America was objectively racist, evil, imperialist, sexist (pick your terms of opprobrium). Oppression was held to be an expression of bourgeois power that, like sin, was all-pervasive. But widespread though it was, the demonic realm of oppression somehow didn't include Eastern Europe under Communism.

Postmodernism was the Indian rope trick of academia—an intellectual slight of hand that can't withstand scrutiny. When questioned about this unstable ménage, some deconstructionists exempted themselves from the criticism they directed at others. Other people—not them—had been irredeemably infected by racism, sexism, homophobia (and later Islamophobia), as well as numerous other ailments native to American society. In identifying the poison, they immunized themselves and achieved a state of grace. Other deconstructionists acknowledged the tension but carried on unperturbed on the grounds that their opinions were at least aesthetically appealing or, even more important, an expression of good intentions. This unhinged conceptual double bind might have been the subject of mirth and satire in an environment where open debate was the order of the day, but on the campuses conditioned by political correctness, those who objected generally kept their heads down.

★ ★ ★

Translated into the political world, the defense of affirmative action, black power, and various other burgeoning "rights" produced a game of "heads I win, tails you lose," as analyst of civil rights law John Rosenberg described it. Through their spokespeople and the clerisy, the protected classes were encouraged to complain of discrimination on the basis of either equal *or* unequal treatment.

Campus liberals promoted unbridled sexual freedom while raising alarms over sexual harassment. Sorting out the charges was either left to the putative female victim or the campus clerisy, which insisted that the rules for rape would be judged by a shifting standard. At the same time, the call for integration was matched by calls for separate black dorms and curricula. The personal was political, except when it was purely private (as in the right to abort a fetus). In the absence of standards, the clerisy, through its influence in the media and the administration of academia, arrogated to itself the right to define each situation by its own lights.

The public responded harshly to these liberal efforts to institutionalize double standards; nasty fights over court-ordered busing and school integration and curricula ensued. While liberals were bent on sniffing out new and arcane examples of discrimination, the utopian promises of the '60s had turned into the dystopian reality of sharply rising crime rates, draconian censorship of free speech on college campuses, and the social disintegration of the cities.

On campuses, Democratic Party presidential candidate Jesse Jackson led students in chanting "Hey, Hey, Ho, Ho, Western Civ has to go." The former SDS co-founder Kirkpatrick Sale was a sought-after campus speaker. Sale rehashed Stuart Chase's 1930s paean to Mexican peasants. Speaking of Western civilization, he told his readers:

> I regard it as a desperately sick and inwardly miserable society that doesn't realize it's suffering from a terminal disease affluenza. . . . [I]t is founded on a set of ideas that are fundamentally pernicious, and they have to do with rationalism and humanism and materialism and nationalism and science and progress. . . . Imagine if it had singing, dancing, laughing, and sex as its regular components.

Back in the late 1940s, Lionel Trilling had regretted the absence of contemporary conservative thinkers who might keep liberals, who had been far more influenced by Communism than they cared to acknowledge, on their toes. Without the "corrective of conservatism," he argued, liberal ideas become "stale, habitual, and inert." But when influential conservative thinkers such as Milton Friedman, Irving Kristol, and Charles Murray entered the arena, liberals circled the wagons rather than engage in debate. Rather than serve as a laboratory for social and political reform, academia clutched its power to credentialize and cut itself off from the corruption of outside influences. Older notions of objectivity, which served as a constraint on political propaganda, were cast aside in favor of emotionally satisfying truths. What emerged was a mixture of bullying, moralism, and interest-group politics as organized claims to victimization came to dominate campus life. On many campuses, professors scolded that the very term "underclass" was a racist slur. And when authors such as Charles Murray accurately described the growth of social pathology in the inner cities, academics dismissed their words as an underhanded attempt to advance a right-wing agenda. On campus at least, reality was to be rewritten. An alternative reality, a coerced consensus enforced by the rising power of academic administrators who, by the 1990s, outnumbered teachers and scholars, took hold in academia.

CHAPTER 14

★ ★ ★

The Clinton Interregnum

Heightened racial tensions and the possibility of yet another Jesse Jackson run for president seemed to doom Democratic hopes for 1992. When rioting broke out in heavily African-American South Los Angeles in 1992 and fifty-three people were killed, it was described in the best PC tradition as a "revolt" or an "uprising." Having learned little, a host of mayors, including Governor Mario Cuomo of New York, who thought government could replace the family, warned of more violence unless Americans poured even more money into the inner cities.

It was in these unpropitious circumstances that Governor Bill Clinton of Arkansas and the neoliberal Democratic Leadership Council (DLC) tried to reconnect the Democratic Party to America's main streets. Just days after the Democrats' 1988 presidential defeat, Clinton took the measure of Dukakis. "No matter how popular your programs may be, you must be considered in the mainstream on the shared values of the American people." Clinton would prove to be a neoliberal with a difference.

Bill Clinton's presidency was made possible by the shattering impact of Michael Dukakis's defeat in 1988. In the three elections of the 1980s

—'80, '84, and '88—Democrats has lost forty-four, forty-nine, and forty-one states respectively. There was even talk of a fundamental FDR-like realignment rightward of the sort that had kept Democrats in power from 1933 through 1948.

In the wake of Dukakis's defeat, the Democratic Leadership Council and its think tank the Progressive Policy Institute, led by Al From and Will Marshall, became a force to be reckoned with. Unlike Charles Peters and the editors of *The Washington Monthly*, From and Marshall's group had an electoral focus. It argued that after three straight defeats, only a southern neoliberal or new type of Democrat could capture the White House. Democrats, said the DLC, had to reconcile themselves to the middle-class American mainstream disdained by liberals.

The DLC's members and the neoliberals were not wholly separate in their interests; in fact, they overlapped, and casual observers sometimes failed to distinguish between them. The DLC, moreover, adopted several key neoliberal assumptions—about the challenge of global competitiveness, the need for more efficient government and market-friendly policies, and the pursuit of economic growth over fairness.

But the focus of the DLC's push wasn't by and large technocratic, and it didn't seek to court the upscale voters pursued by some neoliberals. DLC Democrats emphasized, rather, the more numerous working-class Reagan Democrats. The liberals, From and Marshall contended, had confused the enlargement of government with the expansion of opportunity. From, in line with Peters, said that government had been turned into a milch cow for the wealthy and well-connected. From asserted that all claims on government are not equal, that our leaders must reject demands that are less than worthy. The DLC, and by extension Clinton, insisted that Democrats had to make reducing crime a priority and that government policy, rather than subsidizing a separate way of life for the poor, should help bring the poor into the mainstream.

Speaking for the DLC, Clinton said, "We believe in the moral and cultural values that most Americans share: liberty of conscience, individual responsibility, tolerance of difference, the imperative of work, the need for faith, and the importance of family." Then, acknowledging that the occasionally blunt instrument of the rights revolution made many Americans uneasy, he offered reassurance: "We believe that American citizenship entails responsibility as well as rights, and we mean to ask our citizens to give something back to their communities and their country." With these words, Clinton laid down what seemed a daring marker at the time. "There is an idea abroad in the land that if you abandon your children, the government will raise them," he added, at a 1991 DLC gathering. "I will let you in on a secret. Governments do not raise children—people do. And it's time they were asked to assume their responsibilities and forced to do so if they refuse." Clinton's centrism—he had strong ties to many strains in the party—figured in his support for welfare reforms, even the mention of which angered both the professional racialists and the feminists who had suggested that sex had no social consequences.

Hard-line liberals saw Clinton's rhetoric as a vote-grubbing concession to right-wing Republicanism. Jesse Jackson and Senate liberals led by Howard Metzenbaum denounced the DLC as "Democrats for the Leisure Class." But for the most part, liberals limited themselves to mere grumbling when Clinton—notwithstanding his vice president, the deep-dyed environmentalist Al Gore—embraced economic growth.

On the national level, the political version of the postmodernists' double game was interrupted by the Clinton ascendancy. When African-American novelist Toni Morrison dubbed Clinton "the first black president," Clinton supporters quickly made the label into a laudatory refrain. And a good many feminists considered Clinton one of their own, despite his checkered personal history. But Clinton attempted to rise above identity politics and temper the double game by making an old-fashioned centrist appeal to common values.

But, with some exception on the state and local level, the growing strength of government unionism would pump new life into liberal identity politics.

CHAPTER 15

★ ★ ★

Gentry Liberals and Public-Sector Unions to the Fore

John Sweeney's ascension to the leadership of the AFL-CIO in 1995 was a little-discussed landmark for both the union movement and liberalism. Sweeney, president of the Service Employees International Union (SEIU) that had successfully organized janitors on both coasts, was the first AFL-CIO leader to emerge from the ranks of a heavily public-sector union. The SEIU combined elements of traditional union organizing aimed at low-end workers with a 1960s-style poor-people's movement, as represented by its affiliate ACORN (Association for Community Organizing and Reform Now). The fusion made SEIU a powerful political force. Sweeney won the AFL-CIO leadership by pushing aside its longtime president, Lane Kirkland (1979–95). Kirkland had been one of the architects of American victory in the Cold War. But the declining ranks of private-sector labor in the globalized economy weakened Kirkland, and he was unable to prevent the adoption of the 1994 North American Free Trade Agreement, which organized labor deemed a mortal threat.

Fairly or not, Kirkland also bore the brunt of the blame for the Republicans' smashing 1994 electoral victory that returned the House of Representatives to GOP control for the first time in forty years. In the aftermath of that election, Sweeney teamed up with the American Federation of State, Country and Municipal Employees (AFCSME) to topple Kirkland. While the Republicans were moving right, AFSCME, which had played a key role in electing President Clinton in 1992, hoped to push the Democrats left. Sweeney's performance in leading the rapidly growing SEIU, which had merged with the National Association of Government Employees, seemed to promise a labor revival.

Labor and the New Left had split apart over George McGovern. Sweeney closed that breach by incorporating identity-politics activists into the labor movement. Sweeney exhorted, "We have to reach out energetically to our natural allies in the movements for civil rights and women's rights, as well as the gay, lesbian, and intellectual and student communities."

The Monica Lewinsky affair was the end of Clinton's centrist idyll. Clinton was forced to appeal to the identity-politics clerisy—the public-sector militants, the African-American and feminist leaders, and their academic, political, and media allies—who got to decide whether a particular action was racist or sexist, in order to preserve his presidency from the foolish Republican attempt to impeach him over the affair.

The public disliked the GOP for overplaying its hand; for many Americans, the attacks on Clinton in the name of morality only highlighted the hypocrisy of Republicans, some of whom were having (or had already had) extramarital affairs at the same time they were assailing Clinton for ethical faults. But it was not lost on the public that if the president involved had been a Republican, Clinton's actions in the Lewinsky affair would have been condemned as a classic abuse of male power. Liberal feminists' efforts to exonerate Clinton only reinforced the public's disdain for feminism in particular and liberal double standards more generally. Al Gore suffered the consequences in his 2000 presidential run. The virtual tie of 2000 left liberals angry and convinced that dastardly Republicans had stolen the election.

The game of double standards left Democrats in a vulnerable position when they were forced to confront Islamism after 9/11. For many liberal Democrats, the real enemy, after all, the only one for whom they felt wholehearted hostility, was across the aisle. Loyalty to party had become as intense, or more so, than loyalty to ideology or religion or nation in an earlier time.

The 2004 presidential candidacy of Howard Dean, the standard-bearer of gentry liberalism, brought together in full public view the trends that had been building since the 1960s. It wasn't only that Dean, the heartthrob of upper middle class liberals, disagreed with Republicans on specific issues; his opposition, he told party stalwarts, was rooted in something much deeper: "I hate the Republicans and everything they stand for." Then, in equally fervent tones, he went on to describe liberalism as "our faith." Taking this party loyalty to almost comical extremes, Dean would later proclaim that Saddam Hussein should be presumed innocent pending trial but that corrupt House Majority Leader Tom DeLay should be jailed forthwith for offenses not yet specified.

In the run-up to the 2004 presidential election, half the Senate Democrats attended the Washington premiere of Michael Moore's agit-prop movie *Fahrenheit 9/11*, and laughed and cheered as the movie ridiculed President Bush and denounced American foreign policy in Iraq. Moore's website at the time was publishing the rather unoriginal critique that "Americans are the stupidest people in the world." Trafficking in poses, attitudes, and insinuations—and sometimes outright lies—Moore was part of the Democrats' steady leftward movement.

Massachusetts senator John F. Kerry, the 2004 Democratic Party nominee, had made himself into a JFK facsimile. Wealthy by way of two marriages to rich heiresses, his twenty years in the Senate yielded little in the way of political accomplishments. Like Michael Moore, he campaigned against George Bush's failures in office without presenting a strong idea of what he wanted to accomplish beyond keeping the party's interest groups happy. Novelist Jane Smiley played this decade's Mencken; Kerry lost, she explained because "red-state types, above all, do not want to be told what to do—they prefer to be ignorant. As a result, they are virtually unteachable."

Liberals were left in despair by John Kerry's defeat at the hands of the less-than-impressive President George W. Bush, who was in the midst of incompetently prosecuting a questionable war in Iraq. Kerry's candidacy reopened Vietnam-era wounds and the fundamental question of attitudes toward America. At the time of the Bush–Kerry contest, about two-thirds of all Americans agreed that the United States was a fair and decent country. Virtually all Bush voters agreed. Kerry voters were split down the middle.

CHAPTER 16

★ ★ ★

"What Are Our Convictions?"

After the 2004 election, Paul Starr, editor of the left-wing bimonthly *The American Prospect*, warned, "Liberalism is at greater risk now than at any time in recent American history." Responding to critics who argued that liberalism lacked a navel, Starr urged his liberal allies "to remember their first principles" so they might "rebuild a majority." Starr's fellow liberal Michael Tomasky saw it similarly. After thirty-five years of effort, "what the Democrats still don't have," he wrote "is a philosophy, a big idea that unites their proposals and converts them from a hodgepodge of narrow and specific fixes into a vision for society."

But what were those first principles Starr was searching for? Liberals were united in their hostilities. They were passionate in their opposition to the Republican "dictatorship," to the reviled George Bush and his war in Iraq; they despised the Evangelical "lizzardheads" who lived in "dumbfuckistan"; they detested the Clintons as compromisers whose strategies of triangulation had turned the Democrats, as they saw it, into me-too Republicans chasing after the middle-class vote; they loathed the Democratic Leadership Council and, as Norman Lear put it, "Joe Fucking Lieberman"; and they were sure, insofar as they gave it any thought, that the war on terror was largely a scam that had been sold to the "morons" of Middle America. The billionaire progressives, the suburban MoveOn activists, and the left-wing bloggers were drawn together by hostility not only to Bush and the centrist Democratic Leadership Council, which was driven to extinction, but also to the private-sector middle class they scorned.

It seemed, notwithstanding their claim to be the party of "reason" as argued by Al Gore and Robert Reich, that attitudinizing and name-calling had largely replaced rational argument among postmodern Democrats. Ned Lamont, the son of Thomas Lamont, the co-founder of the J.P. Morgan banking empire, and the left's 2006 candidate for the Senate against Lieberman in Connecticut, caught the essence of the new liberalism: "People," he said, "have different allegiances now...they have allegiances to passions."

Liberals were certain of what they were against. They wanted no part of Bush's misbegotten war in Iraq. They tried in vain, wrote *New York Times* author Matt Bai in his book *The Argument*, to create "some compelling case for the future of an activist American government." The better informed among them understood that the country couldn't go back to the New Deal. Andy Stern, then the president of SEIU, explained lucidly, "I like to say to people who want to return to the New Deal that we are now as far from the New Deal as the New Deal was from the Civil War."

The outcome was unintentionally humorous. One of the partners of the Democratic Alliance, a billionaires' organization funded by George Soros and Peter Lewis, among others, urged a new approach. Speaking of the political virtue of conveying deep convictions, he asked, "What are ours?" Because "once we know them, we can frame them for voters." Andy Stern's "path to a new economic agenda" was an online contest called "Since Sliced Bread" modeled after *American Idol*, in which workaday Americans submitted their ideas to a panel of experts and the winner would receive $100,000. "But the entrants," noted Bai, "offered the same old approaches." When Bai attended a MoveOn brainstorming session to develop an affirmative agenda, he found that the participants, after suggesting such innovations as "fair wages" and "a foreign policy that wins friends," repeatedly slipped into expressing their hostilities. Frustrated, the convener admonished them, "Remember, this has to be positive."

The very idea of politics, the need to accommodate competing but legitimate interests, seemed alien to the Democratic Alliance, whose members were sure that their business expertise, generously donated to the public, could make America once again acceptable in their own eyes. Steven Gluckstern, a onetime leader of the Alliance and a reinsurance fat cat, explained, "One of my friends who's a billionaire says the thing about being rich is that you can do what you want." But how do you accommodate differences among people whose wealth tells each of them they are always right and therefore ought to be obeyed? The Alliance, said Bai, turned into "the political version of a nightmare condo association," because the members assumed that "their wealth conferred on them great vision." Rather than serving as a financial vehicle for politicians, they thought it should be the other way around: Politicians should serve as the vehicles for their brilliant ideas. When the Alliance brought in Judy Wade, of McKinsey consultants, to succeed Gluckstern as the organization's CEO, she quipped to a roomful of Alliance partners: "You know what they say about the difference between a terrorist and a billionaire, 'You can negotiate with a terrorist.' " The joke was not well received. She, too, was deposed.

But why should they compromise? Hadn't their wealth, proof certain of their all-around intelligence, entitled them to dispense orders and have them carried out? "The strange truth was that the zillionaires had come to see themselves, however improbably, as the oppressed," Bai wrote. "They knew what was right about what was best for the country, and if the foolish voters didn't see it as clearly as they did, then it could only be explained by some nefarious conservative plot. They imagined themselves to be victimized and powerless, kept down somehow by the Man."

The gilded resentments of the oppressed wealthy were continuous with the spirit of the 1930s "Penthouse Bolsheviks" and the animating antipathies that Daniel Patrick Moynihan had espied among crusading well-to-do Manhattan liberals in the early 1960s. Wealthy liberals, wrote the young Moynihan, were "frustrated by their inability to translate success in private life" into political success. They "simply do not understand how and why people like" the drab party regulars who dominate elective office. Moynihan worried that the liberals' habit of "impugning the motives of anyone they disagree with" would lead to an intense polarization.

★ ★ ★

The left's "traditional prism of class politics," argues liberal David Callahan, is hopelessly outdated now that wealthy liberals are more than willing to make common cause with the barons of labor. The Democratic Alliance, Callahan notes, has been dubbed "billionaires for big government." Perfectly embodying Eric Hoffer's fears, gentry liberals assume that the same savvy, technical know-how, and cunning that made their fortunes entitles them to a privileged position in the political world. With their contempt for "tea-bagging morons," and sidestepping the egalitarian principle of "one man, one vote," gentry liberals don't understand why the political system doesn't defer to them as a matter of course.

Despite their differences à la *Upstairs Downstairs*, gentry liberals and ACORN activists were united in their disdain for middle-class morality. The real vulgarity wasn't greed but rather a lack of self-awareness. From Randolph Bourne to Susan Sontag and Anna Wintour, a tasteful knowingness was seen as a morality of sorts that exempted the self-aware from the strictures of conventional rules.

Once upon a time, liberals might have distinguished themselves by the methods they offered for producing economic growth. But Democrats' environmentalism left them divided on that score. They were, for the most part, progressives who had given up on progress—material progress, that is. Instead, they saw themselves as representing *moral* progress. They would shortly be swept up in the global-warming fervor, a new version of the Devil that failed.

In 2007, it appeared for a time that the call of former vice president Al Gore for a national and international campaign to fend off the impending catastrophe of global warming might provide the unifying principle liberals were seeking. Like earlier liberal hysterias, such as fears of the population bomb and global winter, global warming gave a patina of science to the socially conservative and internationalist policy positions liberals had long espoused.

The solution, as always, was—right out of H.G. Wells's 1920 opus *The Outline of History*—world government run by the new samurai. Al Gore's Oscar-winning movie *An Inconvenient Truth* brought key players in America's neo-British establishment—Hollywood, Washington, Silicon Valley, and academia—to an unreasoning fervor. But the idea of turning over the future of the American economy to U.N. bureaucrats was unsalable even before the economic meltdown of 2008. And for liberals, perhaps that was just as well. In a few years, scientist James Lovelock, the godfather of modern environmentalism, the very man who conceived of Gaia, noted with asperity that global temperatures since the turn of the millennium had not risen as the computer-based climate models had predicted. Referring in part to the limits of projections based on computer modeling, Lovelock explained: "The problem is we don't know what the climate is doing. We thought we knew twenty years ago." The same could have been said of the economy, which, as the computer-driven models demonstrated, was in fine shape right before it collapsed.

During the run-up to the 2008 election, the rising public-sector unions eclipsed their private-sector brethren, with considerable consequences for the Democratic Party and the country. Private-sector unions had an interest in increasing their share of a growing economy. But public-sector unions, which became the mainstays of the Democratic Party's electoral machinery locally and nationally, are, like their environmentalist allies, extractive. They're interested in the "socialization of private-sector income" regardless of the overall condition of the economy. The gentry liberals and the public-sector unions have become close allies bound by a shared interest in expanding government.

Public-sector unions have become what Andy Stern, president of SEIU until 2010, has described as "the most powerful political force in the country." Their rising influence was virtually undiscussed by the media in 2008. Yet it was the public-sector unions allied with wealthy liberals that funded and ran the effective political campaigns that took control of all the elected branches of government. A Democratic Party dominated by the public-sector unions of the deep-blue states increasingly came to believe that what is good for government is good for society.

In 2008, the alliance of the resentful, extractive, and identity-driven interests resolved the crisis that had dogged liberalism since 1972. The public-sector unions have become the liberals' version of the working and middle classes. Government workers are ideal for liberals. They constitute a group whose wealth depends on increasing the size and cost of government in a sector where considerations of profit and performance are sidelined. They offer an alternative to Main Street shop owners and the private-sector middle class. In the alliance of gentry liberals and public-sector unions, the traditional ideal of self-government has been replaced by a corporatism in which powerful blocs negotiate among themselves to control the real business of government.

CHAPTER 17

★ ★ ★

Conclusion: Obama Versus Main Street

Sinclair Lewis's 1920s never went away. Over time, the emotionally stylized postures of the Twenties produced a politics of affect and affinity that sorted the country into Red/Main Street and Blue/Metropolitan America. The founding liberal fears of the 1920s, goosed by the fecklessness and failures of President George W. Bush, were amplified many times over during his second term. In a replay of a liberal classic, liberals turned Bush into the faux folksy dictator of Sinclair Lewis's 1935 *It Can't Happen Here.* In 2005, *New York Times* columnist Paul Krugman, drawing on the caricatures associated with Sinclair Lewis, detected the creeping fascism of *It Can't Happen Here* when the country-and-western group the Dixie Chicks was boycotted by former fans for songs mocking President Bush. Similarly, former *New York Times* columnist Anthony Lewis, a fan of H.L. Mencken, saw the terrible events at Abu Ghraib as proof that the warning of *It Can't Happen Here* was more than justified.*

---

* The introduction to the 1993 Signet edition depicted Reagan as having been a proto-fascist and then went on to argue that Lewis's "depiction of a fascist future for the United States has a force that grows stronger with each passing year." The author of the introduction, NYU English professor Perry Meisel, argued that what Lewis hated about American provincialism—its gullibility—was mirrored in the success of the Nazis. As proof that the Rotarians were Nazis in the making, Meisel cited Nathanael West's *A Cool Million*, published just a year before Lewis's novel, in 1934: "West narrates the rise of an American fascism by showing the grotesque violence that brings to power Shagpoke Whipple, a dishonest banker and former president modeled upon Ronald Reagan's preferred precursor, Calvin Coolidge."

In 2007, the *New York Observer*'s liberal columnist Joe Conason published *It Can Happen Here: Authoritarian Peril in the Age of Bush*. "For the first time since the resignation of Richard Nixon," wrote Conason, "Americans have reason to doubt the future of democracy and the rule of law." Conason, Krugman, and Lewis were part of a chorus as liberal magazines and newspapers repeatedly riffed on Bush as faux common man and proto-fascist.

Interestingly, though, there is a brief section of *It Can't Happen Here* where Lewis, who had no use for either Communists or Mussolini-like corporatists, anticipated the Obama-era liberal future. The novel's hero, the flinty Vermonter Doremus Jessup (Lewis's alter ego), pronounces from his temporary exile in Canada, where he's fled from the fascism of American corporatism, that the U.S. could "never go back to satisfaction in government of the profits, by the profits, for the profits." The "clever pirates" who raid government "are finished," Jessup says. Then he envisions the government of the future:

> There's got to be a new feeling—that government is not a game for a few smart, resolute athletes like you . . . but a universal partnership, in which the state must own all resources so large that they affect all members of the state, and in which the one worst crime won't be murder or kidnapping but taking advantage of the state—in which the seller of fraudulent medicine, or the liar in Congress, will be punished a whole lot worse than the fellow who takes an ax to the man who's grabbed off his girl.

In other words, the alternative to a fascist corporatism is a liberal corporatism in which men of virtue such as Doremus Jessup run the government. The Obama era's version of the Sinclair Lewis solution has been Chicago-style corporatism. The machine-driven crony capitalism that characterizes the president's hometown of Chicago has, in part, been implemented nationally.

In the seventy-five years since Lewis wrote *It Can't Happen Here*, liberalism has been unable to come to grips with the tension between an increasingly powerful government and self-interest. Croly's ideal of the disinterested expert has come to look less and less plausible, because government and academia have grown so massively that it's hard not to see them as simply two more interest groups.

Liberalism, argued Herbert Croly and his heirs, rested on "disinterestedness." Experts and intellectuals could be trusted, their theory held, because, unlike the Jeffersonian small-business owners, they weren't motivated by narrow self-interest. But with the expansions of the Great Society and onward, much of the public came to see politicians in general and liberals in particular as engaged in the self-interested business of expanding government expressly to secure policies and privileges for themselves and their supporters. The growing importance of public-sector unions has greatly increased the sense that government has gone into business for itself.

Liberalism, which began as a literary construct in the wake of World War I, reached its political apex with the election of Barack Obama, whose personal history as crafted in *Dreams from My Father: A Story of Race and Inheritance* was a literary construct. The alluring political personality of Barack Obama emerged even though he neither presented any new ideas nor even reconsidered old ideas on government reform. Obama, who ran a picture-perfect top-bottom, upstairs-downstairs campaign in 2008, had been opposed to the two successful social-policy reforms of the 1990s. He lambasted both welfare reform and the "broken-windows" policing techniques that did so much—especially in black neighborhoods—to lower crime rates. But he had aligned himself with the rising force in the Democratic Party: the alliance of public-sector unions (including nominally private but heavily government-subsidized health-care unions) and gentry liberals

The biracial Obama, the overwhelming electoral choice of both upper-middle-class professionals and African Americans, was the incarnation of modern liberalism's antipathy to conventional, middle-class America. As a student with a penchant for quoting Nietzsche, Obama was drawn to the writings of Frantz Fanon, assorted writers in the Marxist vein, and T.S. Eliot. Sounding like one of the literary Bolsheviks of the 1920s, Obama told one girlfriend in a letter that Eliot represented "a certain kind of conservatism which I respect more than bourgeois liberalism." As a rising political player, he was drawn to Reverend Wright's black-nationalist church, which espoused a "Black Value System" that had as one of its express tenets "A Disavowal of the Pursuit of Middleclassness," defined as the individual pursuit of economic success. Instead, Wright preached a collective race-based activism that fit in well with the machine politics of Chicago, where Richard Daley expanded crony capitalism to incorporate black power brokers.

In Chicago, a powerful black political presence is entirely consistent with a murder rate thrice that in New York. It's a city where the mayoralty, controlled by Democrats since 1931, has produced an economy in which the largest employer is the federal government, followed by the failed City of Chicago Public School system. In descending order, the next largest employers are the City of Chicago, the Chicago Transit Authority, the Cook County government, and the Chicago Park District.

Obama's magnificent speaking style, with its blend of Ivy League vocabulary and black-preacher cadences, was music to the ears of voters who had grown vexed by the disjointed ramblings of George W. Bush. Obama's TV looks and radio voice, brilliantly deployed in David Axelrod's McGovern-like campaign strategy of racking up delegates in the caucus states, made for a campaign that unfurled like a Hollywood movie with a happy ending. And just as the McGovern campaign had drawn on the anti-Vietnam sentiments of college students, Axelrod mobilized young voters angry over Iraq. Many of these collegians had been raised on Howard Zinn's updating of Nathaniel West's "Pageant of America, or, a Curse on Columbus." Zinn's perennially best-selling version of American history boils down to the following: part one: what we did to the Indians; part two: what we did to the blacks; part three: what we did to everyone else.

Obama and Axelrod's 2008 campaign talk of post-partisanship obscured the candidate's hyper-partisanship and lack of achievement. Obama's policy positions were those of an old-time liberal, but his policy style seemed new. He is the first postmodern presidential candidate: Narratives intended to establish his racial and political authenticity entirely replaced accomplishments. Obama had little to show by way of legislation in either the Illinois legislature or the U.S. Senate, but he had a romance to sell that depicted him as the culmination of liberal reform. That story worked well enough.

Rather than the half-African-American liberal outsider struggling against ingrained prejudices, Obama represented the new American elite that had been anticipated by British author Michael Young in the subtitle of his canonical *The Rise of the Meritocracy*. The 1959 book's now forgotten subtitle read, "The New Elite of our Social Revolution." Obama's

2008 campaign was embraced by this new American elite, which melded Hollywood, Silicon Valley, Wall Street, Washington, and the prestige press. This new alignment, with its whiff of old-world snobbery, bore a striking resemblance to the British establishment, which looked down on manufacturers and shopkeepers. The new configuration was united by its disdain for people aspiring to achieve or hold on to a private-sector middle-class life, people who didn't shop in farmers' markets or know the difference between rice and risotto.*

The new elite was drawn to Obama's style while the nascent Tea Parties were repelled by the substance of his policies. Devoid of new ideas, hampered by an incapacity to rethink liberalism's past failures, Obama's campaign was fueled by kitsch imagery exemplified by graffiti artist Shepherd Fairey's plagiarized HOPE poster, with its evocation of Obama's Che Guevara–like aura. The Czech writer Milan Kundera explained how kitsch works: "Kitsch causes two tears to flow in quick succession. The first tear says: How nice to see children running on the grass! The second tear says: How nice to be moved, together with all mankind, by children running on the grass!" The Obama version went like this: How nice it is to have an articulate, well-educated African American run for president! And how nice it is to know that by supporting Obama we are supporting all those virtuous folks who want to break with our racist past! Randolph Bourne, recall, wanted to "think emotions" and "feel ideas." In his person, Obama offered just such a conflation to his liberal devotees. By thinking well of Obama, his supporters were able to feel good about themselves.

Obama staffed his administration occupationally, regionally, and ideologically on a very narrow basis. Virtually everyone in the administration hailed from Chicago, New York, Boston, or the San Francisco Bay area. Few had any practical or business experience; rather, they were the credentialed "experts," Wall Streeters, and the kind of university-based

---

* "Foodism has taken on the sociological characteristics of what used to be known—in the days of the rising postwar middle class, when Mortimer Adler was peddling the Great Books and Leonard Bernstein was on television—as culture. It is costly. It requires knowledge and connoisseurship, which are themselves costly to develop. It is a badge of membership in the higher classes, an ideal example of what Thorstein Veblen, the great social critic of the Gilded Age, called conspicuous consumption. It is a vehicle of status aspiration and competition, an ever-present occasion for snobbery, one-upmanship and social aggression. (My farmers' market has bigger, better, fresher tomatoes than yours.) Nobody cares if you know about Mozart or Leonardo anymore, but you had better be able to discuss the difference between ganache and couverture." (William Deresiewicz, "A Matter of Taste?" *New York Times,* October 26, 2012)

specialists that Herbert Croly had extolled at the turn of the twentieth century as a natural ruling class. Like the president, they were invested in the sense of their own brilliance and unassailable authority. And like the president, who rejected American exceptionalism, they saw Europe's welfare states, even as they were in throes of crisis, as the model to emulate.

In 2009, liberals controlled all three elected branches of the federal government. The graybeards of the House used that power to try to turn the clock back to 1980 by using the $800 billion stimulus to feed all the interests Ted Kennedy had represented in his presidential run against Jimmy Carter. The stimulus was a striking failure. But aided by a press corps dedicated to advancing his agenda, Obama never tried or needed to make a coherent or sustained case for his economic agenda. Rather, in an expression of the "Chicago way" that he brought to Washington, he told Republicans that he would write the stimulus bill on behalf of Democratic clients. "I won," he explained. What the press largely missed was the striking continuity between George W. Bush's agenda and Obama's—the TARP program to bail out financial firms, the stimulus spending, the easy money from the Fed—albeit in the latter's case, on a vastly expanded scale.

In a country with a functioning press, the president would have been required to explain to the public how feeding Wall Street and his party's already well-compensated interest groups would contribute to an economic revival. Instead, in the least democratic recovery in American history, Democratic clients and contributors prospered while the private-sector businesses of Main Street and the inner city withered, all while the government was piling up massive and unsustainable debt. But thanks to a partisan press, the country had no public discussion of why Keynesianism had failed under Carter and failed again in the 1990s in both Canada and Japan.

After successfully governmentalizing (at least prospectively) the health-care system—one-sixth of the American economy—by way of a parliamentary maneuver made possible by Democratic control of both houses of Congress, Obama suffered a setback in the 2010 elections. The Tea Party movement—a largely grassroots response at first to the federal bailouts of Wall Street and the auto industry, and then to the breakneck expansion of federal power through Obamacare—raised the flag of constitutional government as a constraint on the unmitigated exercise of

Washington's power over its subjects. The Tea Partiers feared the way that big government, big business, big media, and a self-serving academia had coalesced into a Chicago-style bulwark of crony capitalists.

But perhaps more important, the Tea Partiers, although they were relentlessly and baselessly attacked as racist paranoids by the *New York Times*, the *New Yorker*, and their kindred White House–aligned publications, saw that Obama's willingness to pick winners and losers in the economy, often in the name of environmentalism, had frozen small and midsize businesses—the nation's primary job creators—in their tracks. Obama had so successfully put down Main Street that despite a second stimulus, the economy remained stagnant, producing by far the weakest economic recovery of the post-WWII era.

But failure was a success of sorts for Obama, who is often unfairly compared to Jimmy Carter. Carter was defeated in his reelection bid because he had fought against the Democratic Party's reigning interest groups when they demanded reckless spending in the midst of stagflation. Obama catered to these same interest groups, which ensured that he would face no challenge from his left when he came up for reelection. With a consolidated base and a press corps largely devoted to demonizing and defeating his opponent, Obama benefited from the fact that those who were most hurt by the high unemployment wrought by Obama's policies doubled down in their support of the president.

Obama, who had been campaigning virtually full time for two years, successfully used the period of the acrid GOP primaries to paint his general-election opponent Mitt Romney as a money-bags Mormon out of touch with working America. "This is the first president in history who kept his supporters and his grassroots organization," based heavily on public-sector workers, "in place during the course of the presidency," boasted Obama's press secretary Ben LaBolt. With his history at Bain Capital, Romney was the wrong candidate to call out Obama on how the president's faux populism enriched the president's crony-capitalist allies such as Google, GM, and Goldman Sachs while shifting the costs of an ever expanding government onto job-creating small business.

Similarly, Romney didn't effectively rebuke Obama for his insistence that a militant environmentalism would spur economic growth. Obama carried eight of the ten wealthiest counties in the country including the environmentalist stronghold of Marin County, just north of San Francisco, where he won 74 percent of the vote. And in a California version of the top-bottom coalition, the president also won California's agricultural interior where environmental policies that cut off water produced unemployment as high as 30 percent. Not incidentally, wealthy and increasingly stratified California—where many cities (like the state itself) teeter on the edge of bankruptcy due to excesses of the public-sector unions—has been hemorrhaging its middle-class population.

One of the ironies of 2012 was that the onetime liberal bugaboo of the mass media played such a crucial role in reelecting the liberal candidate. A press that was even semi-sentient might have, for instance, acknowledged the problematic quality of the auto bailout. But the scandals of Solyndra and other so-called green companies and the slumping share price for General (dubbed "Government") Motors received scant attention. Instead, the ineffective auto bailout became one of the keys to Obama's narrow but crucial 2012 victories in Great Lakes auto states such as Ohio and Wisconsin. In 2012, the clerisy—composed of the mass media, Hollywood, academia, and the press—were virtually united in their determination to push the incumbent over the top.

The 2012 election continued GOP control of the House of Representatives, while Obama's victory revealed a country deeply divided between what remains of Main Street and the urban heirs of Sinclair Lewis. Party identification had become so deeply attached to personal identity that dating services found that they couldn't match otherwise seemingly compatible singles if one was a Democrat and the other a Republican.

Nearly four years into his presidency Obama was still hammering and blaming George Bush, but he and his fellow liberals have to date never provided a coherent alternative to a market-driven economy and limited government. Obamacare is but an updating of Herbert Croly's plans to turn federal policy over to boards of experts. Their failures notwithstanding, liberals today, like those of the 1920s, still pretend to be the sole keepers of the noosphere. Far too many have invested far too much in liberalism's pretensions to ever abandon it, even in the face of abject policy and electoral failure. Liberals defend their policies today not on substance, but with John Stewart sarcasm (sub-Menckenesque as it is) about the failings of their rivals.

Obama's personal appeal and effective electioneering have obscured the decay of the liberal policy agenda. Over decades, the liberal experts directed the dispersal of trillions of taxpayer dollars to alleviate poverty and improve education—it was the price, they said, that we needed to pay to advance equality. The money flowed, in nearly inconceivable quantities, but the poverty rate today is roughly where it was thirty years ago, and the schools are still mired in failure as academic standards fall prey to collapsing cultural conventions. At the same time, an increasingly bureaucratized and ever larger academia is driving tuition, which continuously outpaces inflation, far higher than the educational results could warrant.

As a matter of policy, liberalism has been a very expensive failure. As a matter of patronage, against which it once rebelled, it has been a considerable success. The founding 1920s liberal hope for a society ruled by an aristocracy of talent has been replaced over time by a concatenation of crony capitalism, credentialism, and contraception. The third, contraception (the promise of sexual liberation being associated with liberalism from the start), has, however, failed to deliver on the once shining promise of creativity corked up only by sexual restraint.

What unites the top and bottom of the Obama coalition is an apparent disdain for the copybook maxims of faith, family, and hard work. Upper-middle-class liberals often live by those very maxims, but they refuse to preach what they practice. To be straightforward about how they live would reveal well-to-do liberals as far more conventional than their pretensions would allow.

With the election of 2012, America has taken a giant step closer to the European model the original liberals of 1919 so ardently admired. But European social democracy, like blue-state America, is imperiled by its sheer costs. "Europe got the American president it wanted—the one who would present no threat to its own delusions," explained the British writer Janet Daley in November 2012. "The United States is now officially one of us: an Old World country complete with class hatred, ethnic Balkanization, bourgeois guilt, and a paternalist ruling elite. And it is locked into the same death spiral of high public spending and self-defeating wealth redistribution as we are."

Liberalism has been the most successful of the turn-of-the-twentieth-century vanguard movements. Its rivals have all fallen. Fascism, reincarnated in the Arab world after WWII, has given way to Islamism. An anarchic version of Communism, though it still attracts campus crowds and Occupy protesters, isn't taken seriously outside the halls of academe. Of the early-twentieth-century isms, only a bureaucratized version of social democracy and liberalism remain. Only liberalism can be said to have been a success of sorts. Its sustained assault on the private-sector middle class and the ideals of self-restraint and self-government have, particularly in the blue states, succeeded all too well in achieving the dream of the 1920s literary Bolsheviks: an increasingly Europeanized class structure for America.

Postscript: One of the central themes of this book's early chapters was the shift between the libertarian-minded liberalism of the 1920s, which reacted to President Wilson's repressive, WWI-era Espionage Act by critiquing government power, and the authoritarian liberalism of the 1930s, which used federal power to impose itself on the nation. In the early years of the twenty-first century, this pattern repeated itself. Liberals responded to the Iraq and Afghan war-surveillance policies of the George W. Bush administration with accusations that made the Republican president out to be little short of a dictator. But when President Obama came to power, liberals fell largely silent about the new administration's continuation of the Bush anti-terror policies. Worse yet, the new administration repressed individual journalists, such as James Rosen of Fox News, through the use of President Wilson's Espionage Act. And as of May 2013, the Obama administration, notes journalist Michael Barone, had "used the Espionage Act of 1917 six times to bring cases against government officials for leaks to the media—twice as many as all of its predecessors combined." Then as now liberalism can swivel from anti-authoritarian to authoritarian modes depending on who is dispensing the rules.

★ ★ ★

Acknowledgments

My family made this book possible. My wife, Jan Rosenberg, listened to me read this entire book out loud—twice. Our son Jacob Siegel was an enormous help in thinking through the arguments. Our son Harry Siegel helpfully edited some of the chapters.

I'd also like to thank Sol Stern, Mark Riebling, Joel Kotkin, Eamon Moynihan, John Rosenberg, Frank Macchiarola, Dan DiSalvo, Lloyd Greene, Fred Ciporen, and Todd Brewster for listening to and commenting on my rambles on the topics discussed in *Revolt Against the Masses.*

The book draws, in part, on my articles that appeared in the *City Journal* thanks to Brian Anderson, Paul Beston, and Ben Plotinksy; in *Commentary* thanks to John Podhoretz and Abe Greenwald; in *The Weekly Standard* thanks to Phil Terzian and Richard Starr; in *The Claremont Review of Books* thanks to John Kienker; in *National Review* thanks to Rich Lowry; in the *Wall Street Journal* thanks to Eric Eichmann, Robert Messenger, and Howard Dickman; in *Telos* thanks to Russell Berman; and in *Minding the Campus* thanks to John Leo. Finally, a longer version of the Appendix on John Stuart Mill appeared in *Society* thanks to its editor Jonathan Imber.

APPENDIX

★ ★ ★

John Stuart Mill and the Clerisy

John Stuart Mill, the mid-nineteenth-century British inspiration for modern American liberalism, was one of the first policy intellectuals of the sort that accompany the arrival of a new administration in Westminster or Washington. In the words of the Victorian poet Alfred Lord Tennyson, these were "the men of the mind," or, as Mill described them, "the pedantocracy" whose conceptual brooms were going to tidy up the political mess in Westminster.

It was fitting, then, that the 2008 election of Barack Obama, of Columbia and Harvard, was accompanied by an extraordinary essay in *The New Yorker*. The magazine anticipated the election of Obama, an American who aspires to be a European, as an event of near providential proportions. On its cover, it similarly celebrated Mill, the iconic British liberal who wished he were French. The magazine's front flap announced a celebratory hymn to THE MAN WHO WAS ALWAYS RIGHT, written by Adam Gopnik, a regular contributor to *The New Yorker.* Discussing a fine biography of Mill, *John Stuart Mill: Victorian Firebrand*, by Richard Reeves, Gopnik presents Mill, in the manner of Maimonides, as a guide for the perplexed. The article's first sentence tells readers, "It is a hard thing, being right about everything all the time." That declaration is softened only slightly a few sentences later to a more reasonable assessment:

"Certainly no one has ever been so right about so many things so much of the time as John Stuart Mill."

What's striking is the disconnect between Gopnik's hagiography and Mill's life. There is a great deal to admire about Mill, who died in 1873 at age sixty-seven, that endures down to the present. One of the founders of modern feminism, he helped midwife the birth of Canada, fought British colonial abuses in Ireland and Jamaica, helped advance parliamentary reform, and defended the right of workingmen to organize on their own behalf. In his most important book, *On Liberty*, he carved out a concept of individual autonomy that continues, at times, to serve as a counterweight to the claims of overmighty government.

But in his rush to pay tribute to Mill as a saint and guiding light for the new liberal future under Obama, Gopnik neglected to come to grips with Mill's life and thought. There were many, often contradictory, Mills, and there were issues on which he was repeatedly wrong.

Mill took his credo from Goethe's insistence that serious problems were invariably "many sided." Henry Cole reported a conversation in that vein with Mills: "With utilitarians, said he, he was a mystic—with mystics a utilitarian—with logicians a sentimentalist and with the latter a logician." But in *On Liberty,* Mills argued for a "single truth" that was "entitled to *govern absolutely* the dealings of society with the individual." In Mill's explication of what came to be called the "harm principle," in *On Liberty*, he argued that neither government nor neighborly opinion had any right to interfere with an individual's self-regarding actions. Yet in writing before and after *On Liberty,* which was published in 1859, the same year as Darwin's *Origins of Species,* Mill was in many ways his own best critic. *On Liberty* insisted that truth was "produced by its collision with error" so that no opinion no matter how half-baked ought to be suppressed. The book famously insisted that "if all mankind minus one were of one opinion, and only one person were of the contrary opinion, mankind would be no more justified in silencing that one person than he, if he had the power, would be justified in silencing mankind." Yet Mill had also made the exact counter case: "I have not any great notion of the advantage of what the 'free discussion men' call the 'collision of opinions,' it being my creed that truth is *sown* and germinates in the mind itself, and is not to be struck *out* suddenly like fire from a flint by knocking another hard body against it."

The Mill who modeled himself on the French philosophes and who deeply admired not the Jacobins but the Girondins of the French Revolution took France, where he spent time as a young man, as "his benchmark and inspiration." He disdained England's fusty balanced constitution, with its continuing role for the aristocracy, and found France, with its revolutionary traditions, "a nation to which by tastes and predilections I am more attached than to my own." In the 1820s, an impassioned young Mill argued: "In England . . . I often think that a violent revolution is very much needed, in order to give that general shake-up to the torpid mind of the nation which the French Revolution gave to Continental Europe. England has never had a general break-up of old associations & hence the extreme difficulty of getting any ideas into its stupid head."

But in his voluminous writings, Mill consistently misjudged developments in France, and that misjudgment was connected to his abstract notions of both history and politics, born of his Benthamite upbringing. While Burkean conservatives worshipped the accumulated wisdom of the elders, the radical Benthamites, anticipating America's '68ers, saw the past as an albatross of ignorance. Breaking with the past, it was argued, was bound to make modern men far wiser than those who had preceded them. It was this perspective, modified to a degree by Mill's personal experiences, that led him to have great expectations for the French revolutions of 1830 and 1848. On both occasions, like '60s radicals rushing to Cuba, Vietnam, China, North Korea, and the Palestinian territories, he made his pilgrimage across the channel to witness the long-awaited rebirth firsthand. "I should not care though a revolution were to exterminate every person in Great Britain and Ireland who has £500 a year," he wrote in the wake of the 1830 upheaval. "Many very amiable persons would perish, but what is the world the better for such amiable persons?" Did Mill include himself? After all, his income of £1,200 from his job as a functionary for the East India Company put him in the top one half of 1 percent of English earners.

Eighteen years later, in his impassioned essay "Vindication of the French Revolution of 1848," a polemical Mill mocked former allies and, almost alone in England, saw great promise for France ahead. Unlike both Tocqueville and Marx, who discerned elements of tragedy and farce in 1848, the solemn Mill took the rhetorical excesses of the French revolutionaries at face value. Mill had spent much of his life mocking the smug certainties of Whig gradualism, but with the rise of Napoleon III's dictatorial regime, he was forced to concede that those who argued that revolution leads to dictatorship were probably right. At that point, rather than reexamine his misbegotten assumptions, he simply ceased writing about France, and his disdain for England endured. "The whole state of Europe," he wrote in 1871, "inspires sadness enough, but that of England contempt." Responding to this comment, Richard Reeves, his sympathetic biographer, writes: "As usual, the contempt was only half-justified: after all, in 1869 the Irish Church was disestablished; in 1870 the principle of universal education was established . . . and in 1872 the secret ballot was established." The franchise was substantially expanded at this time as well, Reeves points out.

As for politics both domestic and international, Mill, as often self-righteous as right, repeatedly misread the situation. In the 1830s, the Tory prime minister Robert Peel, the dominant politician of his age, shifted his party and British politics away from deductive arguments toward practical reforms. Peel's favorite maxim was "There's nothing like a fact." Peel introduced the forerunners of the modern police, England's first significant public-health measures, and the first reforms regulating working hours and conditions. But, notes Reeves, Mill couldn't grasp the idea of a Tory reformer. He denounced Peel as a "third-rate man," full of "low tricks and equivocations," who was "perhaps the least gifted man that ever headed a powerful party in this country." In his waning years, Mill backed Bismarck in the 1870–71 Franco–Prussian war while denouncing the English prime minister Gladstone for allowing the war to happen.

His friend (and first biographer) Alexander Bain wrote of Mill on France that he "dealt gently with her faults, and liberally with her virtues." One can say the reverse about Mill's writing on England. Mill's xenophilia was not the only problematic trait he encoded in his American heirs. Matched against Mill's depiction of autonomy as an absolute good in *On Liberty*, the freest of societies can be condemned as authoritarian, if not worse—as America discovered in the 1960s—and the differences between relatively free and totalitarian societies minimized.

Many of the overwrought arguments that characterized the 1950s New York Intellectual–Frankfurt School critique of mass society, continued by Michel Foucault and enduring into the present in the form of standard-issue Hollywood movies on death by station wagon and back-yard barbecue in suburbia, were laid out in *On Liberty*. At a time when individual freedom was, as Mill later acknowledged, expanding, he hysterically insisted:

> At present, individuals are lost in a crowd. . . . In our times, from the highest class of society down to the lowest, everyone lives as under the eye of a hostile and dreaded censorship. . . . Thus the mind itself is bowed to the yoke: even in what people do for pleasure, conformity is the first thing thought of; they like in crowds . . . peculiarity of taste, eccentricity of conduct, are shunned equally with crimes: until by dint of not following their own nature, they have no nature to follow.

Mill offered little in the way of specifics to justify his claims. Nor could he; in the middle years of Victoria's reign, the public developed an unprecedented appetite for the spirited discussion of ideas, as evidenced by the proliferation of serious and semi-serious journals, including Mill's own *Westminster Review*. Anticipating those such as the Whiggish Macaulay who would rebuke him for "crying 'Fire!' in Noah's flood"—at a time when spirit rapping, debates about evolution, and critiques of religion flourished—Mill contended that the "revival of bigotry" could be just around the corner.

Mill's hyperbole nonetheless endures because it underpins crucial cultural and political claims. Culturally, the tendency to blame society for thwarting individual genius has an enduring allure that captured the founders of American liberalism in the 1920s. It is, on a psychological level, the great guarantor that people of limited talent but an unlimited sense of their own abilities need not face their failings. Politically, Mill, a fervent foe of the English aristocracy, associated democracy with "mediocrity" and "the yoke of custom." His hope was to lead the creation of an alternative elite, what he sometimes described, using the language of Coleridge, as the "clerisy," the "endowed class" of modern meritocrats whose wisdom and intelligence were to produce guided democracy. "The honor and glory of the average man," Mill insisted, lay in their ability to follow the initiative of the intellectual elite composed of men (and women) like him. The clerisy has reappeared in numerous guises since. The concept of a clerisy was adopted by H.G. Wells, influential in both England and America, who dubbed its members "the samurai." In America, it was taken up by *The New Republic* and first came to fruition in the form of the New Deal's Brain Trust. The Brain Trust is in turn the model for the not-so-new liberalism that has accompanied the arrival of the Obama administration.

Mill makes for a problematic liberal saint. He was man of distinctly limited judgment, both a prophet of modern tolerance and the author of *On Liberty*'s absurdities. A constant of Mill's inconstant intellectual and political life was an insistence on the importance of individual character to the well-being of a society. The character of individuals, "the internal culture of the individual," was to him as important as the design of institutions. "The worth of a State," he wrote, "in the long run is the worth of the individuals composing it." That is a Mill who still has something to teach contemporary liberals.

INDEX

★ ★ ★

Page numbers followed by n indicate notes.